A PEDIATRICIAN'S GUIDE TO
Child Behavior Problems

Esther L. Cava, Ph. D.

Supervisor, Student Training PATH, Inc. (CHMC) and
Psychological Consultant
St. Christopher's Hospital for Children
Philadelphia, Pennsylvania

Joseph A. Girone, M.D.   Ruth P. Schiller, M.D.†
Thomas J. Hipp, M.D.   Neil Schlackman, M.D.
Edward P. Rothstein, M.D.   Ronald L. Souder, M.D.‡

Attending Pediatricians
St. Christopher's Hospital for Children
Clinical Assistant and †Clinical Associate Professors and ‡Clinical Instructor
of Pediatrics
Temple University School of Medicine
Philadelphia, Pennsylvania

 MASSON Publishing USA, Inc.

New York•Paris•Milan•Barcelona•Mexico City•Rio de Janeiro

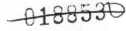

ISBN 0-89352-075-6

Library of Congress Catalog Card Number: 79-88727

Printed in the United States of America

PREFACE

It has been argued that since little is definitively known about the effect of child rearing methods, it is presumptuous to proffer specific advice. Although many of the suggestions made in this book are not based on hard scientific data, parents should not be asked to wait until these data are produced. By utilizing what facts we do have, by accepting, perhaps tentatively, those psychological theories which are plausible, and by applying knowledge gained from experience with children, we should be able to provide parents with reasonably effective recommendations. Of course, as our knowledge about child development increases, changes in the recommendations to parents for preventing psychological disorders and for creating an environment that is favorable for growth and development, may be necessary.

Although the child management advice presented in this book is behavior oriented, the authors are aware of the significant role that psychodynamic factors play in causing and maintaining behavior and thus, stress the importance of intervention by mental health personnel in those situations where the child's problem does not respond to behavior-oriented techniques.

In this book emphasis is on providing parents with suggestions that are concrete and specific: teaching parents to be honest and straightforward with their children, and helping parents create a relaxed and peaceful environment, which is, at the same time, structured and predictable. In general, the goal of this book is to help the pediatricians in their efforts to teach parents and children how to cope with conflicts and stress more adaptively.

Contents

INTRODUCTION

Pediatricians report that requests from parents for child-rearing advice have increased sharply. These requests have made them aware that they have not been prepared adequately to give parents practical advice for dealing with specific child-management problems. In 1973 Tolster and Worley (1976) conducted a survey of 100 pediatricians in the South Florida area on the subject of parents' requests for child-rearing advice. About 60% (of the 100 pediatricians) responded to the questionnaire and 80% of those responding said that at least 10% of their daily calls and/or office visits dealt with questions concerning the child's behavior. The respondents complained that their training in this area was inadequate, and they indicated that they needed practical suggestions for counseling parents who request help in managing their children effectively.

It could be argued that the pediatrician can refer these parents to agencies and practitioners who are competent in this area; however, there are a number of reasons why it is more desirable for the pediatrician to provide these services.

Many parents are reluctant to complete the referral process. The reasons for this are not clear. From what some parents report, however, there is still a stigma associated with bringing a child to a mental health specialist. Parents will also admit to the fear that although they are really only seeking child management advice their own personal lives will be analyzed. Related to this is their concern that seeking treatment from a mental health specialist will require a long-term commitment which can be both financially and temporally expensive. The physician may be able to intervene before a problem becomes so severe that the parent is forced to seek help elsewhere. If the physician can give the parents some anticipatory guidance as well as suggestions for handling those behaviors which have become problems, there might not exist the large age discrepancy (average, 5½ years) between the onset of behavior problems and the admission of the child with those problems to a mental health clinic. (The average age of onset of behavior considered deviant is about 3½ years, while the average age of admission to most clinics is 9 years.)

Because parents view the pediatrician as a person to whom they can go for help when they are concerned about their child, they will consult him first about child-related problems. Even when they are only mildly concerned about the child's behavior, they may refer to it casually while the pediatrician is examining the child. Fuma (1975) suggests that because the relationship between the parents and the child's physician is already a relatively close and trusting one, the physician is in a good position to give child-rearing advice. This book then represents an effort to provide pediatricians with practical suggestions for anticipatory guidance and for helping parents modify their child's undesirable behavior.

There are essentially three separate but closely related functions which the pediatrician can serve in his capacity of behavioral consultant:

1. Primary prevention. By providing parents with anticipatory guidance, the pediatrician may be able to prevent emotional and/or behavioral problems.

2. Secondary prevention. A mild behavior problem for which the parent usually does not seek outside help because he does not perceive it as being serious, can if ignored, become a major problem and a threat to the child's mental health. The pediatrician can frequently detect signs of behavior which, if continued, could interfere with healthy functioning. There is some evidence that major emotional and/or behavioral problems can be prevented by early identification and effective intervention.

3. Identification of those problems so severe or persistent that referral to a mental health agency or private mental health specialist is necessary. (See *Part II—Secondary Prevention,* for criteria for referring a child.)

There is little conclusive evidence indicating that some child-rearing methods are preferable to others. Thus, suggestions in this book are not based on hard, scientific fact. It is felt, however, that decisions on child rearing cannot wait until hard, scientific data are produced. By utilizing some facts, some psychological theories which make sense, and knowledge gained from experience with children, one should be able to give parents some reasonably effective advice.

This book was written to be used as a handbook, a reference book, or as a companion to a book on child development. Essentially, it contains advice on primary and secondary prevention of psychological disorders in children, advice which is specific enough that the pediatrician does not have to extrapolate it before counseling parents. The suggestions are not based on any specific psychological theory; the intention that they will appeal to logic and common sense.

A by-product of parent counseling as suggested in this book is the importance of the parents as the instruments of behavior change. If they successfully carry out the advice, they are likely to feel more adequate in their parenting role, which, in turn, will tend to result in their being more effective in that role.

References

Anderson, J. A.: Pediatrics and child psychology. *J Am Med Assoc,* 1930, **95,** 1015–1018.

Fuma, J. M.: *Pediatric* psychologist . . . ? Do you mean clinical *child* psychologist? *J Clin* Child *Psychol,* 1975 (Fall), 9–12.

Kinsbourne, M.: School problems. *Pediatrics,* 1973, **52,** 697–710.

Routh, D. K.: Psychological training in medical school. Department of Pediatrics: a survey. *Prof Psych,* 1970, **1**(5), 469–472.

Routh, D. K.: Psychological training in medical school departments of pediatrics, a second look. *Am Psychol,* 1972, **27**(6), 587–589.

Schwartz, A. M., and Murphy, M. W.: Cues for screening language disorders in pre-school children. *Pediatrics,* 1975, **55,** 717–722.

Tolster, R. P., and Worley, L. M.: Behavioral aspects of pediatric practice: a survey of practitioners. *J Med Educ,* 1976 (Dec.), **51,** 1019–1020.

PART I

Pediatrician's Role in
Primary Prevention
of Psychologic Disorders

CHAPTER 1

The Effect of Having a Child in the Home

It is probably safe to assume that most parents derive a considerable amount of satisfaction from having children. There is evidence, however, that the presence of children in the home can be a source of great stress for parents, particularly for the mother. These stresses can, if they are not handled effectively, produce psychologic disorders in the child.

The additional financial burden incurred in raising a child(ren) can strain the marital relationship and thus create tension (Crow, 1967; Larson, et al., 1967; Lindgren, 1969; Gray, 1974). Sometimes, because of financial need, the mother returns to work after the infant's birth. In addition to the possible stressful effect this may have on the mother-child relationship, the need to share household chores and child care can strain the marital relationship (Pickett, 1974). Fathers, not accustomed to the role implicit in performing these functions and not having anticipated the need to assume this role, may resist sharing the responsibility for housekeeping and child care. Horton (1974) found that as late as 1974, the average working mother who added the hours she spent working in the home to the hours she spent working outside the home, tended to work a total of 99.6 hours per week.

Crow (1967) and Lindgren (1969) suggest that parents are not always aware that having a child is likely to interfere with their social activities. Some parents have a rather vague notion that they will have to curtail their activities, but they are usually not aware of the extent to which this may occur. Parents having their first child are frequently naive regarding the cost of babysitters, the difficulty of always obtaining them at will, and, because of this, the need to plan social activities

3

in advance. In addition, even mothers who do not work outside the home complain that, because of the additional work in the home and/or because their sleep is interrupted, they are sometimes too tired to go out.

Occasionally the presence of an infant in the home can provoke jealousy in a father who may have derived considerable satisfaction from the attention and care which he received prior to the child's birth and which is now being lavished on the child (Crow, 1967). Crow also suggests that disagreements over how the child should be handled may become a source of marital conflict. Not infrequently there is already an underlying marital problem, and it is less threatening to disagree over the care of the child than to deal with the more basic marital conflicts.

Larsen, et al. (1967) point out that there tends to be a change in the relationship between the new parents and their own parents. Although some of the changes may be positive, there can be conflicts over, for instance, child rearing methods. When these conflicts involve the new parent and his own parents, they do not seem to seriously affect the relationship between the new parent. When, however, the conflicts involve the new parent and his parents-in-law, they can result in marital conflict.

Many parents seeking marital counseling report that their sexual relationship seemed to deteriorate following the birth of their child(ren). This may occur as a result of the stresses described above, or the presence of a child in the home may place an additional stress on an already strained relationship.

Some effects of having a child in the home impinge more directly on the mother than on the father, although the father may be involved. In any case the existence of the problem(s) can result in general family tension. One source of postpartum conflict is the presence of unrealistic expectations (Larsen et al., 1967). Many women not yet pregnant or pregnant for the first time report that they expect to have fewer problems than other mothers seem to have because they intend to be more patient and gentle with their infants; they express confidence that the manifestation of these qualities will produce a happy, contented infant. The conflict arises when the infant, despite the mother's patient efforts to comfort him, continues to cry, when he disturbs the mother's sleep, and generally does not appear to be as happy as it was anticipated he would be. Resentment and anger toward the infant, who has not only frustrated her efforts to comfort him but has thwarted her expectations, may create guilt feelings.

A dependent, immature, needy mother may resent the demands made on her by the dependent, needy infant. The resentment may cause rejection of the child and the potential devastating consequences of that rejection (Ingram, 1974; Hurley, 1967; Horney, 1937).

Larsen, *et al.* (1967) suggest that it might be possible to predict the "postpartum adjustment of mother and baby before delivery" by considering the following factors which they found are related to postpartum adjustment:

1. The capacity of the parents to be aware of the infant's needs, to meet those needs and to at the same time, meet their own needs. Since many parents are either not aware of their infant's needs or have misconceptions concerning them, information to parents prior to delivery or shortly after delivery may prevent or minimize postpartum maladjustment. In addition to the obvious needs, there are needs which if they are to be fulfilled require that the parents recognize their baby's unique temperament (Thomas, *et al.*, 1968).

Common misconceptions which may need correction are: that a child needs the almost constant presence of his parent(s) if he is to feel loved; that a child needs to be protected from all frustrations; and that a child continues to have the same needs throughout his infancy (Ingram, 1974; Glickman and Springer, 1978).

Although it may be easier and more gratifying to meet the infant's needs if one's own needs are met, there are situations where satisfying one's own needs could jeopardize the well-being of the infant, who is wholly dependent on his caretakers. As was noted earlier, responsibility for a child may mean curtailing one's social activities, a limit on the amount of money available for personal luxuries, and the burden of additional household chores. Attention and affection must now be shared with a third individual. And finally a dependent mother who has not had to fulfill the demands of another must now accept the frustration of some of her own needs if she is to care for her infant. How to identify the parent who is not capable of meeting the infant's needs will be discussed at the end of this chapter.

2. The tendency of parents to imitate the parenting behavior of their own parents. Parents report that they find themselves using the same child rearing methods used by their parents even when they deem these methods unacceptable and had consciously decided they would not employ them. It is as though they had unconsciously internalized those parental practices. In cases where these practices are inappropriate or unacceptable, helping the parent become aware of his behavior may encourage him to be more vigilant.

3. As was discussed earlier, prenatal expectations and attitudes are important factors in postpartum adjustment.

4. Past experience with stress. Parents who themselves were overprotected from normal stresses and who, thus, had not been given

opportunities to cope with stress effectively are more likely to find the strain of being a parent overwhleming and unsatisfying. In these situations, suggestions for reducing the stress as well as suggestions for gratifying needs outside the home may minimize the potential for parent-child adjustment problems.

In their studies, Larsen, *et al.* (1965) found that the use of appropriate psychological instruments oriented toward testing for the above factors enabled them to predict at a significant level of confidence those postpartum situations which would be adjustive or nonadjustive. It was their opinion that if vulnerable parents could be identified, some stresses could be prevented and/or minimized by parent counseling.

The vulnerable parent can also be identified informally by noting the presence of one or more of the following conditions and/or characteristics.

1. The mother looks to the infant for gratification of all of her needs.
2. The parents expect the child to keep them together.
3. The parent(s) uses the child to enhance himself, thus exploiting the child.
4. Incongruency between the child's temperament and the parent's temperament or between the former and the parent's expectations concerning how the child should behave (Thomas, *et al.*, 1968).
5. An immature dependent parent may not only be resentful of the child but is often overanxious and ineffective.
6. The home appears to lack a sense of family. Each family member goes his own way, and one senses a general attitude of rejection (Ingram, 1974).
7. The perfectionistic parent who may make unrealistic demands on the child.
8. The mother who is overanxious, overreactive, and overprotective.
9. The mother who rarely holds, fondles, or kisses her baby.
10. The parent doesn't respond to advice and guidance.

Ingram (1974) warns that parents sometimes verbalize attitudes which are not consonant with their actual behavior. Thus, it may be necessary to keep asking questions in an attempt to elicit a report of the parent's actual behavior.

Parents who appear to enjoy watching their child grow, who simply derive pleasure in raising them, are not likely to be vulnerable parents.

Working Mothers

Prior to the 1950s, it was assumed that children who were not cared for by their mothers would suffer irreparable harm even when, in the mother's absence, they were looked after by a reliable adult. This assumption was based, primarily, on studies of children reared in institutions where there were no consistent caretakers. It was found that some of these children were seriously and often irreversibly damaged (Beels, 1976). Kessler (1966) points out that most of the early studies did not control for other variables besides those of separation from mother and consistency of a mother substitute, which may be related to poor development and maladjustment. Since the studies were done in institutions, it may be that infants were just not stimulated enough. In addition to generalizing from results obtained on institutionalized children to children in other kinds of substitute care, the researchers did not distinguish between different types of maladjustment. Although symptoms such as lack of affect are usually associated with maternal deprivation, delinquency and sociopathic behavior are not. In fact, since the latter are often associated with maternal overindulgence, the child is more apt to exhibit symptoms of sociopathy if the mother is in the home.

Since the 1950s there has been a proliferation of studies of the effect of mother absence. The subjects used in these studies have included children residing in institutions as well as children in other types of substitute care. These children have been compared to those being cared for at home by their natural mothers. Following is a summary of the results of such studies:

1. Mothers who employed outside the home and enjoy their work, who are not filled with guilt over working, and who have been able to make satisfactory arrangements for the care of the household, will be as effective in their mothering role as mothers who remain at home. Children whose mothers are not employed outside the home but would like to be, as well as those whose working mothers are unhappy because they must work, tend to develop psychological problems (Beels, 1976; Yarrow, 1962; Lindgren, 1969).

2. In a study of children ages 2–30 months Fowler (1972) found that a significant factor was the quality of care, whether the child was in his own home or in substitute care. When there were several people taking care of the child, as long as those people were warm and affectionate and the environment consistent and predictable, most of the children made strides intellectually and socially. Beels (1976), in reviewing the research done in the 1960s, reports that "most children develop bonds

with several people and it appears likely that these bonds are basically similar" to bonds formed with the mother. Studies by Hecht (1972) in a report to the American Association for the Advancement of Science revealed that it made no significant difference in the child's development whether the child was cared for by his mother full time, by a substitute in the home, or in day care. What seemed to be important again was the quality of the care.

3. Just as the quality of substitute care was apparently the important variable in how the child fared, so the quality of home care seemed to be an important variable in whether the child suffered from having his mother work outside the home. In addition to her satisfaction with her role, an important variable is the stability of the home. If the home is stable, whether the mother works or not, seems to be unimportant. If the home is unstable, however, absence of the mother may increase the instability (Horton, 1974).

4. Lindgren (1969) and Horton suggest that, in some situations, the family seems to benefit from mothers working outside the home. A study done in 1970 by Poenanski et al. (Horton, 1974) found that "children of working mothers were more assertive, more independent, less conforming, and were higher school achievers where stable day care was available."

According to Brazelton (1978) some of the disadvantages resulting from mothers working outside the home are that working mothers tend to be "harried," that they have little contact with their children in the mornings and in the evenings, and that they tend to be irritable and to have guilt feelings because they are not home with their children. Mothers who have, however, carried out the following suggestions for coping with these potential problems, have reported little if any tension resulting from working outside the home:

1. If, during the previous evening, family members choose and put out the clothes they will wear on the following day and if they awaken or are awakened early enough to prepare for the day in an unhurried manner, irritability tends to be reduced. If children dally, they can, after a warning, be sent to bed fifteen minutes earlier that night, one-half hour earlier if they dally on a second day, and so on.

2. To prevent last minute decisions concerning menus and shopping needs, menus for the week can be made up during the previous week.

3. If several meals are prepared on the weekend for the following week, the dinner hour is less hectic and there is more time available for parent-child interaction.

4. The child who has not seen his mother all day may find it difficult, when he does finally see her, to wait until she has finished preparing dinner before he has her attention. If dinner has already been pre-

pared, mother can attend to the child while the meal is being warmed. The child who is old enough to help with the preparation can talk to mother during that time or he can be invited to remain in the kitchen to talk while the meal is being prepared.

5. Mothers who are made aware that it is the quality of contact with their children rather than the quantity that is important, tend to be less concerned that contact is not as frequent as it was when they were not working. Their guilt may also be reduced if they realize that working outside the home need not be detrimental to a child's well-being and may even be beneficial.

Rubenstein *et al.* (1977) did find when comparing mothers and caretakers that mothers "expressed more positive affect, engaged in more playful interactions and offered a greater variety of experiences to the infant" than did the caretakers. Despite these findings, however, the two groups of infants who were from five to six months of age were rated equally on 16 of 17 measures of development. The authors argue that infants are not as vulnerable to separation from mother, at least in the first six months, as one tends to think they are. They found that, as the caretakers continued to tend the infants, they became more responsive and stimulating. They admit, however, that they do not know what the long term effects might be for the child.

Since most of the current research concerned with the effect on children of working mothers reveals that there is, essentially, no difference between those children whose mothers work outside the home and those whose mothers do not, it is important to view psychological problems seen in some children of working mothers as a possible result of other factors (Hecht, 1972; Honig, 1974; Thomas, *et al.*, 1968). Before assuming then that the following behaviors are manifestations of the effects of mother absence, conditions such as interpersonal conflicts within the family and lack of stimulation in the home and/or in substitute care as sources of the problems should not be overlooked:

1. Infants as well as older children may be unusually passive and unresponsive, or if they are responsive, they may be indiscriminate in their attachment.
2. Children at any age may be fearful of others and, as a result, withdraw from contact with others. On the other hand, because their dependency needs may be increased, they may cling to others, particularly adults.
3. Some children respond with restless, unmanageable behavior, and may have trouble concentrating.
4. In situations where stimulation is inadequate, cognitive development as well as social development may be impaired.

5. Sibling incest tends to occur more frequently in homes where the mother is absent (Meiselman, 1978).

The most desirable age of the child at the time his mother enters or reenters the job market depends to a large extent on the availability of satisfactory surrogate care. Some authors have assumed that placing an infant in substitute care before the age of six months would interfere with the development of mother-infant attachment. Honig (1972) cites studies which show no weakening of mother-child attachment in infants placed in day-care programs as early as three months of age. It is suggested, however, that an infant under 15 months of age, because of his particular attachment needs, may require one "special person" to care for him. Fowler (1972) in describing a day-care program reports "that children entering the program before six to eight months of age socialized and adapted more easily" than infants entering at later ages. He suggests that the older infant may have more difficulty adapting not necessarily because of stranger anxiety, but because the older infant has already adapted to his home mileau with which he is familiar. It should be pointed out that the day-care programs mentioned above were designed to include the most favorable conditions for the growth and development of their charges including parent education.

Despite the findings noted above and because substitute care is rarely as excellent as described in the studies, it would seem that if attachment is to develop and if stranger anxiety is not to be exacerbated, the mother should not go to work until the child is 18–24 months of age unless one consistent, warm, and able caretaker is available. In this situation, for the infant to adapt more easily to the surrogate caretaker, it might be more desirable to leave him before he is five or six months old.

The mother should not, of course, start working at the same time that she is trying to wean or toilet train the child or if he is starting school or experiencing other stress.

In summary, it should be emphasized again that the quality of the infant care is more important than whether or not it is the natural parent who provides that care.

References

Beels, C. Christian: The case of the vanishing mommy. *The New York Times Magazine,* July 4, 1976.
Brazelton, T. Berry, in Glickman, Beatrice M. and Springer, Nesha B. (Eds.): *Who Cares for the Baby,* New York, Schocken Books, 1978, p. 16.
Crow, Lester D.: *Psychology of Human Adjustment,* New York, Alfred A. Knopf, 1967.

Fowler, William: Developmental learning approach. *The Merrill-Palmer Quarterly of Behavior and Development*, 1972, **18**(2), 145–175.

Glickman, B. M. and Springer, N. B.: *Who Cares for the Baby*, New York, Schocken Books, 1978.

Gray, N. T.: Family planning in the 1970s: A dynamic force affecting the status of children, in Williams, G. J. and Gordon, S. (Eds.): *Clinical Child Psychology Current Practices and Future Perspectives*, New York, Behavioral Publications, 1974.

Hecht, Kathryn A.: A description of employed mothers and their children in school: An analysis of selected data from the 1970 survey of compensatory education. Paper presented to American Psychological Association, 1972 (Sept).

Honig, Alice S.: Infant development projects: Problems in intervention, in Williams, Gertrude J. and Gordon, Sol (Eds.): *Clinical Child Psychology: Current Practices and Future Perspectives*, New York, Behavioral Publications, 1972.

Horney, K.: *Neurotic Personality of Our Time*, New York, W. W. Norton and Co., 1937.

Horton, Margaret M.: Liberated Women—Liberated Children in Williams, Gertrude J. and Gordon, Sol (Eds.): *Clinical Child Psychology: Current Practices and Future Perspectives*, New York, Behavioral Publications, 1974.

Hurley, J. R.: Parental acceptance—rejection and children's intelligence, in Medinnus, G. R. (Ed.): *Readings in the Psychology of Parent-Child Relations*, New York, John Wiley & Sons, Inc., 1967.

Ingram, G. L.: Families in crisis, in Hardy, R. E. and Cull, J. G. (Eds.): *Therapeutic Needs of the Family*, Springfield, Ill., Charles C. Thomas, 1974.

Kessler, Jane W.: *Psychopathology of Childhood*, Englewood Cliffs, N.J., Prentice-Hall, Inc., 1966.

Larsen, V. L., Evans, T., Brodsack, J., Harmon, J., and Martin, L.: Prediction of early postpartum adjustment. *Am J Orthopsychiatry*, 1967, **37**(2), 397–398.

Lindgren, H. C.: *Psychology of Personal Development*, New York, American Book Co., 1969.

Meiselman, Karin C.: *Incest*, San Francisco, Jossey-Bass, 1978.

Pickett, R. S.: Children and fathers, in Williams, G. J. and Gordon, S. (Eds.): *Clinical Child Psychology: Current Practices and Future Perspectives*, New York, Behavioral Publications, 1974.

Rubenstein, Judith L., Pederson, Frank A., and Yarrow, Leon J.: What happens when mother is away: A comparison of mothers and substitute caregivers. *Developmental Psychology*, 1977, **13**(5), 529–530.

Thomas, A., Chess, S., and Birch, H. G.: *Temperament and Behavior Disorders in Children*, New York, New York University Press, 1968.

Verville, Elinor: *Behavior Problems of Children*, Philadelphia, W. B. Saunders, Co., 1967.

Yarrow, Leon J., in *Annual Review*, 1962.

CHAPTER 2

Birth to Six Months

Birth and Attachment

Most authors agree that interference with initial mother-infant attachment may retard or distort normal development (Ainsworth, 1962; Bowlby, 1969). Klaus and Kennell (1976) summarize the importance of the initial attachment: "this original mother-infant bond is the wellspring for all the infant's subsequent attachments and is the formative relationship in the course of which the child develops a sense of himself. Throughout his life the strength and character of this attachment will influence the quality of all future bonds to other individuals."

Hormonal changes prior to delivery may affect bonding. MacKinnon and Stern (1977) found that in rats an increase in estrogen and withdrawal of progesterone in late pregnancy heighten "maternal responsiveness." Although at present there are no hard data to prove that this same phenomenon occurs in humans, there are many indications to suggest that immediately after birth there is a "critical period" (Salk, 1973) or, as Bowlby (1969) terms it, a "sensitive period" when the mother's response to her infant seems to be stimulated when she holds the infant.

Bowlby (1969) and Klaus and Kennell (1976) suggest that close contact with the infant is crucial during the first hours or, preferably, minutes, following the child's birth. The "critical period" theory implies that if bonding does not occur within a few hours after birth, a degree of maternal responsiveness may be permanently lost. In addition to the importance of immediate contact with the infant, the following behaviors appear to stimulate bonding: looking directly at the infant and talking, smiling, cuddling, and kissing him. Bowlby suggests that by holding him close to her body in a "ventro-ventral position," the mother orients the child "more precisely to her." Klaus and Kennell emphasize the importance of rooming-in and of including the father in the bonding process. They suggest leaving the parents and the infant together for awhile immediately after birth. Some women who have children at home object to rooming-in. They report that the hospital stay temporarily frees them from child care and that rooming-in would interfere with that respite.

"High-risk" infants—premature infants, infants with congenital malformations, infants delivered by Caesarian section, and infants born of diabetic mothers or mothers who are psychologically disturbed—present special problems in relation to attachment. Klaus and Kennell (1976) suggest that if it is known during pregnancy that a mother may have difficulty relating to her infant either because of medical problems or psychological problems, the obstetrician should consult the pediatrician early so that the mother can obtain some anticipatory guidance. They suggest that the obstetrician and the pediatrician together see both parents prenatally to obtain information and to elicit from the parents some of their concerns. The authors suggest that bonding begins prenatally but that it is fragile at that time and, if interrupted following delivery, may not be easily resumed.

Because it is usually necessary to separate the small premature from his parents, bonding becomes difficult following these births. If the parents cannot care for their infant because the infant is too small or too sick, the bonding process may be stimulated if they can be brought into the nursery as soon as possible and as often as possible to look at and touch the child. In instances where the infant must be transferred to another institution, a snapshot which can be developed and printed immediately may be helpful. They further suggest that since, even under these circumstances, the parents cannot have as much contact with their infant as do parents of a full-term infant, they should be encouraged to visit often after the mother leaves the hospital so that they can handle their baby as much as possible and help in his care. The authors emphasize the importance of making the parents aware of the special care which their infant may require and the importance of explaining how their child may be different than a full-term baby.

Klaus and Kennell (1976) suggest that infants with congenital malformations be brought to the mother frequently so that she may begin to focus on the child's normal features and thereby adjust to the child's malformations more easily. The authors point out that parents of malformed babies, particularly mothers, tend to exhibit signs of mourning and that their grief reaction may interfere with their acceptance of an imperfect baby. They caution against the tendency of medical personnel, because of their own guilt or because they are reluctant to face the parents' distress, to delay bringing the infant to the mother, to bring the infant in to the mother infrequently, and sometimes to transfer the infant quickly to another facility.

The effect of maternal neuroses or psychoses on maternal-infant bonding is twofold. According to Zax, *et al.* (1977) in their paper, "Birth outcomes in the offsprings of mentally disordered women," there are more perinatal deaths, lower APGAR scores at 1 and 5 minutes, greater need for resuscitation, and more premature births in infants of mentally ill women. Thus, attachment for these reasons alone may be difficult. In addition, it can be assumed that a psychologically disturbed mother is likely to have more difficulty forming an attachment to her infant.

Mothers of these high-risk infants need specific directions for care of their babies at home. The pediatrician should be alert to signs that the parents are overprotecting their infant, such signs as oversolicitousness, hovering over the infant, having him sleep in the parents' bedroom, excessively regimented management, the rare use of baby sitters, and general overconcern and anxiety over the infant's well-being.

There are infants, without obvious physical problems, whose temperaments are such that they can be considered "at risk." Studies by Thomas, Chess, and Birch (1968, 1970) reveal that children who manifest certain characteristics of temperament are more likely to develop "behavioral and developmental disorders" than children who do not have these characteristics. According to the authors, these individual traits can be seen in the first weeks of life and are apparently not dependent on the quality or quantity of handling or on the parents' personality. These infants seem to be difficult to handle almost from birth; the authors describe them as being "irregular in body functions, and usually intense in their reactions." In general they are irritable infants who tend to cry a great deal. The authors describe as also "at risk" infants who are "slow to warm up." These infants have an unusually low activity level and have in common with the "irritable" infant difficulty in adapting to new stimuli. Anticipatory counseling for parents of these infants make the difference between those infants who will develop psychologic disorders and those who will not.

Both of these kinds of infants seem to require more patience, consistency, and regularity of management than do infants described by Thomas *et al.* (1968) as "easy children." The authors suggest that the pediatrician be aware of the infant's temperament so that he can give the parents of "difficult" infants specific advice. (See sections on "the irritable baby," "crying," and "colic.") Anticipatory guidance related to temperament is crucial because the child's temperament tends to elicit a particular kind of parenting behavior which, in turn, effects the infant's response (Dibble, *et al.*, 1974). Broussard (1976) suggests that the newborn's "innate genetic characteristics" lead the mother to anticipate certain behaviors, an anticipation which may be based on certain misperceptions and which, if not corrected, may "become a self-fulfilling prophecy." Immediate intervention may prevent later problems.

If interference with initial maternal bonding is perceived as early maternal deprivation, infants who have not been able to form this original attachment may have difficulty forming close attachments later in life (Bowlby, 1978; Klaus and Kennell, 1976). Even if present conditions in obstetrical wards do not lend themselves to the development of immediate bonding, it may be beneficial to make the mother aware of how she can, by engaging in those maternal behaviors which stimulate bonding—looking directly at the infant, talking, smiling, cuddling, and kissing him—strengthen the bond between herself and her infant.

References

Ainsworth, Mary D.: Ganda study, in *Patterns of Attachment Behavior Shown by the Infant in Interaction with His Mother, The Merrill-Palmer Quarterly,* 1964, **10,** 15–16.

Bowlby, John: *Maternal Care and Mental Health,* World Health Organization, 1951, pp. 30–36.

Bowlby, John: *Attachment: Attachment and Loss, Vol. 1,* Penguin Books, England, 1969.

Bronfrenbrenner, Urie: *Two Worlds of Childhood, U.S. and U.S.S.R.,* Russell Sage Foundation, New York, 1970.

Broussard, Elsie R.: Neonatal prediction and outcome at 10/11 years. *Child Psychiatry and Human Development,* 1976, **7**(2), 85–93.

Dibble, Eleanor and Cohen, Donald J.: Companion instruments for measuring children's competence and parental style. *Arch Gen Psychiatry,* 1974, **30,** 805–815.

Hansen, Eva and Bjerre, Ingrid: Mother-child relationship in low birthweight groups. *Child Care, Health & Development,* 1977, **3**(2), 93–103.

Kendler, Howard H.: *Basic Psychology,* 2nd ed., Appleton-Century-Crofts, New York, 1968.

Klaus, Marshall H. and Fanaroff, Avroy, A.: *Care of the High-Risk Neonate,* W. B. Saunders Co., Philadelphia, 1973.

Klaus, Marshall H. and Kennell, John H.: *Maternal-Infant Bonding,* C. V. Mosby Co., St. Louis, 1976.

MacKinnon, Diane A. and Stern, Judith M.: Pregnancy duration and fetal number: Effects on maternal behavior in rats. *Physiology & Behavior,* 1977, **18**(5), 793–797.

Salk, Lee: The role of the heartbeat in the relations between mother and infant. *Scientific American,* May 1973.

Thomas, Alexander, Chess, Stella, and Birch, Herbert G.: *Temperament and Behavior Disorders in Children,* New York University Press, New York, 1968.

Thomas, Alexander, Chess, Stella, and Birch, Herbert G.: The origin of personality. *Scientific American,* August 1970.

Zax, Melvin, Sameroff, Arnold J., and Babigian, Haroutun M.: Birth outcomes in the offspring of mentally disordered women. *Am J Orthopsychiatry,* 1977, **47**(2), 218–229.

CHAPTER **3**

The Newborn at Home

Sibling Rivalry

It has been noted previously that, to be most effective, anticipatory guidance should begin before the infant's birth. Unfortunately, this does not usually occur except in instances where the pediatrician is already caring for a child or children of parents who are planning to have another child. In these situations, the parents can benefit from suggestions for minimizing the sibling jealousy which is almost certain to occur.

Spacing of Children

There are no hard data which can be used as a basis for advising parents on how to space their children in order to minimize sibling rivalry. Empirical evidence reveals, however, that where the age difference is small (one to one and one-half years) there is little sibling jealousy at the time of the new infant's birth and for about eight or nine months following the birth. But as the new infant becomes more mobile, sibling jealousy is likely to increase. Although the increase also occurs when the age difference is greater, the jealousy tends to be more intense when children are so close in age that their needs and desires are similar. The nine-month-old and the 20-month-old, being still very dependent on the mother, are more likely to compete for her attention than are the nine-month-old and the four-year-old. When the age difference is small, age-appropriate toys and activities also tend to be similar.

When the age difference is large (four or five years), there appears to be relatively little sibling jealousy probably because the four- or five-year-old who has developed normally is relatively independent of the mother physically and socially, and his interests, toys, and activities are outside the younger child's capabilities. In situations where the

17

older child has not been encouraged to be independent, he may perceive the new infant as an intruder, and sibling rivalry can be intensified.

The three-year-old, following the birth of a sibling, is more likely to
show signs of regression than children at other ages. The following
possible reasons for this have been suggested: (1) The three-year-old, in
contrast to the two-year-old, for instance, tends to be more cognitively
aware of the possible consequences of new situations and, thus, may be
more aware of being displaced. (2) The three-year-old tends to be less
active and more contemplative than he was at age two, possibly resulting in some anxiety over the new family structure. (3) The three-year-
old is on the verge of mastering certain skills such as dressing himself,
remaining dry at night, and playing with peers, all implying some
independence from the parents. Because these skills are not yet
stabilized, it is possible that the stress of a new sibling in the home can
be a source of regression. The immature behavior may then be reinforced by either positive or negative attention. Imitation of the infant
sibling behavior which the older child may perceive as the basis for
parental attention may also be a factor in the older child's regressive
behavior.

Although an age difference of four or five years appears to result in a
reduction of sibling rivalry, parents report that they do not want to
spend so many years raising children. Thus, if the small age differences intensify sibling rivalry, if large age differences are impractical,
and if a difference of three years can result in regressive behavior on
the part of the older child, it appears that a two-year difference may be
the most practical. A two-year-old, although still dependent on his
mother, tends to be actively engaged in exploring his environment and
his interest in the newborn tends to be casual and cursory. Self-care
skills and peer relationships have not yet begun to develop to the point
where regression is likely to be a factor. By the time a new sibling is
mobile, the older child's interests in activities are inappropriate for the
younger child, thus minimizing competition. And yet, the two-year age
difference is small enough to allow for some sibling companionship.

Preparing the Child for the Birth of a Sibling

Because the preschool child's conception of time is faulty (Helms and
Turner, 1976), if he is told about the coming birth too soon, he may
become frustrated and even distrustful when the promised event does
not materialize. Also frustrating to the child may be the disappointment he experiences when the actual birth belies the enthusiastic but
unrealistic picture painted for the child of the joys of having a new

sibling. The preschool child, unless he himself notices his mother's physical change or inadvertently overhears conversations concerning the coming birth and asks about it, may be less concerned if he is told toward the end of the pregnancy and if the information is given casually. Preparing the child for some of the negative realities of having a sibling may minimize the child's frustration and resentment (Helms and Turner, 1976; Rohwer, *et al.*, 1974).

Following are suggestions which, if carried out as soon as the newborn is brought home, can minimize sibling jealousy. The suggestions are relevant only where the older child is age five or under.

1. Mothers report that when they first come home from the hospital, their primary concern is getting themselves and the infant settled, and they are, thus, unable to attend to the older child. Since the older child has been withouthis mother and, in some cases, without his father for several days, and perhaps for the first time, it is important that he receives some undivided attention from the parents when he does see them. For that reason, it might be better if he were not at home when the parents and the newborn arrive from the hospital. If it is not possible to leave the child with others, the parents could arrange to have someone come into the home to attend exclusively to one of the children, preferably to the infant.

2. Crucial to minimizing sibling jealousy is the need of the older child for regular, predictable undivided attention from the parents (Mussen, *et al.*, 1956). He is less likely to demand attention; he is less likely to cling to the parents and to behave in an infantile manner if he knows with some certainty that he will have some time alone with one or both parents.

3. Most authors agree that the child who is encouraged to verbalize his feelings is able to more easily accept a stressful situation and is less likely to "act-out" his feelings (Kessler, 1966; Ellis, 1974; Fagen, *et al.*, 1975; Dreikurs and Grey, 1968). Parents can encourage the child who has difficulty verbalizing his jealousy by:

   a. Verbally expressing dismay or annoyance with the infant in front of the older child. Parents report that when they have done this, this older child tends to express his own negative thoughts concerning his sibling. It is as though he has been given permission, albeit implicit, to experience feelings of jealousy and to express them.

   b. Permitting the older child to help with the care of the infant as well as by granting him special privileges, pointing out in both instances that it is because he is older that he is given these responsibilities and privileges.

c. Taking care that where `possible such stressful procedures as weaning, toilet training, and the child's first separation from mother do not coincide with the arrival of the new baby. It is frequently the sum of a number of stresses, rather than a single stressful situation which can cause problems.

Colic

Brazelton (1962) cites studies which show that most infants have natural daily crying periods, unrelated to any apparent physical problem. It has been suggested that this regular crying serves to release built-up tensions caused by "normal" stimuli impinging on the newborn. It has also been suggested that after the infant arrives home, tensions in the home can intensify the normal crying which can, in turn, be a factor in the development of colic. One source of tension to which the infant may react is that generated by the parent's tendency to view their infant's crying as evidence of their ineffective parenting (Mussen, 1956; Kessler, 1966).

There are newborns who are thought by some (Verville, 1967; Kessler, 1966) to be colicky because they are overresponsive to stimuli. These infants apparently cry for long periods, appear to overreact to ordinary environmental stimuli, and do not respond readily to the usual comforting techniques (see "irritability" below). Brazelton (1962), in discussing some of the factors in the development of colic, found that the presence of the maternal grandmother in the home appeared to add to environmental tension already present. This was due to the grandmother's own helplessness in alleviating the crying, thus reinforcing the parents' concern over the frequent crying. Anxiety and feelings of helplessness over the colic may, in turn, create further tension, to which the infant may then respond with continued distress.

Sumpter (1975) suggests that if parents are told that their feelings of frustration, inadequacy, and ineffectiveness are acceptable feelings, they are less likely to feel guilty. Caplan (1961) suggests that persistent colic during the first few months, when perceptual abilities are developing, may interfere with later ego functioning. The infant who remains distressed for long periods may begin to see the world as hostile and as not meeting his needs. Mussen *et al.* (1956) warn that although there is evidence indicating that maternal tension and anxiety, as well as general tension in the home, are factors in the development of colic, there are large numbers of cases of colic that are not clearly related to these factors. The newborn who tends to be overresponsive and/or irritable, may, as Verville (1967) suggests, cause the mother to feel helpless and incompetent, which, in turn, may then be a

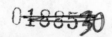

factor in the development of colic. Sumpter (1975) suggests that colicky infants should not be overstimulated. These infants are likely to feel more secure if they are held closely, walked with quietly, and rocked gently.

If the parents have been reassured of the benign quality of the problem and if they have been given some practical advice for handling the problem, they may be amenable to answering questions concerning possible tension-producing conflicts in the home. If they are asked these kinds of questions first, they may feel that they are being blamed for the problem and may become defensive and resistant. Frequently, the parents' awareness of the effects of tension-producing conflicts is enough to motivate them to solve the problem. Where this does not occur spontaneously, they should be urged to seek help.

Sometimes tension is caused by the mother's unconscious rejection of the infant, a rejection which she denies by being overprotective (Kessler, 1966). She may watch over the infant constantly, have excessive contact with him, and be inappropriately and excessively concerned for his well-being even after she has been reassured that the infant is in good health. Where marital conflict is a problem, the overprotective behavior may, instead of indicating her unconscious rejection of the child, represent her attempt to fulfill through the child the emotional needs being frustrated in the marriage. In any case, since overprotection in infancy frequently is continued into childhood, where it can lead to emotional problems, mothers who exhibit this behavior should be referred for intense, long-term psychotherapy.

Spitting Up

Parents report that because of the odor and mess of regurgitated food, spitting up is often offensive and embarrassing to them. Unimportant as this may seem, it can result in subtle expressions of rejection by those who are repelled by the odor and mess. Laupus suggests that, in addition to physical techniques for reducing the frequency of the spitting up, parents handle the infant gently and try to avoid "emotional conflicts." Overfeeding may, in addition to causing regurgitation, create tensions between parent and infant and may, in addition, lead to later eating problems.

Irritability

Kagen and Havemann (1968) described irritable infants as those who "begin to fret, whine, or cry at the slightest provocation, while others do not show this kind of behavior unless their discomfort or pain is quite intense." They further state that these infants, "once they have begun to fret, seem to work themselves up into what looks like a temper tantrum and soon are bellowing at the top of their lungs." Thomas, *et al.* (1968), in their discussion of temperament, find that "difficult children" slept more irregularly, seemed to need less sleep, awakened two or three times a night, had, in general, irregular biological patterns, cried loudly when confronted with new stimuli, cried frequently, and in general reacted intensely. In their longitudinal study, they found that these children later evidenced more behavior problems than did children who did not manifest these symptoms.

Parents who report that their child was an irritable infant describe him as a baby who (1) cried a great deal apparently for no reason, (2) seemed to overreact to loud noises, extremes of temperature, and soiled and wet diapers, and (3) slept little, lightly, and fitfully. These parents report that they had no success in comforting the infant and that they vacillated between feeling that there was something wrong with the infant and feeling that the fault lay in their parental inadequacies. Thomas, *et al.* (1968) found in their studies that parents of these difficult children did not differ from those of "easy children" but that, as the difficult child grew older, the parents appeared to react negatively and at those older ages these parents did differ from other parents. They found that often the mother of a difficult infant began to develop "self-doubts and feelings of guilt, anxiety, and helplessness." Following are suggestions for handling the irritable infant:

1. Stimulation. In contrast to the usual recommendation that parents stimulate their infant, parents of these infants are advised to reduce stimulation. Caplan (1961) suggests that infants be stimulated according to the amounts that they can tolerate. Brazelton, *et al.* (1973), in their discussion of the infant's rhythm and the mother's adjustment to this rhythm, found that the tense, overresponsive infant whose mother increased her stimulation of the infant reacted by withdrawal as if this reaction was necessary for the maintenance of "physiologic and psychologic homeostasis." The authors suggest that parents should be aware of the infant's capacity to "receive and utilize stimuli." It is not implied that parents deprive the infant of stimulation, only that, for these irritable infants, stimulation be confined to the normal handling and vocalization engaged in while the infant is being fed, diapered, and bathed. These infants appear to be able to tolerate increased stimulation without extreme overreaction if, for the first four or five months, they develop in a relatively quiet, calm environment.

Stimulation may not be unidimensional. In addition to stimulation

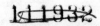

resulting from the noise generated by normal household activities, there is that which accompanies routine care of the infant, such as bathing, feeding, and diapering. There is evidence that the infant's social and emotional development is enhanced when the caretaker talks to and plays with the infant while attending to his physical needs (Klaus and Kennell, 1976; Kessler, 1966; Weisberg, 1963; Brazelton, *et al.*, 1973). As noted above, the irritable infant can tolerate this latter kind of stimulation if it is not intense or too exciting. Multishaped and multicolored mobiles over the crib and playpen are included in the category of quiet stimulation.

It is a second type of stimulation, that which results from disorganized and chaotic activity, which tends to increase irritability. Loud arguing, aimless running around by other children, and continuous high noise levels can result in behaviors which may be construed as defensive. Some withdrawal symptoms, rocking, and head banging are behaviors which may relieve tension in the irritable infant and young child. Because rocking and head banging were frequently found in children from disadvantaged homes, it was assumed that the symptoms were due to stimulus deprivation. Clinical experience with children exhibiting these same symptoms whose parents were, in fact, stimulating their infants made it necessary to revise the previous assumption. Empirical evidence revealed that in the homes where parents stimulated their infants by talking and playing with them and in the homes where parents did not stimulate their infants there was one common factor, namely, the infants in both of these homes were constantly exposed to a disorganized and chaotic environment. These findings are not definitive, and it is possible that the behaviors are multidetermined and a function of temperament as well as random stimulation. Thus, the irritable infant may respond with these behaviors because of overstimulation and/or chaotic stimulation. As was noted by Brazelton, *et al.* (1973), when these infants withdraw, it is as though they are withdrawing from excessive stimulation; when they rock, it is as though they are trying to comfort themselves. The rational for the head banging is not as clear. It is not unreasonable, however, to speculate that this could be a response to frustration.

2. Structure and routine. When, in the clinic, parents of rocking and head banging infants who also stimulate their infants appropriately are questioned about their disorganized households, they tend to defend the lack of organization by expressing their belief that structure and routine are inhibiting and will interfere with the child's creativity, spontaneity, and freedom of expression.

Studies reveal that children of all ages tend to feel more secure and can more easily organize their resources for constructive use in a stable, predictable environment (Thomas, *et al.*, 1968; Klaus and Kennell, 1976). Although the average infant will probably not be seriously hurt by lack of structure, the irritable infant who often appears to be fearful and insecure needs the security that accompanies predictability of structure and routine. Ideally, the infant's environment is, at first, highly structured and then gradually less structured as he seems able to tolerate greater flexibility. When mothers of irritable infants who cry frequently followed the recommendation to use a modified demand feeding schedule rather than feeding on demand they reported that the infant seemed to cry less. Some predictability is involved without the inflexibility of a rigid schedule. It might be added that since feeding on demand means that the parent can only start preparing the food after the infant starts to cry, the delay can be frustrating to an already irritable infant. Modified demand has built into it an approximate schedule so that the food can be ready as soon as the infant signals his hunger. Another advantage is that parents can plan their activities without fear of undue interference. Kessler (1966) cites a study in which it was found that "feeding the baby when he was hungry rather than on a schedule was poorly related to the satisfaction of either the mother or the infant." And Brody (1961) illustrates how, in a family whose routine was disrupted by demand feeding, there was less harassment and resentment toward the infant, after the parents were advised to use a modified demand schedule.

Parent counselors report that when parents have followed suggestions for imposing a sleep routine on their irritable infants, they are able to modify the infants' sleep habits so that they coincide more closely to those of the other family members. Keeping the infant awake during the day with quiet stimulation, without disturbing the total amount of sleep he requires, permits the spacing of his daytime sleeping so that he is awake in the afternoon and drowsy at night. This appears to ease the transition from daytime sleeping and night wakefulness to longer periods of night sleeping. When the infant cries during the night after he has had his night feeding or after he is no longer given a night feeding, he is more likely to fall back to sleep quickly and to sleep through subsequent nights if he is left to cry to see if he will fall asleep again by himself (Brody, 1961).

3. Picking up the irritable infant during the day. Although infants tend to become quiet and relaxed if they are picked up, rocked, and comforted when they cry (Freedman, 1971; Mussen, *et al.*, 1956), many irritable infants, when they start crying, often without apparent cause, appear to "work themselves up" to what resembles hysteria (Kagen and Havemann, 1968). The mother of this kind of infant may feel

guilty when, despite all her efforts to comfort the infant, he continues to cry.

4. Relief of parental stress. Caring for an irritable infant is frustrating, anxiety-producing, and fatiguing even when the parents are following suggestions for reducing the infant's irritability. Thomas, *et al.* (1968) found in their study of "difficult children" that parents of these children obtain relief by going out either together or by each parent relieving the other parent while one of them goes out, particularly during those periods in the day when the infant is most demanding. Some mothers, instead of going out, have hired someone or asked a relative to come in to care for the infant while she rests, or just attends to some of her own grooming needs. If the parents do not seek some relief, feelings of anger, guilt over the anger, and self-pity may interfere with the parent-child relationship.

Thumb Sucking

Why infants suck their thumbs in the first place is not clear. There are, essentially, three basic theories: (1) Thumb sucking is related to nutritional sucking; (2) thumb sucking is a means of reducing tension; (3) thumb sucking is unrelated to nutritional sucking although it may indeed reduce tension, but it is not initiated because the tension is present. Levy (1934) found that infants who spent less time sucking the breast or the bottle, tended to do more nonnutritional sucking than did infants who spent more time in nutritional sucking. Ribble (1944) noted that there was no "marked" thumb sucking in those infants who were not limited in the amount of nutritional sucking they were permitted. Sears and Wise (1950) found, however, that the earlier the infant was weaned, the less nonnutritional sucking he seemed to do. Their definition of late weaning was defined as that taking place after three months of age, and some of the infants studied had been put on a cup from birth and yet did not suck their thumbs. Both findings, although appearing to contradict each other, could be valid if the relationship between nonnutritional and nutritional sucking is viewed as a curvilinear relationship. That is, both too little and too much sucking can result in nonnutritional sucking. Freud viewed both nutritional sucking and nonnutritional sucking as oral activities which were gratifying, implying that the latter was a generalization of the former. He would not have been surprised that infants fed from cups at birth would not then suck their thumbs.

A number of authors imply that an infant sucks his thumb because he is tense and insecure (Kessler, 1966; Bowlby, 1971; Spock, 1957).

Brazelton (1967) believes that infants and children engage in nonnu-tritional sucking just because they enjoy it and that it does not neces-sarily indicate an abnormal amount of stress or insecurity. He does not believe it is necessary to even discuss the "reduction of tension" in relationship to the sucking. Several of the authors cited above also discuss thumb sucking as being pleasurable and gratifying but relate it to relaxation and relief of tension. Flavell (1963) in summarizing Piaget's view says that, initially and for a very short period, the infant will suck his hand if it inadvertently reaches his mouth or if someone puts his hand to his mouth. As he matures, he can keep his hand to his mouth longer and then by the time he is three or four months old he is able to bring his hand to his mouth deliberately. He may then continue to suck his thumb if he does find that it is pleasurable and maybe even tension reducing. But he does not, initially, "consciously," seek out his thumb to suck because he is upset or feels insecure. Although Spock in 1945 suggested that children suck their thumbs because of need, he later modified this to some extent by suggesting that the habit is main-tained because it becomes a habit and not because the child continues to feel insecure.

Kessler (1966), in addressing herself to the question of why some children suck their thumbs and some do not, suggests that thumb sucking may be only one infantile behavior in a generally immature child. These immature children also tend to have difficulty tolerating frustration, are inappropriately dependent, have not internalized con-trol, are irresponsible, and tend to seek gratifications in a manner which is more appropriate to a younger child. Kessler states that one need not be concerned about thumb sucking until after the child is two or two and one-half years of age. It should be noted, however, that since it does tend to become a habit which is not easy to break, and since, when continued beyond the age when society considers it appropriate, it has an effect on the child's self image, efforts to prevent thumb sucking may make sense.

It can be argued that, of all the means for comforting the infant, thumb sucking is the only one over which the caretaker has virtually no control. This means that when parents, in order to foster the child's psychological maturity and the development of independence, want to gradually eliminate some of their own comfort-producing practices as they become age inappropriate, they can do so because they can control the instruments through which the child derives the comfort. They do not have this control over thumb sucking.

It is possible that the infant who derives comfort from sucking his thumb, because he is quiet, may be handled less than an infant who derives his comfort primarily from handling and body contact. Thus, thumb sucking may mask the infant's need for parental attention and stimulation. And because thumb sucking, if not relinquished prior to the eruption of the permanent teeth, can result in dental problems, he should by the time he is four years old, be encouraged to break the habit (Verville, 1967).

If the young child is not engaging in age-appropriate activities, tends to be withdrawn, does a great deal of day dreaming, spends much of his time sucking his thumb, almost as if this were a substitute for other gratifications, and if the thumb sucking is not one of a constellation of symptoms suggesting immaturity, he may be an anxious child who needs help. Since it may not be practical and perhaps not even desirable to feed newborns from a cup, if the goal is to try to prevent thumb sucking, permitting the infant to suck long and hard during feedings so that he is literally too tired to suck between feedings has, when this advice has been carried out by parents, been successful. This means that the person feeding the infant must be patient and unhurried. The caretaker can also try to distract the infant when he is seen to bring his thumb to his mouth. Parents who feel that the infant benefits from sucking his thumb can be reassured that children usually give up the habit themselves without any lasting effects (Brazelton, 1967).

As Verville (1967) suggests, pacifiers have one advantage over thumb sucking. The child's use of the pacifier is controlled by another, and it can be gradually removed when it is felt that the habit should be broken. It is suggested that the habit can be given up more readily if the pacifier is not always available to the child. For instance, Verville suggests that it not be removed from the home. It should be noted that, as with thumb sucking, it may mask the infant's need for physical care, attention, and stimulation. And like thumb sucking, when use of the pacifier continues beyond the age when it is considered appropriate, the child may be perceived as immature and may as a result develop a poor self image.

Crying

As noted during the discussion of colic, infants typically cry several hours a day possibly because it reduces tension from almost continuous stimuli impinging on the infant (Brazelton, 1962). In his study of 80 mothers Brazelton found that during the second week of birth, the first week at home, the median of crying was one and three-quarters hours in a 24-hour period. The maximum number of crying hours occurred at about six weeks when the median was two and three-quarter hours, and then the amount of crying time gradually decreased except in those infants who were called "heavy fussers" who cried as much as four hours at six weeks of age. When the infant was under the age of six weeks, he tended to cry mostly between the hours of six and eleven p.m. (Brazelton suggests that this is because father is home, mother is tired and the siblings are home). At six weeks of age the peak crying hours tended to be from three to twelve P.M. and at ten weeks of age from six to twelve P.M. and five to eleven P.M. Brazelton suggests that parents be reassured that normally infants do this much crying.

Moss (1967) sees the cry as a signal for mother to respond and argues that mother's behavior depends on the infant's state and "activity level," often expressed by crying. Brazelton, *et al.* (1973) in their paper on reciprocity suggest that the mother who is sensitive to the infant's needs and responds to those needs has an infant who is more responsive. They believe that the infant's needs must "shape the mother first." Moss suggests that when the mother responds to the infant first, because he will, in turn, respond to her, she can then later be the one to shape his behavior.

Most of the authors agree that holding and rocking the crying infant will result in a cessation of the crying. Brackbill and Thompson (1967), and Brackbill (1971) found that swaddling was also effective in stopping the infant's crying. Aaronson (1978) found that infants who were swaddled slept more and cried less. She also found that swaddling tended to quiet "irritable" infants. It is often crucial to find a means of quieting the "irritable" infant. Persistent crying can create in the mother feelings of helplessness, guilt, and inadequacy and, in her attempt to compensate for these feelings, she may overstimulate the child which can result in greater stress (Brazelton, 1962; Moss, 1967; Kagan, 1966; Verville, 1967).

Moss (1967) found that mothers tend to respond more quickly to the crying of their female infants than to the crying of their male infants. When asked about this, they justified their behavior by noting that boys need to be tough. On the other hand, they tended to hold their boy infants longer because the boys were more "cuddly." Since these differential maternal behaviors are important to the children's later relationship to others, alerting parents to this tendency may prevent later problems.

Unless nighttime crying is excessive, it usually does not become a problem until the child is about six months old. Parents tend to become more upset when the infant cries at night than when the older child cries probably because they cannot interpret the infant's crying and are fearful, for instance, that the infant might be ill (Sumpter, 1975). Brackbill and Thompson (1967) found that swaddling not only reduced crying but promoted sleep. Before the age of about five or six months after which some secondary gains may be obtained from the crying (see following chapter), most infants will respond to being held for short periods and/or to being rocked.

When one considers that the immediate cause of infant abuse is frequently the infant's persistent crying which parents cannot handle effectively, reducing the intensity and frequency of crying beyond normal limits can be critical (Brackbill, 1971). In addition, it is reasonable to expect that infants who are comforted when they cry are more likely to develop basic trust which is a necessary ingredient of mental health (Erikson, 1950). Infants who learn that they can look to others for comfort when they are distressed are apt to have more satisfactory relationships with others later (Kagen and Havemann, 1968). Aaronson (1978) points out that if the infant's needs are satisfied after his cry signals the caretaker that he is in need, he will feel some confidence that he can exercise some control over his environment and he will not continue to feel helpless.

One last word about mothering and parent-infant interactions in general: Some mothers feel guilty when for some reason they are not able to spend a great deal of time with their infants. Since the guilt itself can create problems, they should be reassured that, in general, it is the quality of mothering and not the quantity that is important to the parent-child relationship. There must be enough time to permit quality interactions but if a choice must be made, the quality of the interaction is the important ingredient.

References

Aaronson, May: *Child Welfare,* 1978 (Mar.), **57**(2).

Bowlby, John: *Attachment and Loss, Vol. 1: Attachment,* England, Penguin Books Ltd., 1971.

Brackbill, Yvonne: Cumulative effects of continuous stimulation on arousal level in infants. *Child Development,* 1971, **42,** 17–26.

Brackbill, Yvonne, and Thompson, George G.: *Behavior in Infancy and Early Childhood,* New York, The Free Press, 1967.

Brazelton, T. Berry: Crying in infancy. *Pediatrics,* 1962 (Apr.), 579–588.

Brazelton, T. Berry: Sucking in infancy, in Yvonne Brackbill and George G. Thompson (Eds.): *Behavior in Infancy and Early Childhood,* New York, The Free Press, 1967.

Brazelton, T. Berry; Koslowski, Barbara, and Main, Mary: The origins of reciprocity, in M. Lewis and L. Rosenblum (Eds.): *Origins of Behavior,* New York, Wiley, 1973, Vol. 1.

Brody, Sylvia: Preventing intervention in current problems of early childhood, in Gerald Caplan (Ed.): *Prevention of Mental Disorders in Children,* New York, Basic Books, Inc., 1961.

Caplan, Gerald: *Prevention of Mental Disorders in Children,* New York, Basic Books, Inc., 1961.

Dreikurs, Rudolf and Grey, Loren: *Logical Consequences: A Handbook of Discipline,* New York, Meredith Press, 1968.

Ellis, Albert: Emotional education in the classroom: The living school, in G. J. Williams and S. Gordon (Eds.): *Clinical Child Psychology,* New York, Behavioral Publications, 1974.

Erikson, Eric H.: *Childhood and Society,* New York, Norton, 1950.

Fagen, S. A., Long, N. J., and Stevens, D. J.: *Teaching Children Self-Control,* Columbus, Ohio, Charles E. Merrill Publishing Co., 1975.

Flavell, John H: *The Developmental Psychology of Jean Piaget,* Princeton, N.J., D. Van Nostrand Co., Inc., 1963.

Freedman, Daniel G.: The impact of behavior genetics and ethology, in Herbert E. Rie (Ed.): *Perspectives in Child Psychopathology,* Chicago, Aldine-Atherton, 1971.

Helms, D. B. and Turner, J. S.: *Exploring Child's Behavior,* Philadelphia, W. B. Saunders Co., 1976.

Honig, Alice S.: Infant development projects: Problems in intervention, in G. J. Williams and S. Gordon (Eds.): *Clinical Child Psychology,* New York, Behavioral Publications, 1974.

Kagan, Jerome: On the need for relativism, Lecture given at Educational Testing Service, Princeton, N.J., January, 1966.

Kagan, Jerome and Havemann, Ernest: *Psychology, An Introduction,* New York, Harcourt, Brace and World, Inc., 1968.

Kessler, Jane W.: *Psychopathology of Childhood,* Englewood Cliffs, N.J., Prentice-Hall, Inc., 1966.

Klaus, Marshall H. and Kennell, John H.: *Maternal-Infant Bonding,* St. Louis, C. V. Mosby Co., 1976.

Levy, D. M.: Experiment of the sucking reflex and social behavior of dogs. *Am J Orthopsychiatry,* 1934, **IV,** 203–24.

Luce, Gay: Hormones in the Development of Behavior, in Julius Segal (Ed.): *The Mental Health of the Child,* Rockville, Md., National Institute of Mental Health, 1971.

Moss, Howard A.: Sex, age, and state as determinants of mother-infant interaction, *Merrill-Palmer Quarterly of Behavior and Development,* 1967, **13**(1), 19–36.

Mussen, P. H., Conger, J. J., and Kagan, J.: *Child Development and Personality,* 3rd ed., New York, Harper and Row, 1956.

Ribble, M.: Infantile experience in relation to personality development, in J.McV. Hunt (Ed.): *Personality and Behavior Disorders,* New York, The Ronald Press Co., 1944.

Rohwer, W. D., Jr., Ammon, P. R., and Cramer, P.: *Understanding Intellectual Development,* Hinsdale, Ill., Dryden Press, 1974.

Sears, R. R. and Wise, G. W.: Relation of cup feeding in infancy to thumb sucking and the oral drive. *American Journal of Orthopsychiatry,* 1950, **20,** 123–139.

Spock, B.: *Baby and Child Care,* New York, Pocket Books, Inc., 1957.

Sumpter, E. A.: Behavior problems in early childhood. *Pediatric Clinics of No. America,* 1975, **22**(3).

Thomas, A., Chess, S., and Birch, H. G.: *Temperament and Behavior Disorders in Children,* New York, New York University Press, 1968.

Verville, Elinor: *Behavior Problems of Children,* Philadelphia, W. B. Saunders Co., 1967.

Weisberg, Paul: Social and Nonsocial conditioning of infant vocalizations, in Yvonne Brackbill and George G. Thompson (Eds.): *Behavior in Infancy and Early Childhood,* New York, The Free Press, 1967.

CHAPTER 4

Six Months to Two Years

It has been suggested that experience during the child's first two years are particularly significant in his succeeding years (Hunt, 1961). More specifically, during the ages of six months to two years, a foundation is being laid for "later intellectual development" (White, 1975). At approximately six months of age, a change in the infant seems to occur, a change which may signal a difference in parent handling. This change may be due to the infant's beginning recognition of himself as an individual. Yahraes (1971) calls this the "separation-individuation" phase, a phase in which the "initial oneness between infant and mother begins to come apart." Bowlby (1971) says that, by this time, the infant begins to perceive contingencies and "knows" what will relieve his discomfort and starts to "plan" his behavior so that these contingencies occur. He says that, although this phase is definitely observable at seven or eight months, in many instances, it can be noted as early as five months. Mothers report that around this age they detect a difference in the infant's cry and some mothers have labeled this new cry as "phony."

This difference in the quality of the infant's cry is relevant to a consideration of the need for children to learn to tolerate frustration and to cope effectively with stress. The part played by early conditioning is crucial to a discussion of frustration tolerance. When the infant "learns" as a result of conditioning that crying will enable him to manipulate his environment, he can gratify his desire to effect his mother's immediate appearance, a desire which may no longer be a function of physical discomfort (Moss, 1967; Millar, 1977, Kagan and Havemann, 1968; Des Lauriers, 1971).

Thomas, *et al.* (1970) suggest that small doses of frustration early in the child's life may make it easier for him to tolerate the necessary stresses of daily life. Animal studies reveal that young animals who were protected from stressful experiences were unable to cope with new situations, while animals who had experiences which were unpleasant were able, as adults, to cope effectively with new situations (Luce, 1971). The author suggests that some stress in infancy may help the infant adjust to stress by a "series of approximations." Verville (1967) emphathizes with parents who want to protect their child from frustration but suggests that it is easier for a child to deal with the stresses of life if he has an opportunity to practice his ability to handle small doses of frustration. Bowlby (1971) feels that after the age of about six months, infants often cry in order to be picked up and that if children are to learn to tolerate frustration it is important that they learn gradually to adapt to stress. None of the authors cited suggest that parents purposely frustrate their infant. They imply, instead, that after the age of about six months, a mother need not immediately interrupt her activity to pick up the crying infant. Moss (1967) suggests that the parent can differentiate between "unlearned" and "learned" crying by noting when the crying stops; if it stops as soon as the mother appears before there has been any holding, rocking, or other stimulation, the crying is probably a learned response.

Sleeping

As has been suggested above, continuing to respond immediately to the crying infant reinforces the crying behavior. This can become a problem in situations where infants and young children are reluctant to go to sleep. Verville (1967) and Sumpter (1975) are specific about the persistence of sleep problems in instances where the parent continues to respond to the child's crying at bedtime. Sumpter suggests that the problems begin at about six to nine months and that parents of these young infants tend to continue to pick up the infants because they are often fearful that the crying signifies distress. Verville is not only concerned that the bedtime problem will continue if the infant is picked up but is concerned that if at the same time attempts are made to amuse him, he will not fall asleep until late and thus be denied of sufficient sleep.

Following are suggestions for preventing and/or minimizing sleep problems:

1. Consistency of bedtimes with changes in the routine gradual and as infrequent as possible.

2. Reading to children after the age of about nine months to a year tends to be relaxing, gives them some undivided attention, and regularizes bedtime. At these early ages the attention span is short enough that five minutes of reading is probably all that the child can

tolerate. From about one to two years, he may be able to attend for ten minutes.

3. Playing the game of peek-a-boo may help in the development of object constancy, the implication being that the child's distress might be reduced as he becomes aware that mother's absence is only temporary (Sumpter, 1975).

4. Verville (1967) suggests that napping is related to bedtime problems. If the afternoon nap time is late so that the nap is prolonged, the child may not be ready for sleep at his regular bedtime.

5. A soft cuddly toy often relaxes the young child enough so that he does not resist going to bed. Bowlby (1971) suggests that the child can give up the mother more easily if he is permitted to attach himself to a substitute cuddly object.

Infants labeled "difficult" by Thomas, et al.—the overreactive, irritable infant who cries a great deal (see previous chapter)—tend to sleep irregularly, to move around frequently while asleep, and to wake up several times during the night. Parents should be told that it is more difficult to develop regular sleeping habits in these children and that it requires more persistence to keep from reinforcing their wakefulness. Going to the child and patting him reassuringly when he wakes during the night is preferable to lying down with him, picking him up, rocking him, or bringing him into the parent's bed. Thomas, et al. also suggest that parents who are made aware very early that their infant fits into this category and that consistent routine is important may be less anxious and less impatient with the child.

Activity Level

Although this topic will be dealt with at greater length later, the recognition that a highly active infant and young child if not handled effectively may have problems later can be crucial to the prevention or, at least, reduction of the seriousness of these problems. Although not documented, there are indications that highly active infants are more likely to be aggressive later (Mussen, et al., 1956). It is suggested that very active infants tend to have a low frustration tolerance, are unable to handle stress effectively, and lack internal controls. These characteristics, which are related to the maintaining of attention, tend to be correlated with the presence of later school problems.

A frequent request from parents is for advice on how to deal with the crawling infant or toddler who is "into everything." Parents seem to know how to handle those situations where the infant can be harmed by what he grabs but are unsure of the degree to which they should restrain the child from touching objects which may not be dangerous per se but which could fall over or be damaged. Parents who choose the option of "baby-proofing" their home are often not aware of the problems this can create if and when they want to take the child to the homes of friends or relatives. Parents report that when they have followed suggestions for teaching the infant not to touch first one object and then gradually other objects, they have been successful in helping the child to internalize controls.

Two additional items related to activity level are relevant: Mothers of irritable infants, especially those who are wakeful and startle easily, report that their infants seem to be stimulated rather than relaxed by their baths. Sleeping problems are reduced when these children are bathed either early in the evening or in the morning, rather than at bedtime. The second situation concerns the very placid infant who rarely cries even when hungry. Wing (1972) suggests that these infants be watched for possible autism. They often do not hold up their arms as a signal that they wish to be picked up, and they seem generally to be uninterested in their environment. Parents are often fearful that these children are retarded; the developmental milestones, however, tend to be normal.

Precursors to Child Abuse

Since the precipitating cause of child abuse is frequently excessive crying, this seems an appropriate place to discuss some of the conditions which can result in child abuse. Wittenberg (1971) suggests the following as frequent antecedents to child abuse: young parents who have their children too quickly; marital conflicts; poverty; a mother who is overwhelmed and lonely; and a baby who was premature or ill in the nursery, the latter due to early separation and failure of "bonding." Bullard, et al. (1967) add to this, those mothers who have difficulty developing a positive relationship with the child and, in the infant, overactivity and colic. Unwanted infants tend to be abused, and parents who themselves have been abused as children tend to abuse their own children. Abusing mothers are often found to be depressed, to have a history of an inability to control their impulses, to have been irritable individuals, and to feel isolated. They are pregnant frequently and react irritably and impulsively to the stress of being pregnant at the same time that they are trying to handle an infant or small child. Another clue to the possibility of future child abuse is the mother's tendency to use physical punishment on very small infants even those under the age of six months, and her tendency to increase the intensity of the punishment as the child becomes older. In some cases these mothers have unrealistic expectations of their infants, revealing that they feel their infants should, by the time they are a year old, have a well-developed conscience.

Stranger and Separation Anxiety

Although parents today may know more about child development than those in the past, there are still a large number of parents who are not prepared for normal stranger and separation anxiety. According to Verville (1967) parents are often embarrassed by their infant's "bad manners" and are also often concerned that his behavior signifies future shyness.

Most writers see stranger anxiety as a positive aspect of the child's growth and development. His ability to make a distinction between his parent and others indicates that he has been able to form an attachment (Kessler, 1966; Mussen, et al., 1956; Freedman, 1971; Kagan and Havemann, 1968; White, 1975). Bowlby (1971) states that stranger anxiety has been observed in infants as young as four months but can be delayed until the infant is a year old. He also suggests that the degree to which the infant is anxious and the intensity with which he expresses his anxiety is a function of the following conditions: how far the stranger is from the infant; whether or not the stranger tries to approach the infant; whether the environment is familiar or not; whether the child is fatigued or ill; and whether the caretaker is near or distant from the infant.

Handling stranger anxiety is not unlike handling any fear. The child should neither be forced to go to the stranger immediately or be withdrawn from the situation. If the child is held in the safety and security of the parent's arms while the parent slowly and gradually approaches the stranger, withdrawing somewhat as soon as the child appears to become anxious, the child's anxiety seems to abate at the same time that he is learning by successive approximations that the stranger need not be feared. Brazelton (1975) points out that infants at this age are also fearful of pediatricians, and he suggests allowing the mother to hold the infant while the infant is being examined and to try to look at the infant directly as little as possible. Goodrich (1961) suggests that it is when the child is capable of moving away from the mother that he begins to realize that it is possible for him to be removed from the mother and that this may engender fear. Mussen, et al. (1956) suggest that the child is fearful because he cannot understand his mother's absence and is not sure that she will return. The child who can see the mother periodically during his explorations appears to be reassured (Yahraes, 1971). Mothers report their annoyance at their young child who while playing outside wants to come in repeatedly. Shortly after he has been brought in and his outer clothes have been removed, he insists on returning outside. Those mothers who have followed recommendations to show themselves to the child periodically report that these forays on the part of the child are minimized. Although separation anxiety begins to abate at about 18 months of age, it is still seen in some children at age two.

For the child to gradually adapt to separation from his parents and for him to learn that his parents will indeed return, it is suggested that the parents separate themselves from the child first for very short periods, gradually increasing the length of the periods of separation. Studies reveal that infants who have been exposed to periods of separation from the mother seem to exhibit less intense separation anxiety (Mussen, et al., 1956). Burlingham and Freud (1967) suggest that when mothers separate from the child frequently, they must reappear frequently; each separation and reappearance seems to lessen the child's anxiety.

Although separation anxiety is accepted as "normal," it can result in conflicts (Kagan and Havemann, 1968). Where separation is not introduced gradually, the shock of sudden separation can be traumatizing. Although a single trauma may not result in long lasting effects, widely separated sudden departures of the parent without warning may create problems. Bowlby (1971) cautions that because the infant seems satisfied if he does not see mother leave, mother should not sneak off unseen. It is also suggested that children do better if they are left in a familiar environment and if they are not left with strangers. If an infant has not experienced frequent separations and is then left for a long period of time especially in unfamiliar surroundings, the result may be either intense attachment or withdrawal. If the child attaches himself intensely for fear that he will be left, he may not be able to separate later when this is age-appropriate, and this inability to separate may interfere with his functioning. Withdrawal from the parent may be a defense against the fear that if he attaches himself, he may be left again and although this kind of child may have no difficulty physically separating himself from the parent, he may have difficulty forming attachments.

Feeding

Sometimes infants have difficulty when they are first given solid foods. If mother sees this as a refusal of the food, conflict over feeding may arise (Verville, 1967). Anna Freud (1965) suggests that mothers tend to equate mothering with food and perceive the refusal of food by the child as a rejection of her. This presumption is often reinforced when mother notes that the child who refuses food from her will accept food from others. Another conflict over feeding may result from the young child's desire to feed himself when he is not quite mature enough to hold the spoon without spilling the food. If this results in a battle between parent and child, the child may either rebel or comply submissively.

In their discussion of "difficult infants" Thomas, et al. (1968) point out that these infants tend to express their hunger irregularly. They will signify their hunger, but when offered the feeding, they may accept just a small portion at that time, only to appear hungry again shortly afterward. Since this can, of course, upset the mother, it may become a source of conflict. The authors point out also that self-demand feeding for these infants does not seem to result in regular feeding habits and that if parents assume that it will, they may continue to be frustrated. A modified demand schedule may be less frustrating to parents of these "difficult infants."

Another possible source of conflict related to feeding concerns the reduction in the rate of weight gain during the second year of life. Most parents are not aware that during this period the child gains only about ⅓ of what he gained during the first year and when they note that the child is eating less, they manifest their concern by giving the child considerable attention for not eating (Verville, 1967). Related to the situation above is that in which parents who have been accustomed to ignoring the child during meals, suddenly become aware that the child who had been eating well in the past is eating less. Because of their concern, the parents then concentrate their attention on the child who at subsequent meals may elicit attention by not eating. Some have suggested that the child learns that he can enliven his day by exciting his parents with food refusals.

Weaning

In situations where the bottle has become a desirable object in itself, weaning, of course, becomes more difficult. Thus, early weaning may prevent the child from becoming attached to the bottle. It should also be noted that the child who still has a bottle beyond the age when this is considered appropriate tends to also be immature in other areas. The immature behavior results in ridicule and can be a source of lowered self-esteem (Verville, 1967).

Early Influences on Intellectual Functioning

Following are some of the early influences on intellectual functioning as summarized by Yahraes (1971), by Mussen, et al. (1956), and by Meyers and Dingman (1967):

1. Children whose parents are overtly concerned that their infants obtain a good education are more apt to achieve higher scores on intelligence tests than are children of parents who appear to be minimally concerned about education.

2. Mothers of achieving children report that from the time their child was an infant, they reinforced the child's attempts to achieve and tended to ignore his request for help.

3. More generally, mothers who tend to respond positively to their infants and to be concerned for their infant's well-being tend to have children who score well on intelligence tests. (It should be noted here that these mothers themselves tend to be well educated so that genetics and/or environment may be a factor.)

4. Children whose mothers tend to respond to their infant's babbling tend later to use more words than other children, to be able to label, and to identify objects and feelings.

Since "mental tests" for infants and those for older children tap different abilities, tests given in infancy and early childhood are poor predictors for future intellectual functioning. Infant tests tap sensory-motor tasks and not memory, abstract ability, and learning, functions which are examined in tests for older children. Even tests given to infants and young children within a period of a year or two have low correlations with each other. It is possible to use intelligence tests in the diagnosis of mental retardation after a child has reached the age of two years (Mussen, *et al.,* 1956; Meyers and Dingman, 1967).

Discipline

As has been noted previously, the 12-month-old may begin to express his independence by rebelling against feeding and sleeping routines. This may require, on the one hand, that parents ignore eating and sleeping refusal while making sure that they are not reinforcing behaviors which are inappropriate for the young child who cannot judge for himself what is in his best interest.

The tendency of children of this age to explore their environment heedlessly requires that they be protected from injury. It may be possible to distract the child, but if he is persistent, it may be necessary to remove him from a dangerous situation. Removing him immediately from the situation to his crib for approximately one or two minutes and increasing the length of time by small amounts, if done consistently, is sometimes an effective conditioning procedure. It keeps the child away from dangerous situations while at the same time permitting him some independence which he could not have if the parent had to watch him constantly. Spanking and/or scolding the child may result in a poor parent-child relationship. If parents do not have some effective technique for dealing with the behavior, they may perceive the child as being purposely defiant. This may, in turn, result in parental behaviors which can, inadvertently, fulfill the parents' prophecy. In addition, parents may see the child as uncontrollable and themselves as inadequate because they cannot control him.

References

Bayley, Nancy: The growth of intelligence, in Yvonne Brackbill and George G. Thompson (Eds.): *Behavior in Infancy and Early Childhood,* New York, The Free Press, 1967.

Bayley, Nancy and Schaefer, Earl S.: Maternal behavior and personality development: Data from the Berkeley growth study, in Gene R. Medinnus (Ed.): *Readings in the Psychology of Parent-Child Relations,* New York, John Wiley & Sons, Inc., 1967.

Bowlby, John: *Attachment and Loss, Vol. I: Attachment,* England, Pelican Books, 1971.

Brazelton, T. Berry: Anticipatory Guidance, in Stanford B. Friedman (Guest Ed.): *The Pediatric Clinics of North America,* 1975, **22**(3), Philadelphia, W. B. Saunders Co.

Bullard, D. M., Jr., Glaser, H. H., Heagarty, M. C., and Pivchik, E. C.: Failure to thrive in the "neglected" child. *Am J Orthopsychiatry,* 1967, **37**(4), 680–690.

Burlingham, Dorothy and Freud, Anna: Young children in wartime: Traumatic effects of separation from parents, in Yvonne Brackbill and George G. Thompson (Eds.): *Behavior in Infancy and Early Childhood,* New York, The Free Press, 1967.

Des Lauriers, Austin M.: Ego psychology and the definition of behavior disorder, in Herbert E. Rie (Ed.): *Perspectives in Child Psychopathology,* New York, Aldine-Atherton, 1971.

Fagen, Stanley A., Long, Nicholas J., and Stevens, Donald J.: *Teaching Children Self-Control,* Columbus, Ohio, Charles E. Merrill Publishing Co., 1975.

Freedman, Daniel G.: The impact of behavior genetics and ethology, in Herbert E. Rie (Ed.): *Perspectives in Child Psychopathology,* New York, Aldine-Atherton, 1971.

Freud, Anna: *Normality and Pathology in Childhood,* New York, International Universities Press, Inc., 1965.

Goodrich, D. Wells: Possibilities for preventive intervention during initial personality formation, in Gerald Caplan (Ed.): *Prevention of Mental Disorders in Children,* New York, Basic Books, Inc., 1961.

Hunt, J. McV.: *Intelligence and Experience,* New York, Ronald Press, 1961.

Kagan, Jerome and Havemann, Ernest: *Psychology: An Introduction,* New York, Harcourt, Brace and World, Inc., 1968.

Kessler, Jan W.: *Psychopathology of Childhood,* Englewood Cliffs, N.J., Prentice-Hall, Inc., 1966.

Luce, Gay: Hormones in the development of behavior, in Julius Segal (Ed.): *The Mental Health of the Child,* Rockville, Md., National Institute of Mental Health, 1971.

Meyers, C. E. and Dingman, Harvey F.: Hypothetical structures of abilities
during the preschool years, in Yvonne Brackbill and George G. Thompson
(Eds.): *Behavior in Infancy and Early Childhood,* New York, The Free
Press, 1967.
Millar, W. Stuart: The effect of social feedback contingent upon a non-social
response in seven- and ten-month-old infants, *Psychol. Res.,* 1977, **39,**
169–184.
Moss, Howard A.: Sex, age, and state as determinants of mother-infant interaction, *Merrill-Palmer Quarterly of Behavior and Development,* 1967,
13(1), 19–36.
Mussen, Paul Henry, Conger, John Janeway, and Kagan, Jerome: *Child De-
velopment and Personality,* New York, Harper and Row, 1956.
Schaffer, H. Rudolph: Objective observations of personality development in
early infancy, in Yvonne Brackbill and George G. Thompson (Eds.): *Be-
havior in Infancy and Early Childhood,* New York, The Free Press, 1967.
Spock, Benjamin: The striving for autonomy and regressive object relation-
ships, in Yvonne Brackbill and George G. Thompson (Eds.): *Behavior in
Infancy and Early Childhood,* New York, The Free Press, 1967.
Sumpter, Edwin A.: Behavior problems in early childhood, in Sanford B.
Friedman (Guest Ed.): *The Pediatric Clinics of North America,* 1975, **22**(3),
Philadelphia, W. B. Saunders Co.
Thomas, Alexander, Chess, Stella, and Birch, Herbert G.: *Temperament and
Behavior Disorders in Children,* New York, New York University Press,
1968.
Thomas, Alexander, Chess, Stella, and Birch, Herbert G.: The origin of person-
ality. *Scientific American,* 1970 (Aug.), 102–109.
Verville, Elinor: *Behavior Problems of Children,* Philadelphia, W. B. Saunders
Co., 1967.
White, Burton L.: What we know about infants and what we need to know.
Paper prepared for Texas Conference on Infancy, Austin, Texas, June
22–24, 1975.
Wing, Lorna: *Autistic Children: A Guide for Parents,* Secaucus, N.J., The
Citadel Press, 1974.
Wittenberg, Clarissa: Studies of child abuse and infant accidents, in Julius
Segal, *The Mental Health of the Child,* Rockville, Md., National Institute
of Mental Health, 1971.
Yahraes, Herbert: Childhood influences upon intelligence, personality, and
mental health; also how the child separates from the mother, in Julius
Segal, *The Mental Health of the Child,* Rockville, Md., National Institute
of Mental Health, 1971.

CHAPTER 5

The Two-Year-Old

Although many of the topics to be discussed in this chapter may be relevant to children ranging in age from 18 months to three years, it is simpler to use the age of two to represent that period when the child exhibits characteristics of development which appear to be qualitatively different than those manifested at earlier ages.

The child, at this age, can anticipate situations which are relatively routine. This may be due, in part, to his rudimentary awareness of cause and effect relationships.

The development of constancy permits him to imitate a model even when the model is not present and to "pretend" without the presence of the original stimulus. Related to this is his greater social sense, which not only results in a greater awareness of others but causes him to spend less time in solitary play.

The two-year-old also has a greater sense of self, as a being separate from another, which leads to greater efforts to achieve independence and autonomy. It is because of these efforts that he begins to experience more serious adult restraints on his activities. His desire for independence creates some intrapsychic conflict as well as parent-child conflict. Although his need to assert himself is great, his dependency needs continue to be significant.

The parent-child relationship is further strained because the child, at this age, seems, almost suddenly, to develop sleeping problems; in addition, he is physically capable of climbing out of his crib. Parents who do not know how to effectively handle these situations may scold and spank the child, communicating to him that he is "bad." The parent-child conflicts initiated at this age may persist (Mussen, *et al.*, 1956; Flavell, 1963; Crow, 1967; Verville, 1967; Yahraes, 1971; Escalona, 1974; Sumpter, 1975; and Whiteside, 1976).

Parents complain most about their two-year-old child's

41

"negativism." If they can anticipate that the two-year-old, because of his apparent need for autonomy, is likely to resist attempts to force him to comply with parental requests, they may be less angry at the child and more amenable to suggestions for handling him in a non-punitive manner. If parents know that the two-year-old tends to be active just for the sake of being active and likes to move objects around just for the sake of moving them around (Whiteside, 1976), they are less likely to assume that the child is engaging in these apparently aimless acitivities in order to irritate them. Yahraes (1971) argues that the negativism often observed in the two-year-old may actually be important for his sense of self. And Verville (1967) suggests that it is a positive characteristic because it signifies the child's striving for independence.

If the two-year-old has frequent access to large open spaces and if there are safe objects on which he can climb (Whiteside, 1976), his activity need not be restricted as frequently. Verville (1967) suggests that in situations where the parent wants the two-year-old to move from one area to another, he should not argue, beg, or give complicated explanations; instead, he should firmly and quietly carry the child to the designated area. This should help to prevent the friction often generated when the parent is trying to persuade the child to comply.

Mussen, et al. (1956) suggest that if the child is to learn the "skills, attitudes, and behaviors" he needs to know in order to enjoy a satisfying life, he must develop inner controls. This implies the imposition of external controls. The authors warn, however, against unnecessary controls which can undermine the child's independence. Most authors stress the importance of firmness and consistency and warn against discipline as a manifestation of parental anger or as an expression of the parent's need to prove his authority.

Sometimes the two-year-old's insistence on autonomy and the frustration he experiences when restraints are placed on his behavior results in temper tantrums. Kagan and Havemann (1968) warn that temper-tantrum-like behavior can continue into adulthood if children learn that tantrums will cause the parent to yield to their wishes. Following are some suggestions for imposing necessary controls on the behavior of two-year-olds:

1. Parents report that they become annoyed when the child refuses to do what he is asked to do. They may not realize the importance of deciding before they make the request whether it is negotiable or not. If it is, indeed, a request and not a demand, the child can refuse, but if it is not negotiable, it should be phrased in the form of a demand which, if refused, can result in consequences which should follow any disobedient behavior.

2. If the two-year-old is given some warning before it is time for him to come in for meals, get ready for bed, or put his toys away, he is less likely to rebel than if he is suddenly told to do something immediately.

3. As noted above, it is better not to argue with him but to just pick him up firmly but gently and do with him what is necessary.

4. Sumpter (1975) suggests that setting very firm and consistent limits and then using such consequences as time-out periods, tends to be effective in controlling the child's behavior. Although the two-year-old may not immediately understand the relationship between his behavior and time-out, if the time-out periods are used consistently, he will begin to make an association between the behavior and the consequences of that behavior. Time-out can, for the two-year-old, consist of a few moments sitting in a chair. Parents report that increasing by small increments the length of the time-out periods for each specific undesirable behavior is more effective than continuing to use the same length of time.

It should be noted that some mothers tend to be overprotective and do not permit their children age-appropriate independence and autonomy. Mussen, et al. (1956) suggest that wherever possible, a child should be given choices. Some of the choices may have to be limited, but the child may still perceive himself as having made the decision. For instance, he can choose between several sets of clothing; he can choose between certain foods for breakfast and perhaps lunch; he can decide whether he wants to sit down or stand up; and, even at this age, he can choose between continuing to behave in an undesirable manner and accepting the consequences or he can change his behavior. Although he cannot yet understand the concept of responsibility for his behavior, he can, after he has made the association between certain behaviors and their consequences, understand what will happen if he continues the behavior. Dreikurs and Grey (1968) suggest that discussing the child's misbehavior with him may generate arguments and may detract from the firmness with which demands are made. It may also delay the implementation of the consequences which tend to be more effective if they are imposed immediately following the undesirable behavior. In general, discussing unacceptable behavior with the child reinforces it, probably because the attention implicit in conversation is rewarding.

As was noted earlier, the two-year-old often appears aimless and disorganized in his play. His attention span is very short and as Whiteside (1976) suggests it is measured, at this age, in seconds rather than in minutes. Parents who are not aware of this normal behavior may make demands on the child which are unrealistic. Parents also often expect that the child at this age should share, not realizing that he is not yet that interested in others. The play of the two-year-old is described as "parallel." Although he is engaging in less solitary play than previously, he is not involved directly with the other child. He is, however, becoming a social creature and actively wishes to be with other children (Crow, 1967). Some mothers become upset because after making an effort to satisfy the child's wish to be with other children, the child does not actually play with them.

Because the two-year-old still has to be reassured that his mother is available, he tends, when away from her, to seek her out frequently. As was noted earlier in discussing separation anxiety in the younger child, friction between mother and child can be prevented if the mother will show herself to the child occasionally. Yahraes (1971) suggests that if mother and child remain too close and the mother has not left the child for gradually longer and longer periods, there may be separation problems at all ages; the problems may even reemerge at adolescence.

Sumpter (1975) suggests that sleeping problems reported by parents of two-year-olds may, in part, be due to separation anxiety. As noted earlier, a soft cuddly toy at bedtime may ease the separation. Sleeping problems at this age may also be due to the parent's reluctance to ignore the child's crying. As suggested in the previous chapter, many sleeping problems seem to begin at the ages of six to nine months, partly because parents continue to respond to the child's crying out of fear that he may be ill. When he is two years old and still cries at bedtime, the parents become frustrated and angry. Even when they have been reassured that the child is healthy, and even though they might let him cry for one or two nights, they will frequently give in either because they cannot tolerate the crying or because of concern for neighbors. Sumpter suggests that parents be reassured that the child will not be traumatized by crying for a long time and that the crying will lessen and soon disappear if they do not respond to it. Sumpter also points out that those parents who tend to continue to resist suggestions to let the child cry should be warned that if they continue to give into the child, they are apt to be successfully manipulated by the child in other ways as well. He suggests that parents of children who crawl out of bed should be reassured that it is all right if the child sleeps on the floor. In a few cases where the bedtime problem is intense, medication for about a week may help.

There is some evidence that, at this age, the child is somewhat more fearful than he was previously. For instance, the two-year-old tends to fear unexpected stimulation; he also "hears things," and even rough and animal-like noises during play with his father, apparently appears real to the child. According to Piaget (Flavell, 1963), a two-year-old begins to be aware of causes and of his surroundings. Verville (1967) suggests that the child is fearful that he will not be able to handle situations which he does not yet understand. It is suggested that he be gradually exposed to sudden movements, particularly those on television; that he have periods of relaxation devoid of frightening activities at bedtime and that, in general, a calm bedtime routine be established.

According to Douglas and Blomfield (1967), mothers in the United States tend to begin toilet training their children at this age even though in Europe mothers tend to train their infants at much younger ages. The authors whose paper was based on research done in England state that "neurologists generally consider that six months is the earliest age that myelination is sufficiently developed to support voluntary control." They do not suggest that infants be toilet trained at this age, but results of their study reveal that, among infants who were trained in the first six months, there were fewer cases of later soiling. When infants are regular in their elimination and when putting them on the toilet at their regular elimination times is done casually and for extremely short periods, the parent can condition the child. If the parent can do this casually, it need not be traumatic.

Much of the literature today is more concerned with the effect of harsh toilet training methods than the age at which toilet training begins. Forman and Hetznecker (1975) state that the effect of toilet training on the child's later mental health has been "exaggerated." They feel that it is only when toilet training becomes an arena for friction between the mother and child can it become traumatizing. Kagan and Havemann (1968) feel that one of the reasons that harsh toilet training methods can have ill effects later is that a mother who uses such methods probably uses these same kinds of methods in trying to elicit compliance in other areas. Mussen, et al. (1956) tend to agree with Douglas and Blomfield (1967) that conditioning may be preferable to a somewhat sudden attempt to try to obtain the child's conscious cooperation in the training. They suggest that it is easier to "shape and reward" the child who is regular by putting him on the toilet when he usually defecates or urinates. And if indeed the two-year-old tends to be "negativistic," isn't this an inopportune time to begin training, which almost by its nature seems to elicit resistance? It is frequently a source of mother-child conflict and may be one of the child's first experiences with discipline, which because the situation occurs daily may make it more difficult for parents to handle than the resistance to other less frequent demands (Kagan and Havemann, 1968).

Parents desirous of training or, perhaps more correctly, conditioning their child who is regular in elimination report that the following technique is effective: the parent takes the child from the breakfast table, for instance, immediately after he has finished eating and places him on the toilet. The parent can read to him or play with him for one to three minutes and if the child defecates in the toilet he is rewarded with mild priase and approval. If he does not defecate and has only one bowel movement a day, nothing is said and the routine is repeated on the following morning. Usually children under the age of one and one-half years do not resist this procedure if it is done in the manner described. However, in the older child who has not been conditioned and who does resist the procedure, it is suggested that toilet training be postponed for several weeks or even several months until the memory of its negative effects have disappeared (Forman and Hetznecker, 1975).

It should be noted that the "difficult" child as described by Thomas, et al. (1968) is usually irregular in elimination. The timing and/or frequency of bowel movements tend to be unpredictable. This makes it more difficult to train him. It is suggested to mothers of these children that they probably cannot successfully condition them. They may have to wait until the child is old enough to make his needs known. The child who has been gradually exposed to some discipline in infancy, and who, therefore, does not experience discipline for the first time during toilet training, is less likely to resist the training than is the child who perceives the situation as a test of his independence.

Although there are apparently no systematic data on sibling rivalry and its special relationship to the two-year-old, experience in child guidance clinics reveals that the two-year-old, because of his curiosity, his tendency to test limits, and his striving for independence, tends to interfere with his older sibling(s). He may annoy his sibling when the sibling is engaged in an activity alone or with his peers or he may take his sibling's possessions. Sibling rivalry is exacerbated when the parent protects the two-year-old, ignoring the right of the older sibling to be left alone if he wishes and to have his possessions inviolate.

One last note about enhancing the development in children of this age: Irwin (1967) in studying children from low socio-economic status homes found that although children under the age of 17 months did not benefit from being read aloud to, children from the ages 17 to 30 months old increased their verbal skills by being read to daily. Parents should be warned, however, that since the young child's attention span is normally very short, particularly so for very active children, the reading periods should be short and the child should not be forced to listen.

References

Bowlby, John: *Attachment and Loss Vol. 1: Attachment,* Great Britain, Pelican Books, 1969.

Crow, Lester D.: *Psychology of Human Adjustment,* New York, Alfred A. Knopf, 1967.

Douglas, J. W. B. and Blomfield, J. M.: Bowel training and bed wetting, in Brackbill, Yvonne and Thompson, George G. (Eds.): *Behavior in Infancy and Early Childhood,* New York, The Free Press, 1967.

Dreikurs, Rudolf and Grey, Loren: *Logical Consequences: A New Approach to Discipline,* New York, Meredith Press, 1968.

Escalona, Sibylle K.: Developmental issues in the second year of life: their implications for day care practices. *Psychosocial Process,* 1974, 3(1), 28–33.

Flavell, John H.: *The Developmental Psychology of Jean Piaget,* Princeton, N.J., D. Van Nostrand Co., Inc., 1963.

Forman, Marc A. and Hetznecker, William H.: Critical developmental issues, in Vaughan and McKay (Eds.): *Nelson—Textbook of Pediatrics,* 10th ed., Philadelphia, W. B. Saunders Co., 1975.

Gesell, Arnold and Ames, Louise B.: The development of handedness, in Brackbill, Yvonne and Thompson, George G. (Eds.): *Behavior in Infancy and Early Childhood,* New York, The Free Press, 1967.

Irwin, Orvis, C.: Acceleration of infant speech by story-reading, in Brackbill, Yvonne and Thompson, George G. (Eds.): *Behavior in Infancy and Early Childhood,* New York, The Free Press, 1967.

Kagan, Jerome and Havemann, Ernest: *Psychology: An Introduction,* New York, Harcourt, Brace & World, Inc., 1968.

Mussen, Paul H., Conger, John J., and Kagan, Jerome: *Child Development and Personality,* New York, Harper and Row, 1956.

Settlage, Calvin F., Psychologic disorders, in Vaughan and McKay (Eds.): *Nelson—Textbook of Pediatrics,* Philadelphia, W. B. Saunders Co., 1975.

Sumpter, Edwin A.: Behavior problems in early childhood, in Friedman, Stanford B. (Ed.): *Pediatric Clinics of North America,* Philadelphia, W. B. Saunders Co., 1975.

Thomas, Alexander, Chess, Stella, and Birch, Herbert G.: *Temperament and Behavior Disorders in Children,* New York, New York University Press, 1968.

Verville, Elinor: *Behavior Problems of Children,* Philadelphia, W. B. Saunders Co., 1967.

Whiteside, Mary F., Busch, Fred, and Horner, Thomas: From egocentric to cooperative play in young children: A normative study. *J Am Acad Child Psychiatry,* 1976, 15(2), 294–313.

Yahraes, Herbert, in Segal, Julius (Ed.): *The Mental Health of the Child,* Rockville, Md., National Institute of Mental Health, 1971.

CHAPTER 6

Ages Three to Five

The differences between the three-year-old and the two-year-old have implications for anticipatory guidance as well as for general child management. The three-year-old can handle mother's temporary absence with less anxiety (Freud, 1965; Bowlby, 1969); although still engaging in some parallel play, he is interacting more with others and is able to sustain this interaction for longer periods (Escalona, 1974; Whiteside, *et al.,* 1976; Mussen, *et al.,* 1956); he talks a great deal at this age, a large amount of this talking tending to be in the form of questions (Verville, 1967; Piaget, 1962); and he seems, at this age, to begin to be aware of differences between the sexes (Kagan and Havemann, 1968; Mussen, *et al.,* 1956; Satterfield, 1975; Bowlby, 1969).

Because the three-year-old is so much more competent than the two-year-old, parents are often unaware that he still has some separation anxiety, that even though he is capable of interacting with peers, he does better with one or two children than in a larger group, and that he still has difficulty sharing and handling interpersonal conflicts (Whiteside, *et al.,* 1976); he has not yet learned to internalize controls (Nicholson, 1970); and he confuses reality with fantasy (Crow, 1967; Kessler, 1966). The three-year-old also tends to regress at times (Freud, 1965; Verville, 1967); and the three-year-old still has difficulty dealing with abstractions (Kagan and Havemann, 1968; Kagan, 1974).

Some parents are upset when their child, who continues to have separation anxiety, refuses to attend nursery school. Anna Freud suggests that the three-year-old who still has separation problems should begin school gradually and that his mother should be available in the event that the child wishes to go to her. These parents can also be reassured that a nursery school experience is not crucial to the child's well-being and that delaying enrollment will not deprive the child. Two alternatives to nursery school where separation is mandatory are: inviting a child into the home where the children can play together in the presence of the mother and/or meeting frequently with other mothers and their children. Both of these alternatives would provide the children with opportunities for learning and developing social skills.

By the time a child is four years old, he should feel secure enough to separate with little or no difficulty. Bowlby (1969) suggests that separation anxiety in the four- or five-year-old should be considered a problem. Even if temporary during these ages, it may signal that the child is frightened, ill, fatigued, hungry, or is being stressed in other ways. The preschool child may be anxious if there is a death in the family, if the mother is ill, if there are marital problems, or if the family has moved recently (Murphy, 1961).

According to Whiteside, *et al.* (1976), for the three-year-old the function of a peer relationship is primarily to fill his "narcissistic needs," and it is only when he reaches the age of four that he manifests a real interest in another child. Not until he is about five can he begin to play cooperatively, understand the point of view of others, and adhere to rules (Piaget, 1962; Mussen, *et al.*, 1956). Since many nursery schools group three- to five-year-olds together, the three-year-old may be expected to interact in a group with the same ease displayed by the four- or five-year-old. He may then be singled out as having a problem because he does not conform. At this age he will interact more effectively with one other child or possibly two other children. It isn't until he is four years old that he can participate in group activities comfortably and effectively (Escalona, 1974; Nicholson, 1970).

The three-year-old's tendency to both talk almost constantly (one study revealed that during the three-year-old's waking day he refrains from talking for a total of about 19 minutes) and his frequent questions sometimes leave parents in a bind. On the one hand they find themselves impatient, but on the other hand they are fearful that if they do not listen to the child and answer his questions, they will dampen his curiosity. Piaget (1962) calls the child's behavior "games of mental exercise" and feels that the child asks questions to entertain himself and to practice his new skill. Verville (1967) adds to these functions two other motives: to obtain "respect" from those who give him a thoughtful answer to his questions, but also to draw attention to himself. Although parents should be aware that not answering the child's questions may indeed cause the child to stop asking questions (Kagan and Havemann, 1968), they should also be reassured that ignoring the child's questions occasionally will not damage the child, especially when they have ascertained that the child is using this behavior primarily as an attention-getting device. At these times, responding with an "oh" or "uh huh" ignores what the child is saying without ignoring the child himself.

Sometimes, because the three-year-old seems to be relatively skilled in his use of language, parents assume that his cognitive development is mature enough to include the ability to handle abstract concepts. Three-year-olds and some four-year-olds are not capable of reasoning unless the subject is concrete (Kagan and Havemann, 1968). Parents are seldom aware that abstract concepts such as death, truth, and morality can only bewilder the child unless these concepts are tied to concrete situations within his sphere of experience. Kagan (1974) suggests that the preschool child can improve his ability to understand concepts if caretakers describe objects for him according to various categories such as color, form, size, etc.

In the area of sensory experience, although exposure to visual, oral, and kinesthetic stimulation is important, some parents and teachers assume that exposure is sufficient for effective stimulation. It is when sounds, sights, and movements are brought to the child's attention that he actually becomes aware of them. Because the child tends to be concrete and needs to place new stimuli in the context of his previous experience, new stimuli, to be most effective, should be verbally and concretely associated with familiar events.

Some parents are eager to stimulate their preschool child's academic potential by teaching him academic skills. They may not be aware that this can result in the retardation of development in other areas. Professor Louise J. Kaplan, director of the Mother-Infant Nursery of New York University Psychology Department, states that teaching academic skills to the preschool child may interfere with the development of his imagination and that it is preferable at these ages to stimulate the imagination. According to Dr. Kaplan "fantasy play fosters creative thinking and has more to do with developing a lively intelligence than early rote learning" (Kramer, 1975). It should also be noted that because the child may not be mature enough to learn how to read for instance, he is more apt to fail which may be detrimental to his self-image. Kramer quotes Michael Lewis, Clinical Professor of Pediatrics at Baby's Hospital at Columbia University Medical Center: "A child's curiosity and his eagerness to learn are as natural as breathing if they are not turned off by too much pressure, crushed by too much direction." Dr. Lewis feels that to "enjoy reading" is more important than to learn to read, and he feels that a preferable way to achieve this is not by using specific kinds of materials or books but by reading to the child and by permitting the child to observe the parent reading.

Parents who are not aware that preschool children, particularly three-year-olds, tend to regress are often both concerned and annoyed when they see their reasonably well-trained child suddenly begin to crawl rather than walk, to soil and wet, to complain that he cannot dress himself. He may also start clinging to mother again. Freud (1965) stresses that these regressions are frequently due to isolated stresses and are usually temporary. Verville (1967) suggests that at times the three-year-old whose skills in these areas have often just been established seems to engage in these regressive behaviors because he feels insecure. It is almost as if he wishes to test the stability of his skills. Verville suggests that if the parents overreact in a negative manner, they may reinforce the regressive behavior. Sudden changes in the environment such as moving, and starting nursery school, are likely to result in regression. This can be minimized by introducing him to these new experiences gradually and/or by preparing him for them well in advance of the actual change. It is the three-year-old who tends to demonstrate regressive behavior at the birth of a new sibling.

Parents become concerned over their child's sexual activity because they are often unaware that, sometime after the age of three, children become conscious of the difference between the sexes (Kagan and Havemann, 1968; Satterfield, 1975). Mussen, et al. (1956) and Satterfield (1975) point out that it is at these ages when the child "exhibits" his own body and manifests his curiosity in the genitalia of others. He begins to ask questions about sex and the parents' requests for advice center around how to handle the child's "masturbation," how to answer the child's questions, and the effect on the child of nudity in the home.

For those parents who cannot accept the normality of masturbation, some help around their own sexual feelings may be indicated. Parents who are embarrassed by the behavior find it difficult to talk to the child about the activity and are often secretive concerning it. They should be advised to casually explain to the child those times and places when masturbation is inappropriate. Satterfield warns that excessive masturbation should not be ignored. A new sibling, separation anxiety, or marital tension may be the source of the stress which is creating tension for the child.

Satterfield states that today most professionals agree that nudity, because it tends to stimulate erotic sensations, may be harmful to the child. He suggests that, in addition, it is often confusing to the small child because what he is being exposed to in the home is restricted outside the home. There is general consensus that the child's questions about sex should be answered honestly and realistically and in a reasonably casual manner. Parents should be advised that before answering the child's question, it is well to ask him for his views so that some of his misconceptions can be corrected. Some parents overwhelm the child with too much information. It is suggested that each question be answered as the child asks it; if he wants more information and knows that his questions will be answered, he will ask further questions as they occur to him.

Reality and Fantasy

Under the age of four, the child has difficulty making the distinction between the real world and the world of imagination. At the age of four he begins to differentiate but still tends to confuse the two (Crow, 1967; Kessler, 1966). Parents are often concerned when the preschool child tells a story which the child seems to believe, and this may become a source of friction particularly when the child is perceived as deliberately lying. Since, to him, the real world and the world of fantasy are one and the same, he may be bewildered when he is scolded or punished for his version of his experience.

This confusion between the real and the imaginary may help to explain the ease with which the preschool child can accept an imaginary playmate as real. Studies reveal that the child who has an imaginary playmate tends to be either a first-born child, an only child without friends, or a child with a sibling but one who is significantly older or younger than he. It is possible that, for the child without peers, the imaginary playmate can serve as a substitute and help in the development of social and language skills. There are data that suggest that the child who has an imaginary friend tends to initiate activity and be involved in a greater variety of play activities. Research in this area is scant, but one study did reveal that creative and artistic boys and creative girls reported greater incidences of imaginary playmates when they were young children.

In children who tend to be withdrawn, an imaginary playmate may reinforce the withdrawal (Manosevitz, *et al.,* 1973). Mussen, *et al.* (1956) and Verville (1967) suggest that some children may use the imaginary friend as a defense against anxiety aroused by a stressful real environment. The child may turn to the imaginary playmate for comfort if he cannot satisfy the parent's somewhat rigid expectations or if his parents are overcontrolling. The child can tolerate the situation by "controlling his imaginary friend." In any case, treating an imaginary playmate as real is a distortion of reality and should not be reinforced, but neither should the child be humiliated or criticized for this behavior. He can casually be reminded that his friend is a "pretend friend."

Nursery School

Despite the opportunities for learning and for practicing social skills afforded by attending nursery school, there is little dependable data concerning the effect on the child of nursery school experience. Studies of the effect on cognitive development are contradictory; some show that nursery school experience is beneficial, some show that it is not. One study revealed that children who did not attend nursery school fared better in kindergarten than children who attended nursery school. This could be due to several factors. First, the nursery school milieu is usually more permissive than the public kindergarten; second, often what the child is asked to learn in kindergarten is redundant and, as a consequence, the child may be bored. Sometimes, however, it is the problem child who is sent to nursery school. Although most children seem to improve in social skills almost immediately after they enter nursery and for the first several months, it appears not to have any long range benefits for the child who is anxious, cries easily and has outbursts of temper (Mussen, et al., 1956). Some parents are disappointed because they expected the nursery school experience to modify the child's behavior. They may need help in handling the child more effectively before the child is placed in a group situation for which he may not be ready.

Mussen, et al. (1956) caution parents to be wary of those nursery schools where there is too little structure and too much freedom; such a milieu is a poor preparation for the public school environment. Sometimes parents have difficulty choosing a nursery school and request help in making the choice. Where the ratio of teacher to children is high, and the teacher can give more individual attention to each child, guiding them and engaging them in personal contact, the children seem to show greater improvement in social relationships. On the other hand, in those schools where the ratio is low, and the children are given more opportunities for independent activity, there seem to be greater gains in cognitive development. The age of the subjects when studied is important since one longitudinal study revealed that although, at age eight, children who had been in nursery school scored higher in academic achievement than children who were not, by age 11 there were no differences, and by age 15 it seemed that the nursery school children did less well.

Another factor that parents might want to consider is whether the nursery school includes in the same program three-, four-, and five-year-olds or whether there are separate activities, perhaps even separate times or rooms for the three-year-olds who have neither the social nor cognitive skills of the four- and five-year-olds and who therefore should probably not have to compete with them. Some nursery schools require the preschool child to remain in school for as long as five hours, which may be too long for the younger preschooler at least. Whether the child should attend morning sessions or afternoon sessions depends on whether he is still taking an afternoon nap or not. (Day care will be discussed in the chapter on Working Mothers.)

Early Identification

As noted in the introduction, although the average age of the mental health clinic referral is nine, the average age of onset of symptoms is about three and one-half. Thus, the identification and treatment of problems at these preschool ages may prevent more serious problems later. Symptoms which can cause learning and behavioral problems later are: aimless activity, persistent fidgeting, impulsivity, frequent outbursts of temper; overreaction with rage to casual demands or alterations in plans. Other symptoms are "marked" distractibility, short attention span especially when the child is in a group, poor coordination, and generally disruptive behavior (Shrier, 1975; Thomas, et al., 1968). Shrier points out that the child who is withdrawn, who avoids novelty, who avoids taking risks, and who is fearful that he might fail, may have a poor self-image. He suggests that the clowning, aggressive, acting-out child may also have a poor self-image. Watson (1967) describes the immature, "babyish" child who cries easily and constantly seeks help from adults as often coming from a home where the parents are overindulgent and overprotective.

The at-risk children described above need environments which are structured and predictable. In addition, they need sufficient supervision to prevent them from failing; they need their activities structured so that they can experience success; and they need support in their attempts to participate in activities and help in learning more social skills. These children do not do well in nursery schools which tend to be unstructured, where children are given a considerable amount of freedom, and where close supervision is not available. Sometimes the withdrawn child becomes more withdrawn if attempts are made to pressure him into becoming something he may, tempermentally, not be able to become, that is, an outgoing, aggressive, active child. Accepting his limitations, while at the same time praising him for some of his strengths and providing him with opportunities to develop skills in the areas in which he is deficient, may enhance his self-image.

According to Piazza (1977), by the age of three, the left hemisphere of the brain is, in a way, "specialized for verbal functions." It is at this age that delayed speech can be considered a problem. It has been found that "speech and language-disordered children" have a greater incidence of psychologic disorders, even though it is not the speech problem that causes the disorders. The speech problem can, however, lower the child's self-image, and the defect in communication can affect the child's peer relationships. Silver, et al. (1967) suggest examining the home environment for factors which may be related to the speech problem: little verbal stimulation and/or the use of language in a punishing manner. Reynolds and Risley (1968) in a study done in a nursery school found that children with delayed speech began to speak when attention and activities were withheld until the children responded to questions about the activities. This helps to confirm anecdotal data which indicates that successful results are obtained by parents who carry out recommendations to withhold the child's request, where it is not crucial to his health, until he verbalizes the request. In most cases, these children are the youngest in a family, where parents, older siblings, and other relatives do not require the child to speak but fulfill his needs either because they anticipate them or because the child points to what he wants.

It is suggested that to help a child with a speech problem, the adult should listen to the child, accept what he says even if he mis-prounounces words, and when he does mispronounce words, to say them casually correctly but not to ask him to repeat the word. He can be taught to distinguish between sounds, and he should be read to and encouraged to imitate. Language should be associated with positive experiences. It is better not to correct him at times when he would be humiliated. He should not be urged to use language that might denigrate him, such as language used in making apologies. If by the age of three and one-half he is not talking at all, if he cannot talk in sentences, or if his speech is unintelligible and the suggestions outlined above are not successful, he should be referred to a speech therapist.

Finally, the preschool child who can anticipate the demands which will be made on him in regular school is likely to adjust to kindergarten or first grade more easily. Some nursery schools, in order to provide the children with an opportunity to play the role of a kindergartner, set aside a period each day for those older children who will be attending regular school the following school term. Parents can follow a similar procedure at home. He can have the child sit still during these, ask the child to respond to questions which the teacher might ask, and generally provide activities which emphasize the use of language. In addition, during discussions concerning school, the emphasis should be on learning and the teacher as an aid to learning rather than on behavior and the teacher as a disciplinarian.

References

Bowlby, John: *Attachment and Loss Vol. I: Attachment,* Great Britain, Pelican Books, 1969.

Cantwell, Dennis P. and Baker, Lorian: Psychiatric disorder in children with speech and language retardation. *Arch General Psychiatry,* 1977, **34,** 583–591.

Crow, Lester D.: *Psychology of Human Adjustment,* New York, Alfred A. Knopf, 1967.

Escalona, Sibylle K.: Developmental issues in the second year of life: Their implications for day care practices, *Psychosocial Process,* 1974, **III**(1), 28–33.

Flavell, John H.: *The Developmental Psychology of Jean Piaget,* Princeton, N.J., D. Van Nostrand Co., Inc., 1963.

Freud, Anna: *Normality and Pathology in Childhood,* New York, International Universities Press, Inc., 1965.

Kagan, Jerome: Preschool enrichment and learning in Williams, in Gertrude J. and Gordon, Sol (Eds.): *Clinical Child Psychology: Current Practices and Future Perspectives,* New York, Behavioral Publications, 1974.

Kagan, Jerome and Havemann, Ernest: *Psychology: An Introduction,* New York, Harcourt, Brace and World, Inc., 1968.

Kessler, Jane W.: *Psychopathology of Childhood,* Englewood Cliffs, N.J., Prentice-Hall, Inc., 1966.

Kramer, Rita: Must the toy fairy have a Ph.D., *New York Times,* 1975, Nov. 16.

Manosevitz, Martin: Prentice, Norman M. and Wilson, Frances: Individual and family correlates of imaginary companions in preschool children. *Developmental Psychology,* 1973, **8**(1), 72–79.

Murphy, Lois B.: Preventive implications of development in the preschool years, in Caplan, Gerald (Ed.): *Prevention of Mental Disorders in Children,* New York, Basic Books, Inc., 1961.

Mussen, Paul H., Conger, John J., and Kagan, Jerome: *Child Development and Personality,* New York, Harper and Row, 1956.

Nicholson, Dorothy: *Toward Effective Teaching of Young Children,* Anderson, Indiana, Warner Press, 1970.

Piaget, Jean: *Play, Dreams and Imitation in Childhood,* New York, W. W. Norton & Co., Inc., 1962.

Piazza, Donna M.: Cerebral lateralization in young children as measured by dichotic listening and finger tapping tasks. *Neuropsychologia,* 1977, **15**(3), 417–425.

Reynolds, Nancy J. and Risley, T. R.: The role of social and material reinforcers in increasing talking of a disadvantaged preschool child. *J Appl Behavior Anal,* 1968, **1,** 253–262.

Satterfield, Sharon. Common sexual problems of children and adolescents, in

Friedman, Stanford B. (Ed.): *The Pediatric Clinics of North America,* 1975, **22**(3), Philadelphia, W. B. Saunders Co.

Shrier, Diane K.: Memo to day care staff: Helping children with minimal brain dysfunction. *Child Welfare,* 1975, **54**(2), 89–96.

Silver, Archie A., Pfeiffer, Elsbeth, and Hagin, Rose A.: The therapeutic nursery as an aid in diagnosis of delayed language development. *Am J Orthopsychiatry,* 1967, **37**(5), 963–970.

Thomas, Alexander, Chess, Stella, and Birch, Herbert G.: *Temperament and Behavior Disorders in Children,* New York, New York University Press, 1968.

Verville, Elinor: *Behavior Problems of Children,* Philadelphia, W. B. Saunders Co., 1967.

Watson, Goodwin: Some personality differences in children related to strict or permissive parental discipline, in Medinnus, Gene R. (Ed.): *Reasonings in the Psychology of Parent-Child Relations,* New York, John Wiley and Sons, Inc., 1967.

Whiteside, Mary F., Busch, Fred, and Horner, Thomas: From egocentric to cooperative play in young children. *J Am Acad Child Psychiatry,* 1976, **15**(2), 294–313.

CHAPTER 7

Some Non-Age-Specific Topics

Birth Order

Although evidence concerning the degree to which birth order is a factor in individual differences is often contradictory, there have been studies which do demonstrate that many mothers do not treat their first born and later born children alike. One of the reasons why some of the evidence may be contradictory is that until recently studies of birth order have not considered sex as a variable. For instance, Jacobs and Moss (1976) summarize a number of studies which revealed that primiparous mothers stimulated their infants more, verbalized more with them, and, in general, spent more non-feeding time with their infants. When the authors, however, compared the mother's behavior toward her first born with her behavior toward her later born child, and considered sex as a variable, it was found that if the first born child was a female and the second born child a male, the latter received as much attention as the first born child. It was primarily when the second born child was a female that the difference between the amount of attention given to the children as infants was different. In any case, because there does appear to be a difference between how the mother handles her first born and later born children, anticipatory guidance may help to minimize these differences in handling, particularly since the differences appear to often involve inadequate mothering for one of the children.

First-Borns

First-born children and only children tend to be more socially responsible than later borns probably because the first born tends to spend considerable time with adults who then become important references for values and behavior. Possibly for the same reasons first borns tend to set high standards for themselves and have high need achievement scores. On the other hand, because of their fear that they will be displaced by their sibling, they tend to be more anxious and to have a high affiliative need. They tend to be resentful of the new sibling and sometimes experience guilt over this resentment. It is felt that, for these reasons, there are more first-born children brought to child guidance clinics than later borns, and frequently the presenting problem is nervousness, withdrawal, and anxiety rather than acting-out behavior often found in later-born children. First-born children often set high standards for themselves not only because they spend so much time with adults but also because of their desire to "regain their position of status" by achieving (MacDonald, 1971; Verville, 1967; Mussen, *et al.,* 1956; Dreikurs and Grey, 1968). Anticipatory counseling of parents with their first child should include, in addition to recommendations for handling sibling rivalry, suggestions that peer relationships be encouraged, that the amount of gratuitous attention paid to the child be minimal so that withdrawal of some attention following the birth of another child will be less traumatic, and that the child be helped to set more realistic standards for himself.

Youngest Child

Most authors agree that the youngest child is usually "babied" and "spoiled" and as a child, if not as an infant, tends to receive most of the parent's attention. The youngest child tends to be more irresponsible, tends to cling to the parent, and the parent tends to protect the child from complaints from older siblings. Because of the overprotection, the youngest child sometimes feels that he cannot be criticized and do whatever he pleases. He often irritates his older siblings knowing that if they should retaliate they will be punished by the parents, and he tends to be more defiant than his siblings (MacDonald, 1971; Verville, 1967; Mussen, *et al.,* 1956; Dreikurs and Grey, 1968).

A consequence of overindulging and overprotecting the youngest child which is not so obvious was noted by Alfred Adler, who suggested that as the youngest child becomes aware that he does not know as much as his siblings and cannot perform as well, he develops feelings of "inferiority." If he is not required to learn or to do things for himself or to assume age-appropriate responsibilities, he has reason to feel inadequate. The result of having these feelings of inadequancy, again according to Adler, is sometimes seen in the youngest child's attempt to compensate for his feelings of inferiority by inappropriate and unacceptable compensatory behavior, such as dominating and attacking others, especially younger children, and cheating in order to manifest achievement. Experience in child guidance clinics with youngest children tends to reinforce Adler's theories.

Implications for anticipatory counseling to parents of youngest children are, of course, obvious, but what is frequently not so obvious is the mother's need to pamper her youngest child. Again, experience in clinics reveals that these mothers are very resistant to recommendations for helping the youngest child to become more independent and responsible. They will frequently project blame for the child's behavior onto the school, peers, his siblings, and even the other parent. If, however, they can be counseled while the child is still an infant, their overprotective and overindulgent behavior might be minimized.

The Middle Child

Although there are no hard data to either support or deny the existence of what many call the "middle child syndrome," empirical observation suggests that personality and behavioral factors characteristic of the middle child are probably at least as valid as those attributed to the first-born and youngest child. Alfred Adler suggested that when the youngest child is born, the eldest child often assumes added responsibilities while the youngest child assumes the role of "baby," thus leaving the middle child without the privileges of either the older or the younger child. Adler argues that this may generate feelings in the middle child that there is "no place for him" (Dreikurs and Grey, 1968). Thus, he may feel rejected. Mussen, et al. (1956) and Verville (1967) suggest that the middle child may, in order to feel accepted, and in his eagerness for demonstrations of affection, try too hard to please his parents. Sometimes this takes the form of efforts to achieve which, if successful, would enhance his self-image as well as please his parents. Experience in clinics with middle children referred for problems suggests that the child either does achieve, academically, for instance, but is not rewarded in the home, or is unable to achieve because of limited ability and finds that by unacceptable behavior he is able to gain the attention he seeks.

The implication for anticipatory counseling to aprents of middle children is, primarily, one that is applicable to each of the children: if each child is treated as a unique individual with a distinct personality and given privileges and responsibilities appropriate to his age, the need to use his siblings as measures of his self-image should be minimized.

It should be noted that there are large numbers of families in which children do not exhibit the birth order differences noted above. How the siblings are treated by the parents, spacing of the siblings as well as their sex may all be factors in the presence or absence of birth order effects.

Sibling Rivalry

Much of the evidence for the relationship between birth order and sibling rivalry is theoretical. There does, however, appear to be considerable face validity for the theory. If one accepts the evidence that the first-born tends to feel displaced, it is reasonable to assume that he will resent the presence of his sibling and feel angry at the sibling and possibly at his parents. If, however, he is given responsibilities and privileges appropriate to his age, responsibilities and privileges which are inappropriate to the younger child, if his unique personality and his individual interests are taken into account, and if he is given regular predictable undivided attention, his jealousy of the younger sibling may be ameliorated. Brody (1961) cautions that occasionally it is the older child who is overprotected so that he will not be jealous and the younger sibling may then feel rejected. It should be pointed out here that in the long run first-born children tend to achieve success and to obtain high scores on intelligence tests (Mussen, *et al.*, 1956).

The later-born child may compare himself with his older sibling who by virtue of age alone is more capable. This is especially true if the differences in age between the two is small (MacDonald, 1971). Dreikurs and Grey (1968) suggest that when the younger child finds he cannot emulate the older child, particularly the older child who is a "good child," he may give up and become destructive because this is one way in which he can gain some recognition. When he is punished for his destructiveness, the older sibling may become a target for his anger.

Although while the youngest child is an infant, the older children may express affection for him and may even be overprotective, when he becomes old enough to provoke them, especially in situations where they know that he probably will not be punished for annoying them, sibling fighting and anger directed toward the youngest child by the older siblings sometimes becomes intense. Experience with families seen in mental health facilities indicates that rivalry between older siblings and a youngest sibling who has been pampered is a common occurrence.

Following are a number of suggestions of minimizing sibling rivalry (see also chapter on the Newborn at Home):

1. Regular, predictable undivided attention to each child tends to

alleviate jealousy. Since fathers are at home infrequently and sometimes take the children out with them on the weekend, taking one
child on alternate weekend days gives each child some undivided attention from father.

2. Children who can verbalize their feelings of anger and resentment at their sibling and/or the parents whom they may perceive as
favoring one sibling over another are less likely to build up their resentment and to act it out.

3. To reduce sibling rivalry, and to encourage the younger children
to mature, older children should be permitted more privileges as these
become age-appropriate. They should, however, assume more responsibility.

4. Each child should be perceived as having a distinct and unique
personality and should be made aware that, no matter how different he
may be from his siblings, he is an acceptable human being. And his
interests as long as they are acceptable interests, should be respected.
This is an area where parents often have difficulty because of their own
needs to have a certain kind of child and their disappointment when
the child does not fulfill their expectations. The most common situation
is that in which a father who wants an athletic son finds it difficult to
hide his disappointment in a son who is cerebral and/or awkward. This
becomes an important factor in sibling rivalry when a second son is
outgoing and athletic. Permitting each child to become successful in
his own sphere of interest, even discouraging siblings to develop similar interests, can minimize the rivalry.

5. Sibling rivalry tends to be reinforced when parents insist that
siblings play with each other when they prefer not to do so. Related to
this is the tendency for some parents to protect the child who does not
have as many playmates as his siblings. Parents may insist that when
an older child has his friends over, he include the younger sibling in his
play, which may cause considerable resentment in the older child. On
the other hand, sometimes the older child does not have playmates and
interferes with the younger sibling's play. Even when the younger
sibling is playing alone, he may, for instance, criticize the younger
child or take his toys.

6. Sibling rivalry tends to be aggravated when children are forced to
share their possessions with their siblings or when possessions are
owned in common. Parents who have insisted that each child can use
his sibling's possession only after having been granted permission by
the latter have reported a marked reduction in sibling fighting. Where
it is necessary that the children own something in common either
because the object is large and expensive or because it has been given
to all the children as a gift, sibling rivalry is reduced when the children

must take turns. Parents also report that when children know that they do not have to give up their possessions to their sibling unless they wish to do so, although at first they may delight in refusing to permit the sibling to borrow his belongings, they later share their possessions readily.

7. A somewhat typical complaint of siblings is the lack of privacy. Usually the older children complain that their younger siblings do not respect their privacy. This is also a problem, however, where two or more children are forced to share a room. In this latter situation, parents who have followed recommendations to somehow mark off the room into two or three separate areas, report that sibling rivalry has been reduced. Dividing the room has the added advantage of making it easier for each child to be responsible for his particular area.

Although a certain amount of sibling fighting is "normal," if children can learn how to settle their differences and resolve their conflicts in more acceptable ways, they are not as likely to abuse each other physically and/or verbally. The danger of permitting siblings to physically abuse each other is not only that they may hurt each other, but they may assume that using physical force is an appropriate way to settle differences. Verbal abuse can be damaging particularly to a child who already may have a poor self-image and who either accepts the abuse as due him or is sensitive to the abuse. In addition, particularly young children who are permitted to express their anger in this way, tend not to be able to discriminate between those situations at home with their siblings, when this is acceptable and those situations in school, for instance, where it is not. Parents are advised to separate the children when they are fighting and to increase the periods of separation if the fighting continues. Parents can also teach the children alternative ways of handling their anger and solving their differences. (See section on Aggression for specific suggestions.) Frequently in their zeal to have their children relate well to each other, parents permit abuse in part because this interaction implies that at least the children are relating to each other, albeit negatively, rather than each isolating himself from his sibling.

A note concerning twins may be appropriate here. It is, of course, much more difficult to treat twins as unique individuals with their own special abilities and characteristics but, on the other hand, because of this, it probably is more important that their uniqueness be emphasized. Parents no longer tend to dress twins alike and schools tend to place them in separate classrooms in an effort to help each twin develop a sense of his own identity. Verville (1967) suggests that since twins do tend to play with each other, they isolate themselves from other children, which deprives them of the practice they need in order to learn to adapt to others. Parents report that they find themselves, as well as friends and relatives, looking for areas of comparison which tends then to provoke sibling rivalry. Another problem is that there is no age difference which parents generally use to rationalize to each child differences in capabilities.

SEXUAL ACTIVITY

As was noted earlier, between the ages of three and four, children become aware of sexual differences and preschool children, in general, frequently engage in activities which involve undressing and sexual play. There is considerable evidence that the developmental period between ages six and puberty is not a sexually latent stage as was once thought. It has been suggested that "latency" age children were considered relatively asexual because of the strict mores of western countries which tended to create a climate in which sexual expression is either inhibited or concealed. In more permissive cultures, sexual activity during these ages is common. More recently studies done in the United States have revealed similar findings (Rutter, 1970).

Johnson (1967) in his discussion of masturbation suggests that it may actually be a good foundation for perceiving sex as something positive and pleasant. In any case, there is no evidence that masturbation interferes with the later enjoyment of sexual activity. On the contrary, there are indications that women who have masturbated tend to experience greater sexual satisfaction in adulthood than women who did not masturbate. Johnson suggests that children who masturbate excessively, that is, while watching television, while in their seats at school and/or instead of participating in social or creative activities are under some stress which is causing them to be tense and anxious. He suggests also that just as parents teach children that certain behaviors involving bodily functions are only appropriate when engaged in in private, so masturbation can be considered one of those functions and children can learn that it is not appropriate public behavior.

Of special concern is "precocious puberty." Some girls may begin their periods before they have been informed about menstruation. They may become confused and frightened. These children are also precocious in nonsexual physical development and sometimes feel justifiably that they are expected to act older than their chronological age, or they may just want to act older. Unless parents of these children obtain some counseling, the results may be early sexual activity, pregnancy, and/or early marriage (Satterfield, 1975). If parents explain menstruation to their daughters early enough, perhaps by the age of nine, both parents and children may be able to cope more effectively with early puberty. According to McCandless (1970), boys who mature early tend to behave in ways which enhance their "manliness," that is, they may become sexually active early, primarily so they can demonstrate their "sexual prowess." They also in general may act older than their years. Although these inappropriate behaviors are undesirable and parents need help in handling them, some of the consequences suffered are not as serious for the boy in part because of the risk of pregnancy for the girl and in part because American Society tends to be more tolerant of precocity in boys.

Following are some suggestions which can be made to parents for dealing with sexual concerns:

1. Related to information concerning menstruation, it is recommended that boys as well as girls be provided with this information and that girls as well as boys be provided with information concerning nocturnal emissions.

2. If by the time a child is seven or eight years old and has either asked no questions about sex or only very simple ones which he asked at a very early age, he should be given general sex information or an age-appropriate book to read. One book which a seven-year-old can read with some help and which can also be used as a reference for answering the younger child's questions is *Growing Up* by Karl de Scheveinitz, published in paperback by Collier Books, a division of Macmillan Publishing Co., Inc., New York. *The Secret World of the Baby* by Beth Day and Margaret Liley and published by Random House in New York is recommended for children ages nine to eleven.

3. Conflicts with neighbors can sometimes be avoided if children who are given sex information are cautioned that some parents may not appreciate that information being shared with their own children.

4. Parents and/or other caretakers who supply sexual facts to children rarely talk about sexual arousal. Children who can anticipate increased arousal experiences as they enter puberty may cope more adequately with the heightened sex drive when it does intensify.

5. Dr. Mary Calderone, who is associated with SIECUS, suggests that most of the trauma following sexual molestation is due to the overreaction of adults rather than to the act itself unless the molestation involves physical pain. She suggests that adults casually and calmly try to help the child discuss his feelings and reassure him but that they not insist or pressure the child to discuss feelings which he may not, in fact, have.

6. When children are observed engaged in sexual play, the parents

can calmly suggest alternate games, explaining to their own child that he can ask questions if he is curious and that those kinds of games are not condoned by most adults.

7. Because it is around the age of three or four that children become sexually aware and begin to evidence an interest in sexual exploration, parents should be advised to discontinue the practice of having male and female siblings sleep together or bathe together after that age. Rutter (1970) feels that permitting sexual activity in children tends to whet their appetite for further sexual activity.

8. Very young children who observe or overhear sexual activity between their parents or other adults may become frightened and anxious. Somewhat older children, those between the ages of seven and ten may become preoccupied with sex and/or attempt to imitate adult sexual behavior. If a very young child accidentally observes his parents' sexual activity, unless there are signs that he is concerned or unless he questions the parent, it is better to ignore the situation than to imply concern. If the child asks questions about what he saw or if he seems disturbed, explaining the situation in simple age-appropriate terms after he has been asked for his perceptions is usually sufficient. (See also the chapter on Sexual Problems.)

ADOPTION

There are no really good controlled studies of the affect of adoption on the adopted child. Thus, it is not clear that the adopted child's problems are due to his adoptive status. They may be due to the same factors which result in psychological problems in any child. As will be noted later, there may be a tendency to blame the child's adoptive status for his problems and after the problems emerge they may be reinforced by factors inherent in the adoptive process. Reece and Levin (1968) suggest that the large number of adopted children in middle class areas who seem to have psychologic problems may be due to the tendency of middle class families to use psychiatric facilities and also to adopt.

Following are some of the circumstances which frequently lead to adoption and which may create problems in the development of the adopted child:

1. Schechter and Holter (1975) suggest that because the adoptive mother does not experience the fetus' rhythms during the pregnancy, the "fit" between the mother and the child may be "at risk." Anticipatory counseling may help the mother deal with the possible "emotional distance" in the relationship between herself and the adoptive infant.

2. Parents may feel defective because of their inability to have a child of their own, and the child's presence is a constant reminder of this defect.

3. Sometimes there are ambivalent feelings about raising another individual's child, and this may be reinforced if the child is obviously unlike the parents.

4. In many cases parents have waited for many years for a child; then when they do finally adopt a child, they tend to be older than the average parents, and sometimes it is more difficult for older individuals to rear a child through the normal but sometimes difficult developmental stages.

5. Parents who adopt children on the "grey market" may be concerned that the release signed by the biologic mother is not binding, a situation which may create anxiety.

6. The lack of prenatal care, alcohol, or drug ingestion and/or severe malnutrition during the pregnancy of the biologic mother as well as guilt sometimes associated with the premarital pregnancy are all factors which can affect the condition of the child and, in turn, the adoptive parents' reaction to him. This can then affect the later parent-child relationship.

7. If there are also natural children in the family, there are often differences in the way the parents treat the children. They may either treat the natural child as though he were a preferred child or compensate the adopted child by treating him as though he were a preferred child. Anticipatory guidance in these instances might prevent this.

Forman and Hetznecker (1975) suggest that the infant be adopted as soon after birth as possible so that bonding can occur. Unfortunately, the adoptive parents are usually not given the opportunity to form an attachment to the infant during the "sensitive period," the first several hours of life (Klaus and Kennell, 1976). Because the biologic mother usually does not see the infant either, bonding is delayed for these infants. This situation may, however, be preferable to a situation where the biologic mother is permitted to hold and feed the infant she knows she will be giving up in several days. Forman and Hetznecker warn against adopting older children because they have perhaps already been traumatized by "emotional deprivation." In addition some of them have already lived in a number of foster homes and may have major problems by the time they are adopted.

Some behavioral reasons why the adoptive child may have problems or why problems are exacerbated by the fact that they are adopted are:

1. After the adoption the parents may be disappointed because the child is not living up to their fantasy image of the child they wanted.

Anticipatory counseling of adoptive parents should help them lay to rest any conceptions they may have of an ideal biological child. It should be noted that if they are too attached to this nonexistent natural child, it may be difficult for them to form a satisfactory attachment to the adopted child.

2. When parents have a problem, possibly a normal developmental problem, with their adoptive child, they may blame the child's heredity, the agency, or the individual who helped them adopt the child for the problem, and they may then be less likely to carry out recommendations for handling the problem.

3. Ideally, the reasons why potential adoptive parents desire to adopt a child are explored and considered carefully before the request to adopt is granted. Sometimes parents who have marital problems hope that the presence of a child will resolve those problems. Some parents may even have an unconscious aversion to parenthood but, either for reasons of status or as a solution to personal problems, feel compelled to adopt a child.

4. Verville (1967) suggests that adoptive parents are either overly strict because of a strong "sense of duty" or very lax because they are afraid that if they discipline the child, he will feel rejected.

5. Some parents overstate the child's "specialness," unaware that children often infer that the parents may overstate the case in an attempt to compensate them for rejection by their biologic parents. Related to this is the tendency to support the child's feelings that he has been rejected. As a result of this apparent confirmation, the child may either pity himself or use his adoptive parents' concern to manipulate them, which can in turn result in overindulgence and/or overprotectiveness by the adoptive parents.

Since the word "adoption" is an abstract concept which the child under the age of six or seven cannot comprehend, he may be confused if he is told about his adoptive status before those ages. If, however, neighbors, or relatives inform the child that he is adopted or if the child overhears conversation concerning his adoption, he should be told as much as he can understand at that age. In general, when the child is told and how he is told depends on his age and his intellectual ability. Although most children initially express little reaction to this information, it is advised that it not be shared with the child during a stressful period in his life. Parents may benefit from knowing that no matter how conflict-free their relationship with the child has been, adopted adolescents tend to have greater identity problems than do adolescents who are not adopted (Schecter and Holter, 1975; Verville, 1967).

OVERPROTECTION

The overprotective parent is one who supervises closely everything the child does and who often performs tasks for the child to protect him from errors or failure. The parent's behavior implies that the child is not capable of doing things for himself, and, as a result, the child may stop functioning in those areas where he has not been permitted to experience success through his own efforts.

The overprotective parent does not permit the child to learn to delay gratification because he immediately complies with the child's desires for pleasure. The child is protected from anything that seems difficult and from any situation which may be uncomfortable.

Because overprotective parents tend to presume that some harm will come to the child, they tend to restrict his activities, both those activities which the child might wish to engage in by himself and those involving other children. The child may thus be prevented from learning social skills. When he is having trouble in school, these parents tend to blame his difficulty on the school and to resent any implication that they bear any responsibility for the child's problems.

It should be noted here that one theory of the etiology of adult depression argues that the people learn that they are helpless and therefore inadequate and ineffective and that these feelings can lead to depression (Blaney, 1977). Overprotective parents may, inadvertently, create these feelings in their children.

REFERENCES

Brody, Sylvia: Preventive intervention in current problems of early childhood, in Caplan, Gerald (Ed.): *Prevention of Mental Disorders in Children,* New York, Basic Books, Inc., 1961.

Blaney, Paul H.; Contemporary theories of depression: Critique and comparison. *J Abnormal Psychology,* 1977, **86**(3), 203–223.

Dreikurs, Rudolf and Grey, Loren: *Logical Consequences: A New Approach to Discipline,* New York, Meredity Press, 1968.

Forman, Marc A. and Hetznecker, William H.: Critical developmental issues, in Vaughan, V. C. and McKay, James R. (Eds.) *Nelson—Textbook of Pediatrics,* 10th ed., Philadelphia, W. B. Saunders Co., 1975.

Jacobs, Blanche S. and Moss, Howard A.: Birth order and sex of sibling as determinants of mother-infant interaction. *Child Development,* 1976, **47**, 315–322.

Johnson, Warren R.: *Masturbation,* New York, SIECUS Publications, 1967.

Klaus, Marshall H. and Kennell, John H.: *Maternal-Infant Bonding,* St. Louis, C. V. Mosby Co., 1976.

Lipton, George L.: Mother is a bad word: The rights of children in law in two custody cases. *Australian and New Zealand J Psychiatry,* 1977, **11**, 19–23.

MacDonald, A. P., Jr.: Birth order and personality. *J Consulting and Clinical Psychology,* 1971, **36**, 171–176.

McCandless, B. R.: *Adolescents: Behavior and Development.* Hinsdale, Ill, Dryden Press, Inc., 1970.

Mussen, Paul H. Conger, John J, and Kagan, Jerome: *Child Development and Personality,* New York, Harper and Row, 1956.

Nash, John: *Development Psychology: A Psychobiological Approach,* Englewood Cliffs, N.J. Prentice-Hall, Inc., 1970.

Reece, Shirley A., and Levin, Barbara: Psychiatric disturbances in adopted children: A descriptive study. *Social Work,* 1968, **13**(1), 101–111.

Richmond, Julius B. and Lipton, Earle L.: Studies on mental health of children with specific implications for pediatricians, in Caplan, Gerald (Ed.): *Prevention of Mental Disorders in Children,* New York, Basic Books, Inc., 1961.

Rutter, Michael: Normal psychosexual development: Paper presented at the British Psychological Society meeting in Leeds, England, November 6, 1970.

Satterfield, Sharon: Common sexual problems of children and adolescents, in Friedman, Stanford B. (Ed.): *The Pediatric Clinics of North America,* 1975, **22**(3), Philadelphia, W. B. Saunders Co.

Shechter, Marshall D. and Holter, F. Robert: Adopted children in their adoptive families in Friedman, Stanford B. (Ed.): *The Pediatric Clinics of North America,* 1975, **22**(3), Philadelphia, W. B. Saunders Co.

Verville, Elinor: *Behavior Problems of Children,* Philadelphia, W. B. Saunders Co., 1967.

CHAPTER **8**

Adolescence

Although the subject of adolescence, if it is to be dealt with comprehensively, requires a book devoted solely to that topic, anticipatory counseling may minimize the problems frequently found in this age group. Parents need to be made aware that children who are handled consistently early in their lives tend to feel more secure and comfortable and appear to be less needy as adolescents (McCandless, 1970). The following are conflicts which tend to be typical of adolescents in our society and suggestions for minimizing them:

1. The need to become independent. Many parents perceive the adolescent's rebelliousness and antagonism as undesirable behavior designed by the adolescent to annoy the parent rather than as the adolescent's need to deny his dependency needs in order to become independent (Muuss, 1969; McCandless, 1970; Carson, 1971). It seems reasonable to assume that when young children are permitted as much independence as they can tolerate; when they are given responsibilities which they are capable of carrying out and when some of their activities, at least, are a real contribution to the family if not to the community, they will have less need to forcibly wrest independence from their parents during adolescence.

Carson (1971) and Offer (1967), the former in a study of adolescents with problems and the latter in a study of normal adolescents found that most problems, including arguments, disagreements, and general rebellion occurred first at around the ages of 12 or 13. Parents who are not aware of the sometimes sudden change in the child may exacerbate the situation by overreacting to this change, which tends then to result in a counteraction from the child. For example, parents are often puzzled by the adolescent who begins to question parental values and beliefs which he previously accepted (Erik Erikson, in Muuss, 1969). It is suggested that parents engage in arguments and disagreements over

71

topics concerning values and opinions, in order to communicate to the child that his views are worthy of discussion. Such arguments also give the parent an opportunity to present appropriate facts and to discuss the rationale for the parent's belief system. In situations where the child wants to act out his new views, he can be permitted to hold those views even if the behavior itself may be harmful.

Anticipatory counseling may prevent parental overreaction to minor, benign rebellious behavior. For instance, parents who either forbid or appear to enjoy the adolescent's inappropriate clothing, distasteful room decorations, and his playing of loud, discordant music are not allowing the adolescent to perceive his behavior as a manifestation of successful rebellion.

Otto Rank (Muuss, 1979) points out that the adolescent, particularly the adolescent boy, is fearful of remaining close to his parents because this makes him feel like a child, a role which he is trying so hard to reject. The parents who are not aware of the motivation behind the child's perhaps sudden coolness may contribute to the worsening of the relationship by trying to force their attention on the child. On the other hand, they may suddenly stop expressing affection toward the child, who may then feel rejected and assume an air of bravado, which can exaggerate his attempts to become independent (McCandless, 1970). The parent's casual acceptance of the adolescent's fear of closeness without either forcing his expressions of affection on the child or suddenly withdrawing the affectionate behavior may help to alleviate the conflict. Gradually expressing affection in more mature ways as children mature prevents the need for the adolescent to suddenly pull away from the parent.

2. Limit setting and controls. Acting-out adolescents who are brought to child guidance clinics tend to fall into two categories: those who cannot be controlled by their parents because their parents do not know how to control them and those whose parents know how to control them but who are defiant and will not accept those controls. The parents of the former report that they have set limits and have been consistent and firm in handling the child; they are presently having problems because they did not anticipate the new behavior. Once they have been given suggestions for handling that behavior, the problem is alleviated. As noted above parents of defiant adolescents may know what to do but are ineffective because the child not only ignores the limits but refuses to accept the consequences of his unacceptable behavior. In these situations, the options are for individual, group, and family psychotherapy.

Parents whose children are not defiant can be supported in their confusion over disciplining the adolescent if they are made aware that although disciplining the adolescent is similar in many ways to disciplining the younger child, there are differences. Perhaps the parent is faced for the first time with a child who wants more freedom to do as he pleases and wants to be left alone to take responsibility for his own behavior. In addition, because of his need to be independent, he is more resistant to restraints on his behavior, and, because of his increased size, it is more difficult to enforce those restraints (Douvan and Adelson, 1966).

Following are suggestions for parents of acting-out adolescents:

a. Parents need to be aware that limits should be age-appropriate as well as appropriate to the individual child's maturity. Some parents need help in evaluating the amount of freedom their child can tolerate. A parent may not know what limits his child needs until the child has abused privileges already granted to him. Criteria for setting limits are not much different from those used for younger children:

(1) behavior which may harm the adolescent or others and/or

(2) behavior which infringes on the rights of others.

b. Parents whose young child required little supervision often cannot understand that the adolescent because of the combination of a desire for autonomy and faulty judgement may need more supervision than the young child.

c. Parents may find it easier to set reasonable limits if they know that many adolescents want external controls both because they can then "save face" with peers by blaming their parents for restricting anxiety-producing behavior and because, if externally controlled, they need not fear their own impulses.

d. If parents respect the adolescent's desire for privacy and refrain from criticizing him for minor annoying habits like itchiness, they will tend to more successful in gaining the adolescent's cooperation with parental controls.

e. If the parent's attempts to help the adolescent understand why his behavior is unacceptable is ineffective and punishment is necessary, deprivation of privileges, if consistently carried out, is usually effective, especially if the duration of the deprivation is short at first and increased as the behavior persists. The number of privileges denied can also be increased.

Some parents are concerned that although they may be able to exercise control over the adolescent's behavior in the home, they cannot supervise him when he is away from home. The adolescent should be aware that the rules governing his behavior also apply outside the home and consequences for infractions of those rules apply no matter where the behavior occurs.

f. In some situations where an adolescent is intractable, the parent may want to remove all privileges and require that the child earn them back, one by one, as his behavior improves. This is most effective if the first privilege earned is the least desirable and if the amount of time spent enjoying the privilege is, at first, small and then increased as the appropriate behavior continues.

Although there is no hard evidence that adolescents whose parents were lax and/or inconsistent in disciplining them when they were younger had more problems than adolescents whose parents had been firm and consistent in their discipline, experience tends to confirm this hypothesis. Some permissive parents are reluctant to discipline their children because of their desire to be "pals" to their children. Parents should be warned that assuming the role of "pal" while children are young may create problems during adolescence. Because adolescent misbehavior can often result in serious consequences, the previously permissive parent may have to set limits and exercise some control which is more likely to be met with defiance if the adolescent perceives the parent as a peer. The adolescent who views the parent as a pal may have difficulty expressing anger toward the parent, and, as a result, he may turn the anger upon himself and become depressed. The adolescent may also become depressed because of guilt over his rebellious behavior, and he may provoke conflicts with his parents to lessen the guilt.

3. Identity problems. If parents are aware of the normal "identity crisis" of adolescence (Erik Erikson, in Muuss, 1969), they are less likely to be disturbed when their apparently stable child begins to change his interests and friends frequently, overidentifies with movie or literary heroes and/or with the leaders of the groups to which he belongs, and if he spends time with "undesirable" peers. If the parents can anticipate these changes and accept them as relatively normal, they may be able to control their tendency to overreact. The instability of relationships and interests and often poor judgement will tend to be temporary and transient if the parents can, with some resemblance of calm, await the end of this period in the child's development.

Because mothers and female teachers tend to be the primary child caretakers of both boys and girls in our society, girls, since they are continually exposed to female models, tend to have fewer problems than boys in sexual identification. Because the father is often the only male model for the young boy, it is important that he be involved with his son throughout the boy's childhood to prevent or minimize sexual identity problems. In situations where fathers are uninvolved and/or passive and mothers are dominant, the male adolescent may actively reject his mother not only to assert his independence but out of fear that he may be identifying with a female. Many mothers report that they become confused when their 12- or 13-year-old son with whom they thought they had a good relationship suddenly, for no apparent reason, turns against them. At the same time that the boy is rejecting his mother, he will try to involve his father in a relationship with him.

4. Sexuality and boy image. Related to identification is the new sexual awareness which Erik Erikson suggests is an important factor in the adolescent's need to form a new identity. Many parents are not aware that their self-assured young child may, in adolescence, feel physically awkward, self-conscious, and sensitive. Kurt Lewin (Muuss, 1969) has suggested that the adolescent is not only concerned with his body in general but is fearful that the primary and secondary sex characteristics might not be normal. Parents and older siblings often become impatient with the adolescent who appears to overreact to teasing and criticism which is directed at his appearance. Otto Rank has suggested that one of the major conflicts in adolescence is between the biological forces and the adolescent's conscience or, more properly, his superego. He has suggested that adolescents whose parents have helped them develop a strong superego from childhood are less likely to be overwhelmed by this conflict.

5. Mood swings. The anxiety generated by the conflicts listed above as well as by concerns over the future contribute to the adolescent's apparent emotional instability. Rorschach responses by adolescents, when compared with adult responses, do resemble those of emotionally disturbed adults. If, however, one considers the probable source of the adolescent's behavior, it is not surprising to find some manifestations of emotional chaos. Anticipatory counseling may help to minimize the instability. If parents have not protected their children from feelings such as anger, grief, and some anxiety and if they have not protected the children from their children's own mistakes, children tend to learn early and gradually how to cope effectively with their feelings and should, during adolescence, be able to cope with the surges of feelings that appear to occur at that time. If parents can anticipate the potential problems of adolescence and can keep from overreacting when problems do arise, there should be less anxiety related to parent-child relationships. All of the suggestions given above for minimizing some of the specific problems should help to minimize the moodiness typical of adolescence.

Parents who are faced somewhat suddenly with an uncommunicative adolescent who seems to want to be left alone, are puzzled, concerned, and feel rejected. Those parents who can anticipate that this may occur are less upset if they let the adolescent know that they are available if needed and then leave him alone as long as he is carrying out his necessary functions at home and at school. In most cases, depression due to a poor self-image, inner directed anger, and/or guilt is an adjustment reaction of adolescence and is temporary.

Parents sometimes dread the onset of their child's adolescence because of the negative characteristics attributed to that stage of development. In addition to anticipatory counseling, they need reassurance that many, probably the majority of, adolescents manage to cope effectively without, as McCandless (1970) puts it, "melodrama." In fact, Piaget states that it is a "duty of the modern adolescent . . . to revolt against all imposed truths and to build up his intellectual and moral ideas as freely as he can."

Although drugs are also abused by younger children, drug abuse tends to reach its peak during adolescence, and some anticipatory guidance may help to prevent abuse. Following are a number of factors which have been found to be associated with drug abuse and some suggestions for prevention:

1. Zuckerman, et al. (1970) found that drug abusers tended to be sensation-seekers. The source of this need may be twofold: (a) It is possible that children who had been protected from feelings or who had not been stimulated to have "peak" experiences may later turn to mood-enhancing drugs. (b) Louria (1971) suggests that for some adolescents drugs relieve boredom and satiation. These adolescents look for new and different experiences, and taking drugs is sometimes the only new experience available to them. Adolescents who as children were overindulged, or who were permitted to engage in activities more appropriate for the adolescent or adult, may find that there are few if any experiences they have not known. And the child whose experiences have been narrow may become easily bored. The child who has been exposed to a wide range of challenging activities, particularly creative activities, may actually turn to those activities in adolescence and is less likely to seek sensation for the sake of relieving boredom.

2. Reilly (1975) and Kaplan and Meyerowitz (1970) found that adolescents whose parents were vague and inconsistent in setting limits, who could not forbid the child to behave in ways which were harmful and undesirable, and who generally did not say "no" to the child, tended to abuse drugs more than adolescents whose parents were consistent, had definite standards, and were able to deny the child privileges or rewards when this seemed appropriate.

3. Parents of adolescents who abused drugs tend to themselves abuse drugs although not always the same drugs abused by the child and not always illegeal drugs (Bowker, 1976; Reilly, 1975; Louria, 1971; and Carson, 1971). Not infrequently the child takes his first drug from the parents' medicine cabinet. These drugs are usually mood-enhancing drugs or tranquillizers. Whether a child will abuse drugs or

not depends less on the parents' lectures than on the parents' behavior.

4. Reilly (1975) in his study found that adolescents whose parents attended to them only when the adolescents engaged in inappropriate or unacceptable behavior tended to turn to drugs. There was little or no emotional attachment between family members and the parents tended to be overcritical. Sometimes these adolescents express the feeling that since they will be criticized anyhow, they might as well "be shot for a sheep as for a lamb."

It has also been found that children who were not permitted to be age-appropriately independent, whose parents were inflexible and had unrealistically high expectations of the child, tended to become drug abusers during adolescence (Kaplan and Meyerowitz, 1970; Carson, 1971).

5. Kaplan and Meyerowitz (1970) and Jessor (1976) found that adolescents who were regular marijuana users placed little value on achievement. Jessor noted, in addition, that the parents of these adolescents neither supported the child nor controlled his behavior. These children also tended to exhibit more general unacceptable behavior than adolescents who were not regular marijuana users.

6. Finally, Kaplan and Meyerowitz (1970) found that the drug abuser tends to cope less successfully with negative feelings related to his self-image and/or with situations which elicit those feelings. They imply that children who have learned, early in their development, how to effectively handle their feelings, and whose parents have not protected them from negative emotions, are more likely, during adolescence, to continue to cope effectively without resorting to drugs as a defense against the anxiety which can be aroused when the adolescent experiences feelings of inadequacy.

In counseling parents of drug abusers, the same methods outlined earlier in this chapter for dealing with acting-out adolescents can be recommended. Adolescent drug abusers who do not respond to parental control may benefit from programs designed specifically for the adolescent drug abuser.

References

Bowker, Lee H.: The incidence of drug use and associated factors in two small towns: A community survey. *Bulletin on Narcotics,* 1976, **28**(4), 17–25.

Carson, Wm. McMillin: Home is where the grounding is, in 1972 pub. by Hamilton Wesley House, Hamilton, Ontario, Canada, The Child Study Association of America (by the staff): *You, Your Child and Drugs,* New York, The Child Study Press, 1971.

Count, Jerome: The conflict factor in adolescent growth. *Adolescence,* 1967, **2**(6), 167–181.

Douvan, Elizabeth and Adelson, Joseph: *The Adolescent Experience,* New York, John Wiley & Sons, Inc., 1966.

Jessor, Richard: Predicting time of onset of marijuana use: A developmental study of high school youth. *J Consulting and Clinical Psychology,* 1976, 44(1), 125–134.

Kaplan, Howard B. and Meyerowitz, Joseph H.: Social and psychological correlates of drug abuse. *Social Science and Medicine,* 1970, 4, 203–225.

Louria, Donald B.: Currents in drug abuse. Paper presented at 138th meeting of the American Association for the Advancement of Science, 1971.

McCandless, Boyd R.: *Adolescents: Behavior and Development,* Hinsdale, Ill., The Dryden Press, Inc., 1970.

Muuss, Rolf E.: *Theories of Adolescence,* 2nd ed., New York, Random House, 1969.

Offer, Daniel: Studies of normal adolescents. *Adolescence,* 1967, 1(4), 305–320.

Reilly, Dennis M.: Family factors in the etiology and treatment of youthful drug abuse. *Family Therapy,* 1975, 2(2), 149–171.

Zuckerman, Marvin, Neary, Richard S., and Brustman, Barbara A.: Sensation-seeking scale correlates in experience (smoking, drugs, alcohol, "hallucinations" and sex) and preference for complexity (designs), in *Proceedings, 78th Annual Convention,* American Psychological Association, 1970.

CHAPTER 9

The Chronically Ill Child

The presence of a chronically ill child in a disharmonious family, although not the primary source of the tension, adds to the already existing stress not only because of his special needs but because he may be singled out as a scapegoat. In families where there is a need for a scapegoat for marital conflict, for instance, the weakest member of the family is usually chosen to play that role.

Problems created by the presence of a chronically ill child in a relatively harmonious family can usually be handled effectively if the parents are given anticipatory guidance and specific suggestions for dealing with particular problems. Because chronically ill children, when compared with physically normal children, tend to have more social and psychological problems (Pless and Roghmann, 1970), it is important that minor problems in the chronically ill are not permitted to become major. The authors of the above study stress, however, that most chronically ill children are socially and psychologically healthy.

In a study of the marital stability in families with a child who has neural tube malformation (primarily children with meningomylocele), Tew, et al. (1977) found that after ten years the divorce rate in the families where the child was still surviving was nine times higher than that for the local population and three times higher than that in families where the affected child had died. It was interesting to note that in those families where conception of the affected child occurred before marriage, the risk of divorce or separation was 50%. The authors conclude that, with this particular chronically ill child at least, the strain on the marriage is great.

Many of the following potential stresses and problems caused by the presence of a chronically ill child in the home can be prevented or, at least, minimized if the parents are made aware of them shortly after the diagnosis is made:

79

1. The most typical problem results from the tendency on the part of the parents to overprotect the chronically ill child. Parents should be aware of measures necessary for protecting the child but should be warned against overprotection. Sometimes even the most knowledgeable parent is unaware that, within the limits of the child's abilities, he can be treated as if he were a "normal" child. Frazier (1977) points out that chronically ill children need to be free to develop and should not be limited by unnecessary protection. He also cautions that children who are protected from stress will not be able to handle stress later and that the overprotected child may continue to seek protection in adulthood. Overprotection may result in continued dependency, immaturity, and in a poor self-image, which has probably already been lowered because of the illness.

2. Related to overprotection are problems resulting from overindulgence and permissiveness (Hartman and Boone, 1972). If parents are permissive, the child may lack self-control and initiative. Travis (1976) suggests that the overindulged child will be "spoiled and arrogant" and warns against the resentment by siblings over the indulgence and permissiveness. Unaffected siblings also tend to resent attention given to the chronically ill child that is not necessary for the child's physical well-being.

3. An overly close mother-child relationship may also result in problems. Hartman and Boone (1972) warn against the separation anxieties resulting from a symbiotic relationship. In addition to the unhappiness this can bring to the mother and to the affected child, there is the possible added effect on the other members of the family, who feel, if not rejected, at least shut out. If father can become more involved, the relationship between mother and child may be less close, and mother would be released to spend time with the other children.

4. The unaffected sibling may need some counseling to help him deal with guilt over being normal and with resentment against the affected child who may require considerable attention. He may also need some help in dealing with the death of the sibling in those cases where early death is anticipated. In cases where the source of the illness is genetic, the nonaffected sibling is often concerned that he may be a carrier and that this will affect his plans for marriage and having children.

5. The chronically ill child who has no obvious psychological problems is faced with a number of stresses:

    a. He is often handicapped, implying restrictions, which in turn, limit his independence.

    b. Many chronically ill children cannot attend school consis-

tently, which interferes with their development of academic skills, which, in turn, can lower their self-images and prevent them from experiencing success in that area at least. Since schoolmates are important sources of social interaction, missing school may result in some social isolation.
   c. Depending on the particular illness, the child may almost constantly anticipate crises which can result in sustained anxiety.
   d. Chronic pain may result in frustration, anger, and depression. The danger of drug addiction should also be considered.
   e. It is not unusual for chronically ill children to resent their parents. They may consciously or unconsciously blame the parents for their condition, and, although they may, on the one hand, be happy at being overindulged, they may chafe at being overprotected. They may also resent their dependence on the parent, and, since overindulgence and overprotection may be a reaction formation by the parent against their own rejection of the child, the child sometimes unconsciously detects the rejection, which may produce resentment.

6. Travis (1976) reports that one of the most frequent questions asked by parents concerning how to manage the chronically ill child is how to discipline him. The tendency to overindulge and overprotect the child is often the source of permissiveness. This is a particular problem in the management of chronically ill children who may use their illness as a means of rebelling and/or expressing anger: they may refuse to take their medication and treatments or they may disregard medical advice in general.

7. In addition to being faced with the foregoing problems, the adolescent is confronted with additional pressures: depending on the specific illness, self-consciousness may be intensified and dating and marriage may be a problem; they are more aware of the seriousness of their disease; missing school is likely to jeopardize their future; depending upon the specific illness, the need to be dependent may result in greater resentment at these ages when independence is so dearly sought; and concern with peer relationships and activities involving peers in which they cannot, because of their disease, participate.

Hospitalization

Tuma (1975) suggests that approximately $1/3$ to $1/2$ of hospitalized children have psychological problems associated with their illness and/or the hospitalization. Most authors agree that preparation for the hospitalization can reduce stress. A tour of the hospital, including learning about the hospital routine, meeting the staff if possible, should help (Lulow, 1967; Dunn, 1975; Kenny, 1975; Travis, 1976). Travis suggests the following books as an aid in preparing the child for his hospitalization: *A Visit to the Hospital* by Francine Chase, published in New York by Grosset and Dunlap, 1958; *Curious George Goes to the Hospital* by Marget and H. A. Rey, published in Boston by Houghton-Mifflin, 1966; and *Johnny Goes to the Hospital* by J. A. Sever, published in Boston by Houghton-Mifflin, 1953.

Travis also suggests that the child might feel less frightened if he can bring his favorite toy to the hospital with him. Kenny (1975) and Dunn (1975) suggest that parents anticipate that the child may perceive the hospital as punishment and/or a rejection of him. This can be minimized if the parents can help the child verbalize his concerns and assure him that his perceptions are not valid.

Kenny also discusses the appropriateness of the child's sadness at being in the hospital. Not infrequently, mental health workers are called in on consultation because a hospitalized child is "depressed" when his unhappiness is appropriate; he is in a strange place; he is separated from his parents, and, depending on his age, he may not be able to understand fully why he is there. Some children are concerned that they will lose parts of their body or that they will be disfigured. Lulow (1967), in discussing children who are to have surgery, cites Anna Freud, who stated that surgery stimulates ideas of "being attacked, overwhelmed. . . ." The anxiety and the physical pain may cause the child to become depressed, withdrawn, and/or angry.

Parents may be less anxious if they can anticipate the possibility that the child will regress as a result of the hospitalization (Brazelton, 1975; Kenny, 1975). The regressive behavior will tend to be temporary if the parents casually retrain the child to again behave in an age-appropriate manner.

How long the mother should remain with the hospitalized child, and the role she assumes while she is with him, depends to some extent on the age of the child, the separation experience of the child, his personality, the degree of his anxiety, the stage of his illness, the relationship between the mother and child, and the needs of the family at home. Kenny (1975) believes that the mother should room-in with any child under the age of two and that she should participate in the care of the child. He suggests, however, that if there are other young children at home whose needs are such that the continued absence would create strong family problems or if she cannot emotionally tolerate remaining in the hospital environs, perhaps she should not stay with the child. It should be noted that some mothers resent being asked to participate in the care of the child. If they can perceive this as benefiting the child rather than as relieving the hospital personnel of their duties, they might be more accepting of this role.

The child who has had frequent and gradually longer separations from the parent is less likely to be concerned if the parent is not with him constantly. In addition, if the child is extroverted and quickly attaches himself to others, he may not be anxious if the parent does not remain with him. It is probably more important for the parent to stay with the child in the acute stages of his illness and when he is terminally ill. There are instances when the mother-child relationship is so poor that the mother's presence is counterproductive. In these latter instances, if the child appears to have a need to attach himself to some adult, there may be another member of the family who could remain with the child. Sometimes assigning a consistent volunteer to the child fulfills that need.

Travis (1976) warns that going home after having been hospitalized in a pleasant, stimulating, nourishing facility can cause the child to experience conflicts over leaving, especially a child who is alone or one who comes from a "disadvantaged" home. Creer, et al. (1974) found that making the hospital stay dull and even unpleasant for an asthmatic boy who tended to exaggerate his symptoms in order to be hospitalized or to try to remain in the hospital longer was successful in preventing further malingering. He was made to stay in his room by himself and was not permitted visitors except necessary staff members. He was not allowed to visit other children on the ward, and he could only read school books; he could not read comic books or watch television. He also had to eat his meals alone in his room and could not go to the patient dining room. When he was outside the hospital, he was praised for appropriate and acceptable behavior and was encouraged to engage in those activities which tended to result in success experiences.

Asthma

Although asthmatic children are vulnerable to potential psychological problems which seem to be unique to asthmatics, they are also susceptible to the psychological problems often found in other chronically ill children. Thus, asthma will be discussed as a chronic illness, in general, and those illnesses which differ in the kinds of potential problems associated with them will be discussed separately.

There are differences of opinion concerning the role of emotional factors in asthma. Most writers believe that emotional stress, although not directly a cause of asthma, can act as a "triggering mechanism" (Travis, 1976; Chong, 1977; Frazier, 1977). Khan (1977) suggests that the child who fears separation may learn that when he has an asthma attack, his mother is closer to him, a situation which then reduces his fear. The author argues that if this pairing of asthma attack and fear reduction continues, the separation fears can, when they are aroused, "trigger an attack." Travis warns that emotional problems in the chronically ill child may be a consequence of the disease rather than the source.

Studies reveal that there tends to be a disturbed relationship between mothers and their asthmatic children (Travis, 1976; Frazier, 1977; Kessler, 1966). Travis suggests that this is due to the child's feelings of insecurity brought about by mother's overprotectiveness. In those situations where the child's need for closeness to the mother is insatiable, the relationship will also tend to suffer. Kessler suggests that the child may be reacting to the mother's unconscious rejection, symptoms of which may be overprotection and overindulgence. In any case, parentectomy, which appears to be effective in the treatment of asthmatic children, is advised in asthma and not in other chronic diseases (Kessler, 1966; Frazier, 1977).

Following are some typical problems found in asthmatics and/or their families:

1. As noted above, there is often a symbiotic relationship with the mother which can interfere not only with the child's striving for independence but with his ability to effectively handle his anger. His strong dependence on his mother prevents him from expressing anger toward her directly. This may result in passive-aggressive behavior or in other maladaptive expressions of anger.

2. Because of the fear of attacks, some asthmatic children are shy and withdrawn. Others, however, tend to repress their fears and appear to be outgoing and undisturbed by their illness. The latter child is more difficult to treat because, despite symptoms of emotional disturbance, he, and frequently his parents, deny that there are problems.

3. According to Frazier (1977) and Travis (1976), asthmatics appear to frequently have their attacks at night, a situation which tends to place a strain on family relationships. Mothers report that fathers tend to sleep through the attacks, which adds to the resentment mothers already may feel at having their sleep interrupted.

4. Depriving the allergic child of a pet can cause resentment in siblings and in the child. In addition, because of pets in other households, the child and/or parents may have to restrict their social activities.

5. As noted earlier, when the child has to miss school frequently, he may not only fall behind in his school work but in the development of his social skills. Related to this are the necessary limits which have to

be placed on the child's participation in even those activities which are safe. The amount of activity which he is permitted may be restricted or the weather may be inclement. Some of the stress may be minimized if the teacher is made aware of the problem, and, in some cases, it is appropriate for the teacher to alert the child's classmates to his problem.

Travis (1976) discusses the potential for secondary gains, which, if realized, may result in problems for the family. Asthmatic children have reported, during psychotherapy, that they use their asthma to avoid school, to try to keep their parents together, and to avoid conflicts with others. They also use their asthma to express their anger by interfering with their parent's sleep and by not permitting their parents to go out. They report that they also use their attacks to avoid punishment. Apparently, these behaviors occur at varied levels of awareness. Some of the children become aware of their motivations only later, and some are aware of them at the time they are engaging in the behavior but control the behavior. When these children have been asked about the possible life threatening results of their behavior, they appear to be either unconcerned or to consider this less important than achieving their immediate ends.

Experience in a mental health clinic attached to a hospital has shown that in families which are basically functional and intact, where parents have had anticipatory guidance, have not overprotected or overindulged their children, and have permitted them to become appropriately independent, there has been a significant reduction in the intensity and frequency of the child's asthmatic attacks.

Leukemia

Although many of the potential problems discussed above are also relevant here, there are some differences. Since it is possible that the child's life span will be shortened, it is more difficult for parents not to overprotect and overindulge their leukemic child. It is also more difficult for them to discipline him. Travis (1976) suggests that when parents overindulge the child, they may communicate to him that he is, indeed, seriously ill, which can increase the child's anxiety. If the child is not disciplined, he may become "a little dictator."

Another potential problem involves the leukemic child's self-image. Loss of hair, for instance, may give the appearance of premature aging which can cause the child to feel different and which can elicit teasing from peers. In this situation it is probably essential that the teacher and/or the principal talk to the other children about the problem. Travis recommends that the child attend school regularly so that he is kept busy and has less time to brood about himself and his condition and so that he can experience some success. (See also the chapter on Death and Dying.)

Juvenile Diabetes

Travis (1976) suggests that injections of insulin which are painful, deprivation of sweets, and the necessity for a very routine life may cause the child to perceive his mother as a punishing individual because she is the one who usually sets the limits. Sometimes testing the urine is embarrassing to the child, especially to the adolescent. He may suffer socially and feel "different" because he cannot stop with other children for a hamburger or ice cream, for instance.

Travis suggests that school personnel and perhaps relatives be informed that sometimes when an insulin reaction is severe, the child may become rebellious and refuse to accept the sugar. In these situations, the administration of glucagon is indicated.

As with so many chronic illnesses, the disease can become a convenient but dangerous outlet for the child's anger and rebelliousness. The rebellious diabetic child, particularly as he enters adolescence, may eat sweets when he knows he should not do so or may refuse to eat after he has already taken his insulin. Some children may insist on doing their own urine tests and then change the results. There is some difference of opinion concerning the age at which a child should be responsible for his care, especially for injecting himself. The consensus is that this be done as early as possible. Younger children, however, will need supervision. Because of their tendency to rebel with little concern for the threat to their health, adolescents may also need supervision. Children who are accustomed to accepting limits and who have a relatively good relationship with their parents are less likely to have problems than are those children who have not developed inner controls and/or whose relationship with their parents is poor or inappropriate. In those cases where the parent-child relationship is stressful, parents should be referred for individual or family psychotherapy if they seem unable to benefit from short term behavior-oriented counseling.

Cystic Fibrosis

Although parents of children with cystic fibrosis also tend to overprotect and overindulge their affected children, the tendency to overindulge is not as great as that which occurs in families where the affected child has leukemia. For some reason, the relationship between mother and child is not as disturbed as that found in families with an asthmatic child. The child with cystic fibrosis does, however, often feel socially isolated. The odor of foul stools and flatulence are embarrassing and may result in rejection because of the repugnance it can elicit in others. The need to expectorate may also be embarrassing and the child may avoid this important function (Travis, 1976). To alleviate some of the embarrassment, it is suggested that, as in other chronic illnesses, teachers and perhaps schoolmates be made aware of the problem. As more and more children with cystic fibrosis are living into adulthood, problems related to self-image, independence, dating, marriage, and having children become more salient.

Parents' groups, as well as groups involving the affected children and the nonaffected siblings, have been generally effective in helping families to cope with the stress created by the presence in the family of a chronically ill child.

Reference

Brazelton, T. Berry: Anticipatory guidance, in Friedman, Stanford B. (Ed.): *The Pediatric Clinics of North America,* 1975, **22**(3), Philadelphia, W. B. Saunders Co.

Chong, T. M.: The management of bronchial asthma. *J. Asthma Res,* 1977, **14**(2), 73–89.

Creer, Thomas L., Weinberg, Eugene, and Molk, Leizer: Managing a hospital behavior problem: Malingering. *J Behavior Therapy and Experimental Psychiatry,* 1974, **5**(3/4), 259–262.

Dunn, J. M.: Role of the physician in prevention of psychologic disorders in the sick child, Vaughn, Victor C. and McKay, R. James (Eds.): *Nelson—Testbook of Pediatrics.* 10th ed., Philadelphia, W. B. Saunders Co., 1975.

Frazier, Claude A.: *Psychosomatic Aspects of Allergy,* New York, Van Nostrand Reinhold Co., 1977.

Hartman, B. H. and Boone, Donald R.: The benevolent overreaction: A well-intentioned but malignant influence on the handicapped child. *Clinical Pediatrics,* 1972, **11**(5), 268–271.

Kenny, Thomas J.: The hospitalized child, in Friedman, Stanford B. (Ed.): *The Pediatric Clinics of North America,* 1975, **22**(3), Philadelphia, W. B. Saunders Co.

Kessler, Jane W.: *Psychopathology of Childhood,* Englewood Cliffs, N.J., Prentice-Hall, Inc., 1966.

Khan, Aman U.: Effectiveness of biofeedback and counterconditioning in the treatment of bronchial asthma. *J Psychosomatic Res,* 1977, **21,** 97–104.

Luce, Gay: Psychodynamics of asthmatic children, in Hardy, Richard E. and Cull, John G. (Eds.): *Therapeutic Needs of the Family,* Springfield, Ill., Charles C. Thomas, 1974.

Lulow, William V.: Preventable psychotic episode. *New York State J Medicine,* 1967, **67**(21), 2882–2885.

Pless, Ivan B and Roughmann, Klaus J.: Chronic illness and its consequences: Observations based on three epidemiologic surveys. *J Pediatrics,* 1971, **79**(3), 351–359.

Tew, B. J., Laurence, K. M., Payne, H., and Rawnsley, K.: Marital stability
    following the birth of a child with spina bifida. *Brit J Psychiatry,* 1977,
    131, 79–82.
Travis, Georgia: *Chronic Illness in Children: Its Impact on Child and Family,*
    Stanford, Cal., Stanford University Press, 1976.
Tuma, June M.: Pediatric psychologist . . . . ? *J Clinical Child Psychology,*
    1975 (Fall), 9–17.

CHAPTER **10**

Problems Related to Death

Loss of a Parent by Death

Many of the concerns expressed by both parents and school personnel indicate some common misconceptions of the effect on children of the loss of a parent:

1. They imply that all children are severely and, unless they receive help, forever emotionally disturbed as a result of the loss. They tend to respond well, however, when it is suggested to them that how the child reacts may be, to a larger extent, a result of the adult's expectations of how the child will or should be effected.

2. They express concern that a boy whose father had died is likely to become a homosexual. They can be reassured that although the presence of a male model in the home may facilitate appropriate sexual identification, it is not essential (Weinraub, 1978). A boy who, prior to the father's death, exhibited feminine characteristics may benefit from a surrogate father: a "big brother," or a close relationship with an uncle or grandfather.

3. The most common misconception is the assumption that a child's behavior problems, appearing at any time following the death of a parent, are due to the child's emotional reaction to the loss. It should be pointed out to the child's caretakers that his unacceptable and inappropriate behavior may be reinforced by their tendency to justify it. When they follow suggestions for dealing with the behavior and when they help the child express his feelings about the death, the child's behavior tends to improve. This is not to minimize the emotional effect of the death on the child. There are studies which do show a relationship between adult depression and early childhood bereavement (Brown, 1966; Birtchnell, 1970); it is suggested, however, that it is the manner in which the loss was handled in childhood which probably differentiates those adults who have problems resulting from that loss and those who do not.

89

It is difficult, without more evidence, to attribute to young children the same feelings and thoughts which adults seem to experience following the loss of a significant person. John Bowlby suggests that infants and young children who lose their primary caretaker do tend to grieve in the same manner that adults do but that this may be more properly a reaction to separation than to death as a permanent loss. Silverman and Englander (1975) suggest that when children have been able to express their concerns, symptoms like enuresis and sleeplessness have been transitory. Melear (1973), replicating a study done by Nagy in 1948 of how children perceive death at different ages, concluded that children between the ages of three and four are relatively ignorant of the meaning of death. Children from four to seven years of age tended to think of death as temporary rather than permanent and irreversible, and, thus, viewed the dead person as someone who can be brought back to life. A few children at the ages of five to seven but most children from seven to ten tended to view death as permanent but indicated they thought that dead people retain their senses. Children over the ages of ten, although there was some overlap with younger children, were able to view death realistically. Parents who do not understand that children and adults do not perceive death in the same way often become upset and express fears that there is something wrong with the child who does not seem to grieve. Many children do mourn in their own way. They will use denial or they will become angry and/or depressed. These feelings, however, tend to be transitory and sporadic or delayed.

Following are some of the more typical problems resulting from the manner in which the death of the parent is handled:

1. Adults who tend to project their feelings onto the child communicate to the child, albeit inadvertently, that the child should be experiencing feelings such as depression. One effect of this projection may be to induce guilt feelings in a child who is not feeling depressed. Another effect of this projection is to elicit pity from adults who perceive the child as being unhappy. There is some evidence that these children may then pity themselves, the result of which can be an overly dependent child who feels helpless.

2. The child who is encouraged to idolize the deceased parent may compare the latter to the surviving parent and thus, of course, find the surviving parent wanting. And there is some evidence to indicate that children who idolize a parent tend to generalize this perception to others of the same or opposite sex and then are disappointed when these others fall short of their expectations.

3. The surviving parent who tries to assume the roles of both mother and father runs the risk of resenting the demands of the child for the

attention the child might receive from two parents. Because of his feelings of resentment, the parent may feel guilty. In addition, his inability to completely compensate for the loss of a parent may generate further guilt.

4. A common problem for which the surviving parent seeks help is related to the necessity for the family, in cases of both divorce and the death of the parent, to live with relatives. The typical complaints center around the conflict over child management techniques. Sometimes bringing all members of the household together for child management counseling results in less conflict. In many cases the surviving parent permits himself to become dependent on the relatives for help in caring for the child and is reluctant to move away and assume full responsibility for the child's care.

5. According to Connor and Doerring (1968) children become angry when they are separated from a "loved one." They frequently perceive the separation as a rejection. If efforts are not made to help the child express his anger, this can create problems both at the time of separation or death and in the future. Pubescent and adolescent children are more likely than younger ones to be angry at the surviving parent because they blame that parent for the death. The younger child is more likely to blame himself for the death. His tendency to engage in magical thinking leads him to the conclusion that the parent died either as a punishment for the child's misbehaviors or as a consequence of his occasional fleeting wish for the parents' death at those times when he was angry at the parent. Koocher (1973) suggests that, to correct previous misconceptions and prevent further ones, one would do well to ask the child to explain in his own words his understanding of the explanations made to him.

6. Data gathered from widows concerning their views of their children's reactions to the death of a parent (Silverman and Englander, 1975) indicate that many boys appear to try to assume the father's role. Sometimes well meaning relatives will tell the child directly that this is now his responsibility and sometimes the surviving parent, in this case the mother, in her loneliness and need to have someone share responsibilities with her, will encourage the child to assume the role of father and often inadvertently, the role of the husband. Where the child is permitted to act as a father to the younger children, the result is, as might be expected, an intensification of sibling rivalry. The women taking part in this survey did not report having this same problem with their daughters. It has been suggested that the boy's need to become less dependent on his mother becomes more difficult to fulfill when the father is not present to assume some of the parental responsibility for him. Thus, by assuming the role of the male member

of the household, the boy can still free himself from his dependency on mother. (See section on Dating and Remarriage for the effects of father absence on children.)

Girls as well as boys may suffer serious consequences in instances where the surviving parent becomes overly close to the child, sometimes the oldest child or more usually an only child. When these mother-child pairs are observed in the clinic setting, even where the child is a female, the interaction between them resembles more that of a married couple than that of a parent and child. If the relationship is not changed, it can have the effect of preventing the child from developing age-appropriate social and recreational skills; it can also intensify reactions to the surviving parent's dating and possibly remarriage. The gratification that both the parent and the child derive from this relationship is considerable, and many parents are resistant to suggestions for changing it. Possibly because there are many more widows than widowers and in divorce mothers still tend to have custody of the children, there is little available information concerning the relationship between father and child in mother-absent homes. In one clinic case, the father was trying to be a mother to his 12-year-old son and as a result was infantilizing the boy.

7. The widows questioned by Silverman and Englander (1975) report that some children express the fear that the surviving parent would also die. This can result in school phobia and other separation problems. Although this fear is not unusual, it tends to be persistent in the child who, prior to the parent's death, tended to be somewhat fearful, clinging, and overdependent for his age.

There is, presently, a consensus that if children are adequately informed about the parent's death and are permitted to talk about the death freely and to express their feelings, many of the problems often associated with the death of the parent could be prevented or at least minimized (Silverman and Englander, 1975; Stitt, 1971; Connor and Doerring, 1968). Because of the concern with the expression of feelings, sometimes pressure is placed on the child to experience and express feelings which he really may not have. As has already been noted, the surviving parent and other adults sometimes express the fear that there is something wrong with the child because he is not reacting as these adults feel he should react. Following are some further suggestions for preventing or minimizing adverse reactions to death:

1. The free flow of conversation about the deceased parent in addition to the presence of photographs permit the child to keep the parent's memory alive so that he can more easily handle the loss as he matures and becomes aware of the permanence of the separation.

2. If explanations are given to the child honestly and openly, in

addition to satisfying the child's need to know, the parent is giving the child permission to talk about the loss. Connor and Doerring (1968) suggest that explanations to the child be couched in concrete terms, in language that he will understand. Dr. Albert Solnit emphasizes the need to adapt the explanations to the age of the child—"smaller amounts of reality for a three-year-old than for an eight-year-old." He also suggests that the proper terms, "death" and "dead" be used, not euphemistic terms which may confuse the child. Most importantly, children are more likely to talk about their feelings if they can be reassured that whatever they feel, even anger toward the deceased parent, is acceptable. There is considerable evidence that if the child can verbalize his angry feelings he is less likely to act them out maladaptively.

3. A child who has been encouraged by the parent to talk about death may find that when he does, he elicits positive attention from the parent. As a result, he may continue to discuss the death and to express feelings concerning the death which he claims to have. Parents of these children will frequently seek help because they find themselves resenting the amount of attention the child's behavior demands and because they suspect the child may be manipulative. The parents are usually seeking permission to ignore some of the child's verbalizations; they also want suggestions for ignoring the behavior without tuning the child out completely.

4. Some parents try to protect the child from grief by avoiding discussions concerning the deceased parent and by trying not to cry in front of the child (Silverman and Englander, 1975). Intense, uncontrolled, and/or prolonged expressions of grief by the surviving parent may upset the child, but, without some adult expression of sorrow, the child may feel reluctant to express his own feelings.

Answering the Child's Questions About Death

As was noted earlier, most authors stress the importance of couching explanations in concrete terms. Koocher (1973) emphasizes the need to answer children's questions in a language which is appropriate to their stage of cognitive development. Since children under the age of about ten tend to have difficulty understanding abstract concepts, answers to their questions should, to insure concreteness, wherever possible be related to the child's own experiences. Sometimes, asking the child his opinion before answering his question can help the parent correct some misconceptions the child may already have. After answering his questions, he should be asked to explain what has been said; this may help to insure that the answer is not being distorted by him. In order not to overwhelm a child who may not be ready to assimilate more than small amounts of information at a time, it is suggested that answers be given to his specific questions without adding further information which he has not yet requested. Following are some of the more typical questions that children ask their parents following the death of someone significant in the child's life:

1. Will I die when I grow up? Mitchell (1967) has found that most young children appear to be satisfied with being told that everyone dies someday.

2. Questions such as, are you going to die too? What will happen to me if you die? Mitchell (1967) suggests reassuring the child by telling him that he, the parent, hopes he will go on living with the child for a long time. She suggests that if the child persists in trying to find out what will happen to him if the surviving parent does die, the parent should, indeed, explain who would care for the child in that event. If no arrangement has been made, the child may be quite satisfied with being reassured that he will not be abandoned.

3. Questions concerning life after death. Because children tend to be concrete in their thinking, explanations which equate death with such common occurrences as sleep and illness, for instance, can create disturbing fears in the child (Kessler, 1966).

Kessler (1966) points out that preschool children tend to ask a number of "why" questions in general because, at those ages, they do not think in terms of chance occurrences. At the same time, children at these ages appear to be quite satisfied with a simple answer to their question even if the answer is incomplete. When children seem very concerned about death, the concern tends to be based more on looking for a cause than on feelings of sympathy or compassion. The surviving parent will often express concern that the child's preoccupation with death is an expression of the child's anxiety or depression and is sometimes resistant to the notion that the child's concern with death is not much different than is his concern with any new phenomenon which he does not understand.

Answering Parent's Questions About Death

In addition to their requests for information about how to answer their children's questions, parents express the following concerns:

1. Questions about discipline tend to center around the parent's fear that the child's inappropriate or unacceptable behavior, which he previously was able to handle, is related to the death and that disciplining the child may traumatize him. Glick, *et al.* (1974) in their studies found that, after the death of a parent, the surviving parent tends to become

lax in discipline partly because he has difficulty functioning normally, but partly to protect the child. According to Silverman and Englander (1975), another concern related to discipline is the surviving parent's (in this study, the mother's) apprehension over her ability to effectively discipline the child without the support of the deceased parent.

2. The surviving parent, frequently because of his own loneliness, will either encourage or permit a child to sleep with him. Suggesting to the parent that this practice, if continued, can interfere with the child's progress toward independence will frequently result in the cessation of the practice.

3. One of the most frequent questions concerns the effect on children of taking them to the funeral. Connor and Doerring (1968), without specifying the age of the child, suggest that the child who does attend the funeral can benefit from watching how adults handle grief. They feel that this will help the child express his own feelings. Dr. Solmit suggests that the child even take part in the funeral arrangements. When one considers the age of the child, however, the effect on a preschool child, whose inability to understand the full meaning of the events, may be confusing and even frightening if manifestations of grief are intense. On the other hand, a mature preschool child who expresses a desire to attend the funeral, if he is not permitted to do so, may perceive death as mysterious and secretive, which could create more anxiety than that which might result from his attending the funeral. The average seven-year-old, according to Piaget, is capable of integrating his experience, of thinking logically and realistically and is at the stage in his congitive development when he can understand many abstract concepts. He probably should be encouraged to attend the funeral. Schowalter (1970) suggests that the child who attends the funeral will feel more secure if he is accompanied by an adult who is not too emotionally involved, someone who can act as an "interpreter" of the proceedings.

A number of concerns which have been discussed previously relate to the parents' apprehensions over the effect that their own grieving will have on the child and to questions concerning the child's feelings.

Dating and Remarriage

Although single parents indicate concern over the effect on their child of dating and/or remarriage, there is a dearth of literature on how children react to these events. The following suggestions are based on empirical evidence gathered from experiences with single-parent families. It seems that a child who is appropriately independent for his age, who engages in age-appropriate activity, and who has satisfactory peer relationships and thus is not dependent on the parent for his social gratification, is less likely to be upset over the parent's dating and even remarriage than is the child who is overly close to the parent and who may have been used, albeit inadvertently, to assuage the parent's loneliness. When children have been asked what bothers them most about their parents' dating, they complain about their uneasiness over frequent demonstrations of affection between the parent and the parent's date; they complain about being disciplined by this relative "stranger"; and they express anger at being left alone or being left with a babysitter when this occurs frequently. Advice to the parent is designed to help him deal with the child's complaints, some of which may be justified, without the parent martyring himself.

Some present-day single parents are concerned about the effect on the child of the parent's "girl friend" or "boy friend" living in the home. Again, there are no systematic studies of how this arrangement affects the child. Empirically there are indications that, as one might expect, how the child reacts will depend on the child's ego strengths and on his relationship with the parent. The child who tends to cope adaptively with most situations and whose relationship to the parent is an age-appropriate independent one seems to accept the situation with ease. The preschool child who is not yet aware that this is not the usual and perhaps not quite acceptable arrangement tends to adjust more easily than the child who is past the age of six or seven and who is not only aware that the two people with whom he is living are not married but who may be concerned for what others think. It is not unusual for a child in this situation to tell school personnel and friends that the person living with him is his parent, even when he himself knows that this is not so.

It might be well to discuss the effects of father absence before discussing the effects of remarriage. Weinraub (1978) summarizes the findings of a number of studies designed to evaluate the effect of father absence. The results are not as clear cut as one might expect. Although several studies report that boys from homes without fathers do tend to be more dependent and less aggressive and manifest a "weaker masculine sex role orientation and preference," these differences between boys from father-absent and father-present homes tend to be small. What may, to some extent, contribute to these small differences is the finding in some studies that boys from father-absent homes manifest greater masculinity, the suggestion being that this is "compensatory masculinity." The author suggests another reason why it may be difficult to ascertain whether the differences between these boys can be attributed to the absence of the father: how the child reacts to living in a father-absent home may depend to a large extent on how the mother relates to and handles the child. A more significant difference found in children of father-absent versus father-present homes is the effect on daughters. There seems to be a greater effect on the femininity of the daughters than on the masculinity of the sons. It is suggested that considering that most fathers do not spend a great deal of time with their children, his effect on the child's development is probably a consequence of the quality of his relationship with the child rather than the quantity of his contacts.

It is felt that the father tends to be perceived as a model for interacting with the world outside the family while mother is perceived as playing a more "expressive, nurturent" role, and that where father is absent, children may have problems dealing with the outside world. Hetherington (1973) found that girls whose fathers had died or, in some instances, whose fathers had completely separated from the family, tended to be inhibited by men and to avoid them, the implication being that they felt rejected by their fathers and were fearful of being rejected by other men. Weinraub summarizes the findings that fathers are important by essentially suggesting that two parents can more adequately and effectively meet a child's needs than can the single parent.

The foregoing, however, are not absolutes, and studies continue to show that the effects of father absence are influenced greatly by maternal characteristics. One might add that the child's ego strengths and past history of success are also important in his ability or inability to cope with not having a father. Weinraub summarizes the importance of the maternal role: "the mother's perceptions of her ability to cope, her attitude toward the father, and her attitude toward the child seem to be critical determinants of the child's emotional adjustment to father absence."

As has been noted earlier, there is little available information concerning the effect of mother absence. Clinical experience suggests that very young children who were close to their mothers tend to exhibit symptoms of separation anxiety and reactive depression which, depending on the stability of the environment and on their relationship with their fathers and new caretakers, is often transitory. There are indications from a very small sample of widowers who are members of TLA, an organization for widows and widowers, that their children when compared to those of the widows tend to be relatively self-sufficient and often take over the housekeeping duties and the care of younger children when there is no housekeeper.

Again, because of the dearth of studies on the effects of remarriage on children, the following suggestions are based on experiences with single-parent families. Despite the findings that a two-parent family enhances the child's development, there are a number of problems associated with remarriage which can negate the advantages. During premarital counseling, parents are advised that, because of the problems, they should not remarry in order to supply the child with a second parent. On the other hand, the parent is advised not to refrain from marrying because of some of the attendant problems. How the child will adjust to the remarriage depends to a large extent on his age, on how close he has been to the surviving parent, and on his ability to cope effectively with stress. The child under the age of three or four years tends to be resilient, and, even though there may be stresses in the beginning of the remarriage, he tends to cope with the stress rather well. The five- to ten-year-old may not adjust as easily as the younger child, but he will be more adaptable than most adolescents. Following are some of the potential problems:

1. Jealousy of the stepparent. Even children who do not depend entirely on the parent for their gratifications, resent having to share their parent's attention and affection with someone else. Children will not infrequently complain that after the surviving parent has remarried, most of the parent's attention is directed towards the stepparent. Some children seem to experience guilt over their jealousy, and those who can verbalize their feelings are less likely to act out their resentment.

2. The parent and stepparent will sometimes complain that the child appears to resent being disciplined by the stepparent. When questioned about the reasons for the resentment, the answer most often is that he cannot accept the stepparent as someone who should be legitimately disciplining him. At other times, however, he resents the stepparent's method of discipline which is different than that of the parent who died and different from that of the surviving parent. Sometimes, in his effort to be accepted by the child, the stepparent is inconsistent and delays disciplining the child as long as possible until he may then explode and become punitive.

3. Some children fear that, by responding positively to the stepparent, they will be disloyal to the deceased parent.

4. Sometimes the stepparent, again in an effort to develop a close relationship with the child, will try to either force expressions of affection from the child or buy the child's affection by overindulging him.

5. The parent and stepparent who would like to have a child of their own are often concerned about the effect this might have on the child of the surviving parent. Typical sibling rivalry can be exacerbated by the stepparent's inadvertent but rather normal more positive feelings toward his own child. If a child under the age of six or seven has not adjusted well to the remarriage, having a baby before that time may be

more stressful than having a baby when the child is less family oriented because of his outside interests. Also, the older child is usually able to verbalize his resentful feelings more easily.

6. Where the stepparent shows a preference for his own child or where the stepparent is trying so hard to seem impartial that he shows a preference for his stepchild, stepsibling rivalry is intensified. Sometimes parents, because they anticipate problems, overreact to conflicts between stepsiblings which may, in reality, be no different than those which arise between natural siblings.

Perinatal Death

It has been found that, in about one-half of perinatal deaths, mothers develop symptoms of severe psychopathology (Culberg, 1972). Klaus and Kennell (1976) suggest that even if there has not been any face-to-face contact between the mother and the baby, many mothers begin to form an attachment to their infants during pregnancy and to, thus, mourn the loss as though there had been a face-to-face attachment. Following a study by Kennell, et al. (1970), it was found that most mothers wanted to be away from the maternity division because it caused them so much distress. This same study resulted in suggestions that the mother herself should decide whether she wants to touch the baby or not. Apparently, some mothers want to and some do not. The authors suggest that mothers be encouraged to handle their infant because it makes the death real and may thus shorten the denial period of mourning. They also suggest that instead of prescribing tranquilizers which tend to dull and delay the mourning process, mother should be encouraged to express her grief.

Contact with the parents after they return home can help them work through their grief. Some anticipatory counseling may be helpful: The parent(s) may have some somatic symptoms; they may have difficulty sleeping, and they may have little appetite. They also may need some help in communicating with each other. Klaus and Kennell (1976) find that American fathers tend to deal with their grief in a different way than their spouses do and that this can cause difficulties. They suggest that the American father often will become much more active, accepting additional work, and may become somewhat irritated at his wife whom he perceives as indulging in her feelings of depression. They theorize that fathers may indeed not feel the same amount or intensity of grief since they may not have formed an attachment. They warn against assuming, in general, that because a parent seems not to mourn that he is not mourning in his own way. The authors recommend that parents be contacted after about three to six months to make certain that they are working through their grief. Lindemann (1944) suggests the following as abnormal reactions: overactivity; somatic complaints, particularly those related to the infant's illness; psychomotor symptoms; problems in interpersonal relationships; and withdrawal.

When mother comes home from the hospital, the child(ren) who is at home is not only concerned that the promised new sibling is not with her but may see the mother as changed because of her depression and preoccupation. Klaus and Kennell (1976) suggest that the mother, particularly, may have suffered a loss in self-esteem and that encouraging her to be effective in caring for the child(ren) at home may help her to regain it.

The effect on the child at home of the infant's death depends not only on how the parents handle their grief but on the age of the child. A young preschool child may be quite satisfied with the information that the baby died. If he does pursue the matter, it is more likely to be related to his disappointment that he does not have the playmate he anticipated rather than to his concern with the death. At this age, expressions of sadness or anxiety are probably indications that the child is being affected by the parent's depression. Since young children tend to be concrete, they are not likely to react as they might after having had some physical contact with the child. Again, although children should be encouraged to express their feelings, they should not be made to feel that there is something wrong with them if they do not grieve at that time.

Informing Parents of a Child's Fatal Illness

It is generally agreed that even in cases where parents are separated or divorced, both parents should be present when the parents are being told that their child has a fatal illness (Easson, 1972; Howell, 1966). This is important so that parents can comfort each other but also so that the risk of misunderstanding is minimized. The only situation which might contraindicate the presence of both parents is that where the physician knows that the separated or divorced parents are so angry at each other that the news would elicit recriminations and general projection of blame. Easson (1972) points out that the parents are likely to be so shocked at the first interview that they might not have any questions at that time. Thus, it becomes important to set up a second interview within a week or two when some of the shock has worn off and questions can be elicited.

Before giving information to the parents, all reasonable tests should have been done, results should be available, and the results should be given to the parents. If the conclusions are as firm as possible when they are presented to the parents, there is less likelihood that the parents will continue to deny the diagnosis and "shop around" for a more acceptable one. Howell (1966) suggests, however, that parents should be given as much hope as is realistic and advised of the importance of encouraging the child to live as normally and as actively as he is physically able.

Easson (1972) points out that if parents know that they are likely to progress through the mourning stages upon hearing that their child has a fatal illness, they may be able to cope more effectively with the feelings experienced during those stages.

There is some consensus that hospital personnel are not as helpful as they might be because of their own problems in dealing with death. Klaus and Kennell (1976) suggest that guilt feelings of staff members interfere with their effectively helping the family to mourn. Easson (1972) says that although members of the family may feel "alienated" by doctors who appear to be cold and unempathic, the family members feel even more uncomfortable and insecure by doctors who are uncontrolled in their expression of their feelings. Parents may feel that the professional to whom they look for help and support is, in effect, looking for some support from the family. Some family members express annoyance that medical personnel who are not members of the family are reacting with what they consider to be inappropriate intensity. On the other hand, there are some family members who are not disconcerted by the somewhat uncontrolled expression of feelings by medical personnel and may even welcome this.

When, as part of normal mourning, the parents experience anger, it is not unusual for this anger to be directed at medical personnel. Occasionally, those persons to whom the anger is directed will react as if it is directed at them personally and will then retaliate. Easson (1972) suggests that the anger should be understood for what it is and tolerated unless it interferes with the treatment.

A very common tendency for parents anticipating a loss of a child is to treat the child differently than he has been treated in the past. There is a tendency to overindulge him, to behave secretively with others when he is around, and to overprotect him (Green and Solnit, 1964; Howell, 1966). (See the chapter on the chronically ill child for a more detailed discussion for this problem.)

Two somewhat typical defenses utilized by parents faced with the knowledge that their child is fatally ill, are:

The tendency to withdraw from the child emotionally before the child actually dies. Although this may be a necessary part of the mourning process, because the child is still alive, the parents may need help to, as Easson (1972) puts it, "reinvest meaningfully while the child still lives." Green and Solnit (1964) in their study of families' reactions to the anticipated loss of a child suggest that some parents, particularly the mother, are unable to relate closely to the child following their awareness that the child is fatally ill. The mechanism described is very similar to that used by individuals who, having been rejected by others, anticipate future rejection and prevent this, in a sense, by withdrawing.

A second defense is that of planning for a replacement child (Klaus and Kennell, 1976; Naiman, et al., 1976; Legg and Sherick, 1976). In planning to have another child before the death of the fatally ill child, the parents may be again trying to withdraw their emotional investment from the living child. Although having a replacement child is much more common following the death of a child, particularly the unexpected death of a child, anticipatory counseling may be appropriate for those parents who indicate, after they had been told that their child is fatally ill, a desire to have another child. (See the section on telling parents about the death of their child for further discussion of the replacement child.)

The Fatally Ill Child and His Siblings

According to Naiman, Rolsky, and Sherman (1976), the siblings of the fatally ill child tend to experience the same stress that their parents experience but, in addition, they tend to resent the attention being paid to the ill child. The guilt which may result from this resentment is sometimes difficult for them to handle, and, depending on the age of the siblings, they may even think that they also are at risk. Their guilt may be compounded because they can engage in activities not permitted their sick sibling and because of the times before the illness when they may have wanted to be rid of their sibling. Helping the siblings express their feelings, in addition to helping the parents to refrain from overindulging and overprotecting the affected child, tends to minimize the siblings' resentment and guilt. (See a further discussion in the chapter, Managing the Chronically Ill Child.)

Pediatricians differ among themselves over whether to tell a child that he is terminally ill. The effects of withholding this information vs. telling the child has, apparently, not yet been studied systematically. Naiman (1976), as a result of considerable experience with fatally ill children, suggests that most children over the age of eight can be told about their illness, not that they are going to die but that they have a serious illness with emphasis on the hope that current treatments of the disease will change its course. He points out that some parents do not want their children to know. Experience in a cystic fibrosis clinic revealed a number of parents who refused to permit medical personnel to tell the children about their illness. Suggesting to the parents that they may, inadvertently, communicate to the child their concerns about him, that they may withdraw from him, or that the child might learn of his diagnosis or prognosis accidentally, and that all of this may cause the child more anxiety than being told, may induce the parents to relent.

Dr. Naiman suggests that children are often much more concerned with the discomfort of the treatment procedure and, if they are in the hospital, their separation from their families than they are with thoughts of their own deaths. It is when they are responding to the overconcerned behavior of others toward them that they may become fearful.

Telling Parents About the Death of Their Child

Parents tend to react in the same way to being told about the death of a child as they react to being told that their child has a fatal illness. One of the differences is that the former is a fact and leaves no room for hope while, in the latter, particularly during the denial stage, parents may look for signs that the diagnosis is an error. Another difference is that the hope that new treatments may result in a cure for the disease no longer exists.

Parents of a child who has died after a prolonged illness which they knew would probably be fatal are often able to handle the death relatively easily because they have almost completed the mourning process. It is when a death is unexpected that the family has much more difficulty coping. The Sudden Death Syndrome appears to result in added stresses: lack of explicit knowledge concerning what caused the death; guilt feelings due to thoughts that the infant died through their neglect; and continued emotional attachment to the infant who died, which is often hard on siblings who have to try to cope with the jealousy of a child who is dead (Stitt, 1971; Beckwith, 1975).

Suggestions for helping parents of SIDS victims include: efforts to notify the family of autopsy results as soon as possible; giving the parents as much information as possible about what is known about SIDS; and suggesting they contact the national foundation for Sudden Infant Death, 1501 Broadway, New York, New York, for information about the location of a local chapter which may be available to them. The local chapter can provide literature on the current status of the syndrome as well as a list of parents who have had the same experience who would be willing to visit the parents.

There appear to be two opposite reactions from parents who have experienced the unexpected death of a young child or an infant: either they do not want another child for fear something will also happen to that child or they are very eager to replace the dead child with another child as soon as possible. Legg and Sherick (1976) give the following reasons for discouraging the replacement of an infant who dies: (1) having a new infant in the home too soon after the death of the deceased infant may delay the mourning process; (2) the new child will be born into a home of mourning; and (3) probably most importantly the new infant is likely to have identity problems. There is a suggestion that the replacement child may begin to have some feelings of guilt because the child whom he is replacing had to die before he himself was conceived. Sander (1962) points out that if one considers the importance of mothers responding to their infants' rhythms, responding to the rhythms of the replacement child may be difficult because the mother may try to impose the deceased child's rhythms on the new child. Kohut (1971) suggests that if the replacement child is born before mourning is complete, mother may still be so preoccupied with the deceased child that she is unable to respond adequately to the new child. And, of course, there is always the possibility that the parents may understandably be overprotective of the replacement child, fearing that they might lose him too.

Symptoms of Emotional Problems Related to Death

Enuresis, nightmares, withdrawal, depression, and sometimes aggressive behaviors are some of the more common reactions to the death of someone significant in the child's life. Even very young children, who do not understand the concept of death, may exhibit the symptoms as a reaction to the tension around them. Usually, in young children and in pre-adolescent children, these symptoms are temporary, lasting for several weeks or perhaps for one or two months. The persistence of the symptoms may be due to: lack of opportunity for the child to talk about his feelings; continued intense and frequent manifestations of depression and general distress by significant others in his environment; and occasionally a need, albeit unconscious, to fulfill the parent's expectations that he will be distressed.

Parents and those mental health workers who have been involved with families where a child is fatally ill or has died all seem to agree that one of the most effective measures for helping these families is regular meetings of a group of parents, sometimes including other family members in the group, to meet on a regular basis both for purposes of learning more about the disease their children have or had and for support from others having or having had similar experiences.

References

Beckwith, J. Bruce: The Sudden Infant Death Syndrome. U.S. Dept. HEW DHEW Publication No. (HSA) 75-5137, 1975.

Birtchnell, J.: Depression in relation to early and recent parent death. *Brit J Psychiat,* 1970, **116,** 299–306.

Brown, F.: Grief and mourning in infancy and childhood. *Brit J Psychiat,* 1966, **112,** 1035–1042.

Connor, Walter, N. J. and Doerring, Paul L.: Meanings of death to young children. *Offspring,* 1968 (Fall), 5–14.

Easson, William M.: The family of the dying child. *Pediatric Clinics of North America,* 1972, **19**(4), 1157–1165.

Easson, William M.: Management of dying child. *J Clinical Psychology,* 1974, 25–27.

Glick, I. O., Weiss, R. S., and Parkes, C. M.: *The First Year of Bereavement,* New York, John Wiley and Sons, 1974.

Green, Morris and Solnit, Albert J.: Reactions to the threatened loss of a child: A vulnerable child syndrome. *Pediatrics,* 1964, 58–66.

Grollman, Earl A. (Ed.): *Explaining Death to Children,* Boston, Beacon Press, 1967.

Hetherington, E. M.: Girls without fathers. *Psychology Today,* 1973, **6,** 47–52.

Howell, Doris A.: A child dies. *J Pediatric Surgery,* 1966, **1**(1), 2–7.

Kennell, John H. and Klaus, Marshall H.: Caring for parents of an infant who dies, in Klaus and Kennell (Eds.): *Maternal-Infant Bonding,* St. Louis, C. V. Mosby Co., 1976.

Kennell, J. H., Slyter, H., and Klaus, M. H.: The mourning response of parents to the death of a newborn infant. *N Engl J Med,* 1970, **283,** 344–349.

Kessler, Jane W.: *Psychopathology of Childhood.* Englewood Cliffs, New Jersey, Prentice-Hall, Inc., 1966.

Kohut, H.: The analysis of self. *Psychoanalytical Study of the Child* (Monograph 4), 1971.

Koocher, Gerald P.: Childhood, death, and cognitive development. *Developmental Psychology,* 1973, **9**(3), 369–375.

Kubler-Ross, E.: *On Death and Dying,* New York, Macmillan, 1969.

Legg, Cecily and Sherick, Ivan.: The replacement child—A developmental tragedy. *Child Psychiatry and Human Development,* 1976, **7**(2), 113–126.

Lindemann, E.: Symptomatology and management of acute grief, *Am J Psychiat,* 1944, **101,** 141–148.

Melear, John D.: Children's conceptions of death. *Genetic Psychology,* 1973, **123,** 359–360.

Mitchell, Marjorie E.: *The Child's Attitude to Death,* New York, Schocken Books, 1967.

Naiman, J. Lawrence, Rolsky, Joan Taksa, and Sherman, Susan B.: The effects of fatal illness in the child on family life, in Vaughan, V. C. and Brazelton, T. B. (Eds.): *The Family—Can It Be Saved,* Year Book Medical Publishers, Chicago, 1976.

Sander, L. W.: Issues in early mother-child interaction. *J Am Acad Child Psychiat,* 1962, **1**, 141–166.

Silverman, Phyllis and Englander, Sue.: The widow's view of her dependent children. *Omega,* 1975, **6**(1), 3–19.

Stitt, Abby: Emergency after death. *Emergency Medicine,* March, 1971.

Schowalter, John E.: How Do Children and Funeral Mix? *J Pediatrics,* 1970, **89**(1), 139–142.

Vachon, Mary L. S.: Grief and bereavement following the death of a spouse. *J Can Psychiatric Assoc,* 1976, **21**, 35–43.

Vore, David A. and Wright, Logan: Psychological management of the family and the dying child, in Hardy, R. E. and Cull, John G. (Eds.): *Therapeutic Needs of the Family,* Springfield, Ill., Charles C. Thomas, 1974.

Weinraub, Marsha.: Fatherhood: The myth of the second-class parent, in Stevens, J. H., Jr. and Mathews, M. (Eds.): *Mother/Child Father/Child Relationships,* New York, Natl. Assoc. for the Education of Young Children, 1978.

Willis, Diane J: The families of terminally ill children: Symptomatology and management. *J Clinical Child Psychology,* 1974 (Sum.), 32–33.

CHAPTER **11**

Prevention of Psychological Problems in Children of Divorced or Separated Parents

If marital problems are severe enough for parents to consider separation, is the child less likely to be traumatized by living with those parents or by living with one parent in a household relatively free of conflict?

In spite of the large increase in the divorce rate, there has been very little research on how divorce/separation affects children. The research thus far has been done on very small samples, and in several instances there is little or no evidence that the problem behaviors manifested by these children were not present before the separation. Marital conflict prior to the separation may have already traumatized some of the children being studied. Because of the parents' preoccupation with their marital problems, they may have been unaware of the child's reaction to the stress and, when questioned by the investigators, may have dated the onset of the child's problems from the date of the separation. According to Thomas Sullivan, M.D., if turmoil in the home is chronic and severe, the child will feel insecure and may become a scapegoat for the marital tension. There is evidence that a child who continues to live in an unhappy home may be reluctant to form close and intimate relationships with others for fear that such relationships will result in unhappiness. Yahraes (1971) reports that Lidz's investigations into the role of the family in schizophrenia reveals that "in more than half the families with a schizophrenic offspring" there was "chronic disequilibrium and discord." On the other hand, if one parent is disturbed, it is felt that the child would suffer less in a home with both parents, so that the parent who is not disturbed can contribute some stability to the child's environment. The effect on children of father absence has been discussed in the previous chapter on The Effect on Children of the Death of a Parent. Although no hard evidence exists for the conclusion that if marital discord can be reduced, children fare better in a home with two parents, those who have investigated the effect of separation on children recommended counseling for married couples considering separation, because the effect of the separation on the children appears to be traumatic.

The few studies on the effect of divorce/separation on children (Wallerstein and Kelly, 1975; McDermott, 1968; Briscol, et al., 1973) indicate, as one would expect, that the way a child is affected depends on: (1) the degree to which marital conflict resulted in turmoil in the home; (2) the presence and intensity of overt aggressive behavior between the parents; (3) the age of the child; (4) the mental health of the parent assuming custody of the child; (5) the post divorce/separation relationship between the parents; and (6) the post divorce/separation relationship between the child and the parent(s).

Following are problems which frequently result from divorce. Anticipatory counseling and/or intervention at the onset of symptoms may prevent or, at least, minimize the effects of the separation:

1. For reasons which are not entirely clear, many children under the age of seven or eight express fears that if the parents divorce, they will be abandoned by both parents. It is possible that this is due, in part at least, to the parents' preoccupation with their own concerns just prior to and/or immediately following the separation. During this time they may emotionally and even physically withdraw from the child.

2. Children of all ages frequently express the feeling that it is they who are being rejected by the parent who is no longer in the home. Young children, under the age of seven or eight, because they cannot yet conceptualize the meaning of divorce, are likely to feel "betrayed, angry, and hurt" (Toomim, 1974).

3. Children, not infrequently, feel responsible for the separation either because of arguments the parents have had over child-rearing practices, because the parent who leaves has, at times, complained that the child is "bad," or because the child has, when angry, wished that the parent would leave. Toomim (1974) suggests that these misperceptions can generate guilt in the child as well as anxiety over his power.

4. Although most professionals are aware of the overwhelming need children have to bring their parents together again, many parents are unaware of the lengths to which children will go to accomplish this end (Toomim, 1974). In cases where separated parents have communicated with each other only when the child presents a behavior problem, acting-out behavior has been reduced or eliminated after the parents have followed recommendations to communicate with each other through a third party or when the child is not present.

5. Presently, there is no evidence indicating whether children do better in the custody of their mothers or their fathers. Studies of the effect of father absence, however (Hetherington, 1967; Carlsmith, 1964), suggest that the continued tendency for courts to award custody to mothers may be detrimental. For boys, there is the problem of sex identification. It is difficult for a father to be an adequate male model when contact with the son is limited. And for girls there are problems in future relationships with men. (Effects of father absence have been discussed more fully in the chapter on the effects of the death of a parent.) Mother absence has been rare but is occurring more frequently as more fathers are seeking and obtaining custody. (Leon Friedman, *New York Times,* 1972 reported that fathers were awarded custody in 38% of contested cases in Minneapolis.) Recently some parents have requested and been granted "shared custody," the child living with one parent for half of the week and with the other parent for the remainder of the week. It is too early to evaluate the effects of this procedure. Some possible disadvantages, however, are inconsistent child-rearing practices and feelings of insecurity in children, particularly preschool children who seem to be more comfortable when they have a familiar home base; and unless both parents live in an area served by the same school, it may be difficult for one parent to transport the child to a distant school.

6. The regularity of visits which can be anticipated appear to be more important than the frequency. Young children, those under the age of seven or eight, tend to become anxious and confused if they cannot predict when the noncustodial parent will visit and/or when the parent promises to visit but does not appear. Older children tend to be angry when visiting is irregular. Children who refuse to visit with their noncustodial parent complain that during these sometimes short and infrequent visits they are asked to share the parent's attention with the parent's girl friend or boy friend or with the children of these friends. They complain also that they are often left with the grandparents and see little of the parent. Toomim (1974) suggests that because the visit with the parent must end at predetermined times, the child may fear becoming close to the parent.

7. In a study of the effect of divorce on preschool children (Wallerstein and Kelly, 1975), it was found that in those cases where conflict continues after divorce, the child's prognosis for mental health is poor. The prognosis is also poor where mothers have custody and continue to be angry, hurt, and depressed. Sometimes the conflict continues because each parent fears that the life style of the other parent will harm the child: in any case, the child is a pawn in the parental conflict. The tendency for the custodial parent to gratify his needs through the child (Toomim, 1974); the tendency for the parent to try to compensate for the absent parent by assuming a dual role; problems involved in living with relatives; potential problems resulting from dating and remarriage; and problems associated with the custodial parent's need to work are discussed in the previous chapter on the effect of the death of a parent.

If it has not been possible, through anticipatory guidance, to prevent some of the problems related to divorce, intervention following the onset of symptoms may be effective if the primary emphasis is on teaching the child and the parent more effective coping mechanisms. It should be pointed out that historical information frequently reveals that the child has had behavior problems prior to the separation and/or that the child has always been emotionally vulnerable. Symptoms may have been ignored either because they were not serious prior to the separation or because they served the function of keeping the marriage intact. When the parents separate, however, and the behavior no longer serves this function, it becomes a target for concern. Whether the behavior is caused by the separation or not, the stress of the separation can exacerbate existing problems.

Suggestions to parents should include the following:

1. Suggestions for encouraging the child to express his feelings about the separation, including his complaints concerning custody and visitation. If in response to the general open-ended question about how the child feels, the child denies having any unusual feelings, the following question can be productive: "Do you sometimes feel responsible for the divorce?" If this is denied and the child is then told that many children do feel this way, they will often admit to the feeling. They can then be reassured that this is not so. One can bypass the questions and just state that some children have these feelings and that they are not realistic. This does not require a response from the child even though it is reassuring. To encourage the child to verbalize his feelings, the parent should try to elicit a verbal response from the child.

2. Suggestions for handling the actual problem behaviors. If the source of the behavior is the acting-out of feelings, the parent and child may need to learn more adaptive methods for expressing feelings.

Sometimes the problem behavior is a result of the parent's reluctance to discipline the child either because the child's behavior is perceived as caused by hurt feelings over the separation or because the custodial parent feels guilty or is inadvertently indifferent during his preoccupation with his own emotions.

3. Suggestions to the parents for coping with their own problems related to the divorce/separation. They may need help in handling their guilt so that they do not try to compensate by trying to assume the role of both parents, by overindulgence and overprotectiveness (Toomim, 1974).

Wallerstein and Kelly (1975) in their study of how children at different ages respond to divorce, found that:

1. The 2½- to 3½-year-old child tends to regress: although toilet trained, he will begin to soil and/or wet; he will tend to be irritable, fearful and may develop sleep problems.

2. Regression in the 3½- to five-year-old is not as typical probably because skills in self-care are more stable. Children at these ages tend to be tearful, whiny, and irritable. More than the younger children, probably because of greater cognitive awareness, these children may seem somewhat confused at the change in the family structure. Aggressive behavior related to the separation is not unusual at these ages.

3. The five- to seven-year-old seems to understand the situation more clearly and can verbalize his feelings even though there is some anxiety and acting-out of anger.

4. The latency age child, following separation, tends to either exhibit symptoms of anxiety such as withdrawal, nervous behavior, and sleep problems or to act-out his feelings by fighting and by defying authority.

5. The adolescent, even when he is depressed, tends to react with aggressive and antisocial behavior, poor academic performance, and, in general, with symptoms of frustration and anger.

Since children under the age of five have such a poor time concept, it is suggested that parents not inform these children of the impending separation until shortly before it actually occurs. At these young ages, children appear to be satisfied with the information that the parents are separating because they, like many people, do not get along. Older children may want more details. If children are asked how they understand the separation, their misperceptions can be corrected. And if the planned living arrangements are explained concretely, some of their anxiety may be alleviated.

The child whose parents behave as though the separation is permanent and who has been given the message that he must adjust to two households and two parents, each of whom may make opposing demands on him, is likely to accept the situation and to use his energies constructively. The child who receives messages which can lead him to infer that the separation is temporary may spend considerable emotional, intellectual, and even physical energy trying to find ways to either bring the parents together or create friction between them (Toomim, 1974).

Toomim (1974) suggests that for children adjustment to divorce takes a long time because they have to work through their feelings repeatedly as they mature both emotionally and cognitively.

References

Briscol, C. W.; Smith, J. B.; Robins, E.; Marten, S., and Gaskin, F.: Divorce and psychiatric disease. *Archives of General Psychiatry,* 1973, **29,** 119–125.

Carlsmith, L.: Effects of early father absence on scholastic aptitude. *Harvard Educational Review,* 1964, **34,** 3–21.

Hetherington, E. M.: Effects of familial variables on sex typing, on parent-child similarity and on imitation in children, in Hill, J. P. (Ed.): *Minnesota Symposia on Child Psychology,* Minneapolis, University of Minnesota Press, 1967, Vol. 1, pp. 82—107.

McDermott, J. F., Jr.: Parental divorce in early childhood. *Am. J. Psychiatry,* 1968, **124,** 1424–1432.

Sorosky, Arthur D.: The psychological effects of divorce on adolescents. *Adolescence,* 1977, **XII**(45), 123–136.

Sullivan, Thomas M.: Family and marital problems. Unpublished communication.

Toomim, Marjorie K.: Child of divorce, in Hardy, Richard E. and Cull, John G. (Eds.): *Therapeutic Needs of the Family,* 1974, Springfield, Ill., Charles C. Thomas.

Wallerstein, Judity S. and Kelly, Joan B.: The effects of parental divorce: Experiences of the preschool child. *J. Am. Acad. Child Psychiatry,* 1975, **14**(4), 600–616.

Yahraes, Herbert: Parental behavior and the origins of schizophrenia, in Segal, Julius (Ed.): *The Mental Health of the Child,* 1971, Washington, D. C., Public Health Service Publications.

Part II

Pediatrician's Role in Secondary Prevention of Psychologic Disorders

CHAPTER 12

Definition

When to Intervene

Following are criteria which can be used as guidelines for intervention:

1. The behavior is inappropriate for the child's age and/or specific situations. Typically, the behavior is considered inappropriate because the child is behaving in an immature manner. Behavior which is precocious, however, can also be considered inappropriate and can create problems.

2. Poor or inadequate functioning in school, with peers, with family members, and/or with adults outside the home. Some specific behaviors which can interfere with a child's functioning and thus put him at a social disadvantage are fighting, defiance of authority, delinquent behavior, school refusal, excessive shyness, poor academic performance, soiling, and day-time wetting.

3. Signs of pathological anxiety. In addition to the presence of overt nervous behaviors, and behaviors such as enuresis and nightmares, the existence of defense mechanisms suggests underlying anxiety. A behavior such as masturbation, when it is excessive, may indicate the presence of anxiety.

4. Indications that a child has a poor self-image. Although the child who is embarrassed, ashamed, and has a negative attitude toward himself is probably also anxious, these feelings can sometimes be handled more easily than anxious feelings because, unless longstanding, they are often attached to specific characteristics within the child or specific situations in his environment.

5. Signs of depression. Kessler (1966) suggests that the kind of depression one finds in adults is rare in children. Adults who turn their aggression inward become depressed while children may feel that they are bad and/or inferior and may try to punish themselves. The child

115

who is accident prone, and/or whose blatant misbehavior seems designed to elicit punishment, may be unhappy with himself. Some children are unhappy because of unexpressed sibling jealousy, feelings of rejection, or fears associated with marital conflict. Because these feelings are often vague and unlabeled, they tend to elicit anxiety and are expressed as anxiety reactions. Frequently expressions of anger reflect a child's unhappiness over unfulfilled needs.

6. The presence of a number of symptoms, each of which alone may not be cause for concern; the more symptoms the child exhibits, the more he is handicapped. One symptom, however, like school phobia, can, by itself, even in the absence of other symptoms, be disabling.

7. Persistence of behaviors which, as described by Lapouse and Monk, "occur as transient developmental phenomena in essentially normal children" (Kanner, 1961). It is not unusual for children to become enuretic or to have nightmares following the birth of a new sibling, following the initial separation from the parent, or as a reaction to other stressful situations. When these behaviors persist, however, intervention is recommended.

8. Behavior which suggests conflicts about sexual identity. Indications that a child is not accepting his gender role are revealed in his insistence on only wearing clothes appropriate to the opposite sex, on restricting his activities to those of the opposite sex, and are revealed by his expressions of the desire to be a member of the opposite sex.

9. Passive-aggressive or passive-resistant behaviors which are frustrating to parents and other authority figures. These behaviors suggest that the child has not learned how to express his anger appropriately.

10. Behaviors characteristic of the child often described as an "isolate" or "loner." He is not psychotic but lacks the social skills and/or the positive self-concept necessary for satisfactory peer relationships.

11. Psychosomatic disease and complaints of physical symptoms for which there appears to be no physiological basis.

When to Refer Children to a Mental Health Specialist

Cases of child abuse, instances of mental retardation, and cases involving suicide attempts and gestures should be referred. Following are other criteria for referring children to agencies where they can be evaluated extensively and where plans can be made for appropriate treatment:

1. When intervention by the pediatrician is not effective.

2. Where a child is phobic and his phobia is incapacitating; for in-

stance, the child who is fearful of buses, cars, and other means of transportation is usually in such great distress that frequent and intensive treatment is necessary.

3. Signs of "early infantile autism." Kanner (1943) described this syndrome after his findings that, according to mothers of autistic children, the children had not withdrawn contact with others but had always been withdrawn. The first signs of infantile autism are lack of the social smile, "no physical reaching out," and "no imitation of gestures or sounds." Clancy and McBride in 1969 report that mothers of autistic children whom they questioned described essentially these same behaviors in the first year of the child's life. Even if, as is suggested by some authors, the interaction between the child's temperament and the mother's response is the probable cause of autism (Clancy and McBride, 1969; Thomas, Chess, and Birch, 1968), the symptoms place the infant at risk.

4. Signs of psychosis or severe neurosis. Here the concern is with the child who is shy because he lacks social skills and/or has a poor self-concept. The withdrawn child who cannot make contact with others, who is seclusive, and who spends considerable time daydreaming which, when interrupted, results in extreme irritability, should be referred. Other symptoms which are frequently precursors of psychosis or severe neurosis and are often found in the withdrawn child are: bizarre behavior; an abnormal need for sameness and familiarity; and the need to engage in ritualistic behavior which, if interrupted, results in an extreme reaction from the child. Loose associations and persistent regressive behaviors are also often associated with withdrawal and are indications for referring the child.

5. Extreme aggressive behavior which, if not interrupted, could be dangerous to the child and/or to others. Children who engage in self-destructive behavior or who use weapons when attacking others should be referred.

Suggestions for Making Referrals

Some parents resist completing a referral. They may feel guilty, and, because of the anxiety their guilt arouses, they may deny that a problem exists. They may also fear that others will learn that there is something "wrong" with their child and rather than risk the possible stigma attached to having a child with a mental health problem, they will minimize the problem. Kessler (1966) suggests that if the emphasis is placed on the effect of the child's behavior on the child rather than on the inappropriateness of the behavior, parents tend to be less resistant. They are also less resistant when it is made clear to them that they are not to blame for the child's problem. They should also be reassured that confidentiality is closely guarded.

If the child is at least seven years old, the age when, according to Piaget, he has a relatively coherent cognitive system with which he can deal somewhat reasonably with the world around him, the need for the referral can be discussed with him honestly. Children at these ages will often respond positively to the concern expressed for their well-being.

Parents report that it helps to allay their anxiety when the referring individual describes the referral process to them. Sometimes parents request that the referring individual call the agency or mental health specialist for them. Most agencies prefer that the parents call them directly; some agencies insist on this. They do, however, appreciate a call from the person making the referral. Parents can be told that they will be asked to give a psychosocial history, that the child will be interviewed, using a play technique if necessary, and that the child may be given some psychological tests if it is felt that testing is appropriate.

There are advantages to referring the child initially, at least, to a clinic rather than to an individual practitioner. Most clinics employ psychiatrists, psychiatric social workers, and psychologists. Although, there is an overlap of function, particularly in the area of treatment, each also has a specific function.

Methods of Intervention

There are two major methods for intervening in attempts to alleviate a child's problem. One is oriented toward the family and/or child dynamics and the goal of treatment is to help the family and/or child gain insight into those factors which created the problem. By its very nature this method implies long-term, intensive psychotherapy, and is not only time-consuming but costly. Presently, there is no evidence that, in the treatment of pre-adolescent children with minor behavior problems amenable to intervention by nonmental health specialists, the aforementioned dynamic approach is more effective than the second method, counseling parents and/or children in an effort to change the child's behavior. In many mental health clinics, intensive, long-term treatment is reserved for children who have major psychological problems or for whom less intensive therapy has been ineffective.

There is mounting evidence that counseling parents on how they can more adequately handle their child's minor behavior problems is effective in dealing with many of those problems (Wahler, *et al.,* 1965;

Hawkins, *et al.*, 1966; Bernal, *et al.*, 1968; Patterson, *et al.*, 1970). Parents who have successfully carried out recommendations for handling the child's problem report that the experience made them feel more confident about their role as parents. They also report changes in the family dynamics: as a result of the implementation of the recommended child management techniques, the child's behavior is more appropriate, more acceptable, and less frustrating, resulting in more positive responses toward the child who, in turn, responds by behaving more acceptably (Patterson and Reid, 1973). Although not documented formally, parents and school personnel report (Bernal, 1969) that the child appears to have an improved self-image. In an unpublished informal study of children who had been referred by schools for behavior problems and whose parents, after implementing child management advice, reported improvement in the child's behavior at home, schools reported that the child's behavior in school had also improved (Cava, 1974). Bernal (1969) finds this same generalization of counseling effects in her studies.

Most parents are capable of effectively carrying out suggestions which are concrete and specific. Some parents report that their efforts have been ineffective. Following are several possible reasons for this:

1. They have not fully understood the suggestions. A behavior diary kept for two or three days detailing the child's behaviors and how the behaviors were handled will often reveal the source of the difficulty.

2. The symptoms have been present longer and/or are more severe than it had seemed initially, and the child should be referred.

3. Some parents are resistant to the notion that they can be the instruments of change either because for them this implies that they are to blame for the child's problems or because they feel that something needs to be done to the child by an outside agent. Some parents are so angry and frustrated over the child's behavior that they are unable to carry out the suggestions calmly and without anger.

4. In a family where there is marital conflict or where the primary caretaker has intrapsychic problems, the parents are often unable to carry out the suggestions consistently. Where there is marital conflict, the child is sometimes used as a scapegoat, and, while he is in that role, the parents do not have to face the issue of their marital conflict. The child's behavior problems serve the funciton then of keeping the parents together.

References

Bentler, P. M.: A typology of transsexualism: Gender identity theory and data. *Arch. Sexual Behavior,* 1976, **5**(6), 567–584.

Bernal, M. E., Duryee, J. S., Pruett, H. L., and Burns, B. J.: Behavior modification and the brat syndrome. *J. Consulting and Clinical Psychology,* 1968, **32**(4), 447–455.

Bernal, M. E.: Behavioral feedback in the modification of brat behaviors. *J. Nervous & Mental Disease,* 1969, **148**(4), 375–385.

Cava, E.: One-shot therapy. Paper presented at AAPSC annual meeting in Chicago, Ill. Nov. 1974.

Clancy, H., Dugdale, A., and Rendle-Short, J.: The diagnosis of infantile autism. *Dev. Med. Child. Neurol.,* 1969, **11**, 432–442.

Clancy, H., and McBride, G.: The autistic process and its treatment. *Child Psychology & Psychiatry,* 1969, **10**, 233–244.

Hawkins, R. P., Peterson, R. F., Schweid, E., and Bijou, S. W.: Behavior therapy in the home: Amelioration of problem parent-child relations with the parent in a therapeutic role. *J. Experimental Child Psychology,* 1966, **4**(1), 99–107.

Kanner, L.: Autistic disturbance of affective contact. *Nervous Child,* 1943, **2**, 217–250.

Kanner, L.: Everyday problems of the everyday child. *Current Medical Digest,* 1961 (Sep.), 47–53.

Kessler, J. W.: *Psychopathology of Childhood,* Englewood Cliffs, N. J., Prentice-Hall, Inc., 1966.

Money, J.: Cytogenetic and other aspects of transvestism and transsexualism. *J. Sex Research,* 1967, **3**(2), 141–143.

Patterson, G. R., Cobb, J. A., and Ray, R. S.: A social engineering technology for retraining the families of aggressive boys. Paper presented at Georgia Symposium in Athens, Georgia, May, 1970.

Patterson, G. R. and Reid, J. B.: Intervention for families of aggressive boys: A replication study. *Behavior Research & Therapy,* 1973.

Rosen, A. C. and Teague, J.: Case studies in development of masculinity and femininity in male children. *Psychological Rep.,* 1974, **34**, 971–983.

Thomas, A., Chess, S., and Birch, H. G.: *Temperament and Behavior Disorders in Children,* New York, New York University Press, 1968.

Wahler, G., Winkel, G. H., Peterson, R. F., and Morrison, D. C.: Mothers as behavior therapists for their own children. *Behavior Research & Therapy,* 1965, **3**, 113–124.

CHAPTER 13

General Behavior Problems

As has been noted in a foregoing chapter, treating children for behavior problems by training parents to become more effective child "managers" is economical, is more apt to insure generalization to the environment outside the home and permits the parents to learn what factors produce inappropriate and unacceptable behaviors in their children and what techniques extinguish those behaviors. In addition, if the parents are successful, they, as the change agents, may feel more adequate and effective as parents, which, in turn, may improve the parent-child relationship.

It is not always necessary and there may even be disadvantages to insisting either that the behavior problems are due to deep intrapsychic conflicts and/or that in order to handle the child's problems effectively, the parents and/or children must change their intrapsychic states. Often it is the interaction between temperament and environment which is at the source of problems. Anna Freud herself stated that she "refused to believe that mothers need to change their personalities before they can change their handling of their child."

Sometimes the anxiety which a child exhibits is a result of rather than a cause of the problem behavior. A child who does not participate in group activities may feel insecure, but he may also have a "temperamental tendency" to "warm up slowly" (Thomas, *et al.,* 1968). If this is not understood and the child is made to feel that there is something wrong with him because of this tendency, he may indeed become and feel insecure. If parents, in their mistaken belief that they should always be looking for unconscious motivation as a basis for the child's behavior, keep questioning the child for reasons for his behavior, the child in self-defense, if you will, may begin to intellectualize; he may also lose some of his spontaneity if he feels that whatever he does is being analyzed. Both parents and children may feel more adequate and

121

effective if their ego strengths are utilized in teaching them how to cope instead of emphasizing the problem and the possible pathology. In addition, a child who grows up believing that it is his frustrations and conflicts and disappointments which are at the basis of his behavior and expects life to be conflict free, will have difficulty believing that he can exercise some control over his behavior (Thomas, *et al.*, 1968; Kessler, 1966; Clement, 1974; Ingram, 1974; Karoly and Rosenthal, 1977; Mira, 1970).

Eating Problems

It is possible that minor eating problems, which might otherwise be ignored and thus possibly extinguished, are reinforced and become more significant because of the symbolism attached to oral ingestion. Most religions have some oral symbolism as part of their dicta or ceremonial rites; mothers by their own reports appear to equate food refusal by the child with rejection of the mother. From empirical evidence, it seems that food is related to dependency and, in this sense, it is interesting that the term "nourishment" is often used as a synonym for love and affection and the fullfillment of dependency needs.

As has been noted earlier, sometimes eating problems begin as a result of ignoring the child who appears to be eating reasonably well and then focusing attention upon him when, for some reason, he is eating less. Some passive-aggressive children discover a very effective means of expressing anger toward their parents who become angry and upset if the child dawdles or refuses to eat. The child may not be completely aware of his motives.

Giving children very small servings initially, permitting them to reject those foods they do not like as long as they are eating a reasonably well-balanced diet, and including them in the family conversation during the meal tends to minimize the emotional reaction which can occur when the subject of eating arises. Adults who are "finicky" eaters report that this characteristic can be restrictive and even embarrassing. It is for this reason that parents are advised to give the child minute servings of foods which the child does not like—one pea for a child who does not like peas—and to casually suggest that the child taste the food. He may refuse to do so, and he need not finish it after he has tasted it.

Dreikurs and Grey (1968) suggest that if a child isn't eating, is playing with his food, or is dawdling, his uneaten food should be removed from him, and he should not be given any food until the next meal. Warning the child before actually removing the food places the responsibility of the consequence squarely upon him. They warn against bribing the child or giving rewards to the child for eating his meal. Parents are often not aware that when they bribe the child with dessert as a reward or when they threaten to withhold dessert as a punishment, the child may get the message that if he eats the unpleasant main meal, he will receive something far better than that, thus reinforcing the desirability of what are often the least desirable foods.

The child who is late for dinner may eat; but if he has not completed his meal when the rest of the family has completed theirs, he may not finish his meal or have a snack, and he may not have food again until the next meal. Evidence for the sometimes irrational perception of the significance of food is revealed in the experience with a large number of parents who quite casually will inflict pain by spanking their children but are outraged at the suggestion that, as a logical consequence of a child's dawdling or not eating, he be deprived of food just until the next meal.

Although some children will vomit as a reaction to stress—starting school, being confronted with new situations, the birth of a new sibling—the problem is usually temporary. Verville (1967) suggests that persistent vomiting may be a reaction to persistent fears and that helping the child to become aware of his fears and then helping him to cope with them should eliminate the vomiting. If, however, he has received a great deal of attention because of the vomiting, he may use the behavior as an attention-getting mechanism. The child who is forced to eat foods he does not like or the child who is forced to eat all of his food whether he is hungry or not may either intentionally or unintentionally vomit after eating.

Those children with persistent vomiting who have been brought to child guidance clinics after physical examinations have proved negative tend to be immature, inappropriately dependent, and have a limited repertoire of coping behaviors. They generally have at one time in their lives vomited for a protracted period because of an actual gastrointestinal problem, and during that period they have received considerable attention. The precipitating cause of the present vomiting as well as a history of other episodes of persistent vomiting usually reveal a situation which is stressful either because it is frightening or because demands are made on the child which he feels he cannot fulfill. The vomiting is reinforced by parental attention, sympathy, protection from the source of fear, and/or withdrawal of the demands that were made on the child. Helping the child to become more appropriately mature and independent, teaching him more effective coping mechanisms, encouraging him to verbalize his fears and feelings of inadequacy, and ignoring the vomiting will tend to alleviate the problem.

The child who is permitted to become obese may develop a poor self-image, in part because of teasing by peers and in part because he may have difficulty participating in physical activities with peers. Some children, in an attempt to compensate for their poor self-image will become bullies; others may withdraw. The child who withdraws may then use food to reduce his anxiety, and the entire process can become cyclical. Sometimes a mother may press her child to eat either because she feels that it is a symptom of health or because of her need to see the child eat the food she has placed before him. Verville suggests that a mother may overfeed her child because of her remorse for having punished the child. Frequently, one finds a high correlation between obesity in children and inappropriate dependency needs. This is consistent with another finding that children who are obese often have overprotective mothers.

Even parents who are themselves obese and are aware of the difficulty of effectively reducing weight tend to ignore the difficulties the child will have if he continues to be obese. If they are obese themselves, by admitting the problem they are admitting their own weakness; even if they are not obese, by admitting the problem they would have to relinquish the gratification of providing the child with large amounts of food and perhaps the satisfaction derived from fulfilling the child's dependency needs. Many parents who have tried to moderate the child's food intake have found it difficult because they cannot accept the child's displeasure and resentment.

Some mothers are receptive to the suggestion that since they are the ones who buy the food, cook it, and serve it, they have some control over the child's diet. Even a young child can be involved in learning to change his eating habits. Verville suggests teaching the child to count his calories and reducing the number of calories by about 100 each week so that the reduced intake is gradual. The child can also be responsible for keeping a graph; he can help with the menu so that he can choose foods which he prefers, and he can be given extra privileges for small decrements in weight the privileges to be increased as he continues to lose. It is recommended that these children develop physical skills within their limitations to enable them to participate in physcial activities. A YWCA or YMCA is a good resource for the development of these skills. Exposing the child to other sources of pleasure besides eating, helping him to become more independent, and helping mother to be less protective may also help in combatting obesity. In some obese boys, an improved relationship with their fathers appears to be effective.

Problems Associated with Sleep

Although there appear to be individual differences in the ease and immediacy with which children fall asleep and in how deeply they sleep (Thomas, *et al.,* 1968) the importance of training should not be overlooked. Many problems associated with sleep found in the elementary school age child result from undesirable habits rooted in infancy or early childhood. Parents who are made aware that they themselves develop undesirable sleeping habits, which then are difficult to break, tend to be receptive to suggestions for trying to change their child's sleeping habits.

One of the most frequent problems is the child's resistence to going to bed. In this context, the word, "bed" is more appropriate than the word "sleep" because the child cannot be directed to sleep only to remain in his room and in bed and to go to the toilet or have a drink of water if necessary without informing the parent (Thomas, *et al.,* 1968). Parents who have followed this advice report that when the child does indeed realize that the demands will be enforced, he tends to actually fall asleep soon after he has gone to bed. It should be noted that it is the "wakeful child" who, in order to relax, needs to have some quiet by himself. If he is not made to remain in bed quietly, he will become more and more wakeful as he is stimulated by either getting up frequently or by altercations with his parents about his getting up (Verville, 1967). Verville suggests that some children comply with bedtime because they are aware that they can get out of bed when they wish.

Children appear to do better if they have a regular bedtime hour which is rarely changed. Even on weekends when the child may be able to stay up later, a regular later hour should be enforced. Also effective is the establishment of some routine associated with bedtime; quiet games or stories are often relaxing. Some parents perceive the child's getting out of bed frequently as a sign that the child needs attention. Regular, predictable, and undivided attention from the parent each day often before bedtime is usually sufficient to fulfill the child's needs. The child who resists going to bed or who leaves his bed after he has been directed to remain there often responds well to the logical consequence of having to go to bed earlier and earlier each night following those nights when he did not comply with reasonable ease.

The child who seems fearful can be given the choice of lying in his bed quietly with the door open and a light burning or, if he is unwilling to stay in bed quietly, of having the door closed and the light off. The fearful child should, of course, be encouraged to express his fears and taught how to cope with them. The child who tends, while in bed, to brood over problems, should receive help in verbalizing his concerns.

Sometimes a casual discussion of what occurred during the day, including possible problems and solutions, would help. Sometimes children who find it difficult to fall asleep quickly can be permitted to read or listen to the radio for five or ten minutes while they are in bed.

One of the questions parents frequently ask is how to handle a situation where siblings who must sleep in the same room stay awake talking or even fighting. Since one child is usually older than another, and since it is important for the older child to have special privileges especially those associated with age, he should be permitted to stay up longer than the younger child. Sometimes this is sufficient to solve the problem, but if the children are very close in age, the difference in their bedtimes may not be large enough to permit the younger child to be asleep before the older child comes to bed. In these situations, allowing the siblings five minutes to talk and then insisting that they be quiet after that time is sometimes effective, especially when they will have to go to bed earlier the following night if they are not quiet. An alternative is to put the older child in the parent's bed until the younger child is asleep and then to transfer the older child to his own room.

Verbal reports from mental health workers who have been called in to schools to observe children who were having learning problems or who seemed withdrawn reveal that a number of these children are just not getting enough sleep. When questioned about the child's sleeping habits, parents have confirmed this.

Nightmares are often a temporary reaction to transient stresses, such as starting school, being exposed to new situations, and/or the birth of a new sibling. Nightmares can persist if the parents reinforce these temporary strains by themselves reacting with anxiety, by making an issue of the nightmares, by sleeping with the child, or by bringing the child into the parent's bed. Persistent nightmares may also indicate that the child is reacting to unrelieved stress. Demands on the child which either because of age or temperament he cannot fulfill, underlying conflicts between parents, intense and frequent marital fighting, and/or feelings of rejection are examples of stressful situations which if not alleviated can result in continued nightmares.

Verville suggests that, in the handling of nightmares, it is important to try to identify and then reduce the particular external stress. The parent can help the child verbalize and overcome those fears which are not real. Children who have nightmares should not be overstimulated by, for instance, permitting them to watch frightening television programs. If the reasons for the nightmares are being attended to, going into the child's room, patting him gently, reassuring him for a moment, and then leaving him is often all that is required to effectively deal with the nightmares, particularly if the child knows that no additional attention will be paid to them. The same suggestions for handling nightmares can be used in cases of night terror and somnambulism. In these latter cases it is important to be sure that the child is awake.

Enuresis

Enuresis is usually not considered to be a problem unless it occurs after the age of five years (Kessler, 1966; McDonald and Trepper, 1977). It is interesting to note that twice as many boys as girls are enuretic. There are a number of factors which may be related to the onset or persistence of the condition. Euresis may be just one symptom of general immaturity. Even when the primary concern of the parent is the child's enuresis, rarely is it the only problem. Not infrequently, one finds that the enuretic child exhibits "immature" behaviors such as thumb sucking, temper tantrums, and immature speech. Crow (1967) and Kessler (1966) suggest that enuresis can be an expression of anger or hostility. If the behavior is reinforced, it can also become a means of gaining attention. Verville (1967) suggests that sibling rivalry may be a source of the behavior; the child can obtain attention not given to a sibling, or the child is imitating the behavior, albeit unconsciously, of a younger sibling who is not yet toilet trained. Sometimes enuresis appears to be a reaction to "punitive toilet training."

Although emotional conflict may be a factor in enuresis—and the possibility that it is should certainly be explored and where tension exists, attempts made to reduce it—conditioning techniques for alleviating the problem have been so successful that it is almost unnecessary to be concerned that an enuretic child may have a psychological disorder. The immediate goal of treating the enuretic child by using classical and/or operant conditioning is to insure that the child remains dry. If the enuresis is persistent, the child's feelings of immaturity tend to be reinforced; his self-image suffers, and he may, as a result of the enuresis rather than as a cause, develop neurotic symptoms (Kessler, 1966). The child who wakes up wet in the morning may become anxious, which may create tension, which, in turn, may result in further wetting.

Suggestions commonly given to parents include restricting fluids after the evening meal and taking the child to the toilet before the parents go to bed late in the evening (Verville, 1967; Kessler, 1966). Some authors and mental health workers do not agree that these steps are necessary. Allowing the child to have fluids in the evening and not taking him to the toilet late in the evening seems, however, to be loading the dice against him. Actually, reports from parents who have brought their enuretic children to child guidance clinics reveal that these two steps are all that are necessary for eliminating the enuresis, especially in younger children. It is always possible, of course, that just seeking and obtaining help for some of the child's other problems may, in itself, reduce tension sufficiently to eliminate the symptom. McDonald and Trepper (1977) suggest that the child also keep a chart and be rewarded, if only with stars or praise, for being dry.

If restricting fluids and toileting the child late at night is not sufficient to stop the enuresis, conditioning with a mat and bell or an alarm clock can be added. Using an alarm clock has the advantage of placing the responsibility on the child. The alarm clock is set for some arbitrary time towards morning and if the child is already wet when the alarm awakens him, he would set the alarm for an earlier time the following night until he awakens dry, toilets himself and returns to bed. Some parents report that after a period of two or three weeks, the child awakens without the alarm clock before he is wet and toilets himself. Kessler suggests that just as the child is fully awake during the night, he should be fully awake when his parents toilet him before they go to bed so that he will know what he is doing and again will have some responsibility for his own toileting. He should not disturb his parents during the night and should always rinse out his nightclothes and bedding when they are wet either at night if he is uncomfortable or in the morning. The method outlined above is usually successful within several weeks or, at the most, several months. There is no evidence of symptom substitution.

One suggestion for increasing the ability to control the frequency with which he has to void is to have the child, during the day, hold the urine in the bladder for five minutes, gradually increasing the amount of time between the urge to void and the actual voiding (Kimmel and Kimmel, 1970; Kessler, 1966; McDonald and Trepper, 1977). Another suggestion is to have the child, when he is voiding during the day, stop in midstream. A study by Harris and Purohit (1977) revealed, however, that training in bladder control, although increasing bladder capacity, did not significantly decrease the frequency of the bedwetting. Samaan (1972) reports successfully treating an enuretic child by having the parents get the child up at night, give her candy and "a hug" immediately after she voids and then gradually making the reward intermittent as the child began getting up by herself.

Although daytime wetting sometimes accompanies nighttime wetting, it tends to be much less common. When it does occur some of the same factors may operate. It may also occur, however, because the child does not want to interrupt his play or because he is fearful that his friends will not wait for him or he may just be preoccupied. Sometimes the child resents being constantly told to go to the toilet and rebels by continuing to wet. Verville (1967) suggests that it is sometimes necessary to retrain the child by insisting that he go to the toilet every two hours.

Encopresis

As in the case of enuresis, encopresis is not usually considered a problem unless it occurs after a child is four or five years of age. Five times as many boys as girls are encopretic. Also as in enuresis, encopresis is frequently a means of expressing anger or of gaining attention (Crow, 1967; Kessler, 1966). Other possible factors are:

1. Incomplete bowel training. This is sometimes due to punitive training methods to which the child reacts with resistance.
2. Fear of the toilet flushing in small children who must use an adult toilet.
3. Preoccupation with play that the child does not want to interrupt in order to go to the toilet.
4. Regression due to jealousy of a younger sibling who is not yet toilet trained.
5. A response to separation anxiety.
6. A few children are fearful of having a bowel movement because of a misconception that babies are lodged in the gastrointestinal tract and are then expelled in the same manner that feces are expelled.
7. Constipation. In the vast majority of instances, constipation occurs for one or more of the foregoing reasons.

Wright (1973) points out that encopresis can be the source of psychological problems as well as the consequence of them: the symptom can interfere with satisfactory interpersonal relationships and can create a poor self-image which, in turn, may result in psychological distress. Thus, the encopresis may persist even though the reasons for its onset are no longer relevant.

There is evidence that in families where boys are encopretic, fathers are either psychologically or physically absent (Schaengold, 1977). Whether the unexpressed anger often found in these boys is related to this fact or not is not clear. Sometimes the anger, whether due to the lack of father participation in the child's life or not, is expressed by means of encopresis because it has previously been effective. In those few cases of encopresis in girls referred to child guidance clinics, conflict between the child and her mother seems to be an important factor in the maintenance of the symptom. Secondary gains cannot be ignored: aside from the attention it elicits, it may prevent the child who is encopretic in school from attending school.

Although, like enuresis, conditioning can be successful without treating the possible underlying causes, it is not as successful as frequently as it is in the treatment of enuresis. For instance, where the parent-child relationship continues to be poor, where there is indeed greater attention given to a younger sibling, where encopresis as a means of expressing anger is effective, where the father who is physically present in the home does not attend to the child, and/or where the father is not present and there is no male substitute, conditioning, by itself, may fail. Helping the child either directly or by counseling the parents to express anger more appropriately, making sure that the child is receiving some undivided attention from the parents, permitting him additional privileges for being older than his younger sibling, impressing upon a father who is present in the home the importance of becoming involved with his encopretic child, and obtaining a "big brother" for the boy in a father-absent family, should help in eliminating the symptom.

When using conditioning in treating the child, many parents prefer to try first a positive contingency reinforcement system and to employ a retraining system only if the former is not successful. The child can be given stars for each day that he has defecated in the toilet and has not soiled. The reward for a certain number of stars can be in the form of extra privileges or special time with the parents. Instead of stars, the child can be given tokens which can then be used for buying toys or other objects (Wright, 1973). Pedrini and Pedrini (1971) report the successful treatment of an encopretic boy who liked to read. He was given coupons for each day that he did not soil, and the coupons were then converted into money for buying books.

If the use of rewards does not result in the elimination of the symptom, retraining may be necessary (Verville, 1967). Retraining which has proved to be successful more often than not includes the following: The child is placed on the toilet immediately after breakfast and since the motive for this is not a punitive one, he may read or look at a book while he is on the toilet. How long he remains there depends on the age of the child. If the child is under the age of six, five minutes, which often seems like an hour to children at this age, is sufficient. If he is left there longer, he can become frustrated and angry, and the training may be counterproductive. The older child should remain on the toilet for ten minutes. If he defecates in the toilet, unless he regularly has more than one bowel movement a day, he need not sit on the toilet any more that day. If he defecates in the toilet and then later soils, the soiling should be ignored except that he must rinse out his own underclothing and clean up any mess that he has made. At this point in his retraining, there should be no punishment for soiling.

If the child has not defecated in the toilet, he should be made to sit on the toilet again immediately after lunch even if he has soiled between breakfast and lunch. If he defecates in the toilet at this time, it should be treated in the same way that defecation in the toilet after breakfast is treated. If he does not defecate in the toilet either after breakfast or after lunch, he is again put on the toilet immediately after dinner. Even if he has soiled during the day, if he has not defecated in the toilet he is placed on the toilet at each of these times. To keep from making an issue over having a bowel movement in the toilet, a casual "good" may be all that is necessary as a reward for using the toilet appropriately.

Wright (1973) suggests that the encopretic child be put on the toilet after breakfast, but that if he does not defecate in the toilet, he should be given a suppository or an enema to make sure that he has a bowel movement at a regular time each day. He is then weaned away from the suppositories and enemas. It would seem that decreasing the child's dependence on these supports may, in itself, become a problem, and the present authors do not, themselves, recommend enemas or suppositories.

Only if all else fails should the child's behavior be modified by the use of punishment. Considering the possible role of anger in encopresis, and the risk that punishment is likely to produce more anger in the child, unless he has learned to express this anger more appropriately, the encopresis may be reinforced. If he is to be punished, he can be deprived of privileges, increasing the number and frequency of privileges lost as the encopresis continues. He can be given extra chores, and again punishment seems more effective if the number of chores is increased as the inappropriate behavior continues. One child for whom playing baseball and the respect of his team members was so important had to miss first one practice and then an increased number of practices as his encopresis persisted; after missing three practices and learning that he still had sufficient time to participate in the actual game, he relinquished his symptom.

It should be noted here that, in many "disadvantaged" families, fathers are often not in the home, the remaining parent is often harassed with a large number of problems, and successfully treating the encopretic child becomes much more difficult. Although retraining by itself may not be successful, sometimes bringing in a male relative as a surrogate father or obtaining a "big brother" is sufficient to extinguish the symptom.

References

Clement, Paul W. Parents, peers, and child patients make the best therapists, in Williams, Gertrude J. and Gordon, Sol (Eds.): *Clinical Child Psychology: Current Practices and Future Perspectives*, New York, Behavioral Publications, 1974.

Crow, Lester D.: *Psychology of Human Adjustment*, New York, Alfred A. Knopf, 1967.

Dreikurs, Rudolf and Grey, Loren: *Logical Consequences: A New Approach to Discipline*, New York, Meredith Press, 1968.

Harris, Leonard S. and Purohit, Arjun P.: Bladder training and enuresis: A controlled trial. *Behavior Research & Therapy*, 1977, 15(6), 485–490.

Ingram, Gilbert L.: Families in crisis, in Hardy, Richard E. and Cull, John G. (Eds.): *Therapeutic Needs of the Family*, Springfield, Ill., Charles C. Thomas, 1974.

Karoly, Paul and Rosenthal, Mitchell: Training parents in behavior modification: Effects on perceptions of family interaction and deviant child behavior. *Behavior Therapy*, 1977, 8, 406–410.

Kessler, Jane W.: *Psychopathology of Childhood*, Englewood Cliffs, N. J., Prentice-Hall, Inc., 1966.

Kimmel, H. D. and Kimmel, Ellen: An instrumental conditioning method for the treatment of enuresis. *J Behavior Therapy & Experimental Psychiatry*, 1970, 1, 121–123.

McDonald, James E. and Trepper, Terry: Enuresis: An historical, cultural, and contemporary account of etiology and treatment. *Psychology in the Schools*, 1977, 14(3), 308–314.

Mira, Mary: Results of a behavior modification training program for parents and teachers. *Behavior Research and Therapy*, 1970, 8, 309–311.

Pedrini, Bonnie C. and Pedrini, D. T.: Reinforcement procedures in the control of encopresis: A case study. *Psychological Rep*, 1971, 28, 937–938.

Samaan, Makram: The control of nocturnal enuresis by operant conditioning. *J Behavioral Therapy & Experimental Psychiatry*, 1972, 3, 103–105.

Schaengold, Marilyn: The relationship between father-absence and encopresis. *Child Welfare*, 1977, 56(6), 386–394.

Thomas, Alexander, Chess, Stella, and Birch, Herbert G.: *Temperament and Behavior Disorders in Children*, New York, New York University Press, 1968.

Verville, Elinor: *Behavior Problems of Children*, Philadelphia, W. B. Saunders Co., 1967.

Wright, Logan: Handling the encopretic child. *Professional Psychology*, 1973(May), 137–144.

CHAPTER 14

Specific Problems
Appropriate for Secondary
Prevention

The Immature, Dependent, and/or Shy Child

Although it is well known that long separations from parents or parent substitutes during a child's early development can result in immaturity, inappropriate dependency needs, and separation problems (Crow, 1967), most of the literature emphasizes "too much mothering" as a precursor of prolonged immaturity in the child (Bowlby, 1969). This kind of mother, according to Bowlby, seems compelled to bestow upon the child an abundance of affection and attention. She tends to be overprotective and insists on being both physically and emotionally close to the child. As has been noted earlier, a mother who overprotects her child may, in fact, be defending against the anxiety aroused by her rejection of the child (Kessler, 1966).

Mussen, *et al.* (1956) cite evidence to the effect that the mother who constantly rewards and almost never punishes dependent behavior causes her children to remain dependent. Negative reinforcement or lack of reinforcement of this kind of behavior extinguishes it. The authors go on to say that children who continue to ask for help when they do not need the help, who seek "attention, recognition, approval, reassurance," and who cling and are reluctant to separate from others, particularly adults, have probably, in the past, been rewarded for these behaviors. Verville (1967) believes that immaturity and dependency are a result of a mother-child relationship where, long after it is appropriate, the parent continues to help the child and to protect him from stress and, thus, from opportunities to become an independent individual. This kind of child avoids tasks which are difficult and experiences which may be uncomfortable. The result may be a child who is reluctant to try anything which requires work and perseverence.

Verville suggests a number of reasons why a parent may behave in this way. A well-intentioned parent may not understand the importance to a child's development of exposure to some stress. Other reasons are: the parent may envision raising the ideal child/adult; the parent may be basically controlling; the child may be a source of love and companionship for a parent whose spouse is dead, separated from the family or unresponsive; or the parent may just not know what a child is capable of doing for himself.

The immature, dependent child tends to be egocentric, to blame others for his problems, and to give up easily. This kind of child frequently has somatic complaints, which often then permit him to withdraw from tasks and experiences which are uncomfortable. He often prefers being with adults rather than peers. Sometimes these children will withdraw when they become aware that they lack certain skills; they may feel inadequate and ineffective. On the other hand, some of these children may become aggressive because they resent their inability to compete successfully. Although their anger may actually be directed at their parents, they will often attack others because they are too dependent on their parents to attack them. Studies by Baumrind and Black (1967) reveal that making demands on the child for self-discipline, encouraging independent behavior, and permitting the child to make decisions whose consequences would not harm the child helped the child to become responsible and independent. The authors point out that there was no correlation between firm and consistent behavior on the part of the parent and punitiveness or coldness.

It has been suggested that children who are socially immature are more likely to learn social skills if they first learn to play with younger children. They might not be accepted by their peers or they might resist playing with peers because of the fear that they would not be accepted. As they are accepted by the younger children, they could gradually be exposed to older children.

As noted above, the immature, dependent child may withdraw because of his awareness that he lacks skills and cannot compete effectively. According to Mussen, et al. (1956), if a child is permitted to continue to withdraw, because it reduces his anxiety, he may have great difficulty overcoming this behavior. Kessler (1966) agrees that withdrawal may be a defense against the anxiety aroused by anticipated social failure but suggests that it can also be a reaction formation against "unconscious aggression." She suggests that the child may, albeit not consciously, be afraid that others will be able to perceive his hostility if he participates in activities.

Thomas, *et al.* (1968), in discussing the child who does not participate, calls attention to the "slow to warm up" child who, temperamentally, tends to be reluctant to participate in activities. The authors believe that if this kind of child is permitted to participate at his own pace, he will finally respond positively, but if he is pressured to participate quickly, he will tend to withdraw and cling to adults. The authors also suggest that this kind of child be exposed to new situaitons frequently but without being pushed. The parent who tends to be impatient will be more likely to become upset with this kind of child, and as a result friction between parent and child may develop. Crow (1967) suggests that in addition to overprotection as a source of shyness, rigid and exacting parents may, albeit inadvertently, cause a child to be shy. He also suggests that often there is a conflict between the child's wish to take part in activities and the fear of being rejected.

Crow emphasizes that shyness is multidetermined and that the factors involved, temperament, environmental situations, and experiences, result in differences in the degrees of "ascendance or submissiveness." He argues that there are children who derive gratification from being self-sufficient and from making decisions for themselves concerning their desire to participate or not. These are often children who for one reason or another have been alone and have experienced satisfaction from doing things by themselves. The implication is, of course, that these children have developed in a secure environment so that they can feel comfortable engaging in activities which require them to use their own resources. These children who often prefer being alone or with one other child often do better if they are permitted to engage in noncompetitive activities and in noncontact sports.

If parents can anticipate that the "slow to warm up" child will participate in group activities if he is not pressured, if they permit the child to practice social skills frequently, and if they can anticipate that some children temperamentally may tend to have relatively little need to be with others, they will be less concerned about their child's "shyness" and encourage his self-sufficiency while at the same time helping him to develop some social skills.

General Disobedience

Verville (1967) outlines some reasons why some children are persistently disobedient:

1. Inconsistency in the enforcement of rules. One parent may be

inconsistent from time to time or the two parents may be inconsistent with each other. In the latter situation, one parent may even protect the child when the other parent tries to punish the child for his misbehavior.

2. Making rules which the parents cannot enforce. Related to this is the tendency on the part of many parents to make idle threats.

3. Some parents tend to lay down a large number of rules either to satisfy their own perfectionistic needs or because of their need to dominate the child.

4. Parents who feel inadequate in their parenting role may, because they don't trust themselves to discipline effectively, permit the child to disobey.

5. Concern that the child will stop loving the parent who disciplines him and/or that limit setting will make the child unhappy.

6. Some parents tend to use their children as servants. The child may to some extent justifiably rebel against the parent's request that the child interrupt his play in order to fetch something for the parent which the parent can often get for himself.

7. Sometimes children who have been punished for expressing anger verbally learn that passive-resistent behavior elicits anger from the parent and their tendency to "forget" instructions becomes a vehicle for expressing their anger.

8. Some parents with several small children or one extremely active child may just give up because they seem unable to succeed in securing the child's cooperation. The finding that parents of children with behavior problems tend to be more "rejecting and hostile toward their children" (Schulman, et al., 1967) may reflect a result rather than a cause of the child's misbehavior.

9. Verville (1967) argues that "permissiveness" is the most prevalent cause of persistent disobedience. The child has discovered that he need not obey unless he wishes to do so and that disobedience will not be penalized.

Swift and Spivack (1975) suggest that instructions to the child be specific and unambiguous and that the child be directed to repeat the instructions. This latter is to help prevent the child from saying that he misunderstood the directions. These authors suggest that if the child tends to forget the instructions, he be told to write them down especially if they are somewhat complex and if there is an appreciable lapse of time between instructions and their execution. As has been noted earlier, the child should be given the option of refusing a request if what he is being told to do is indeed a request. And if he does comply with the request, acknowledgment of his compliance should be forthcoming.

In situations where the child is persistently disobedient, parents should be made aware that changing the child's behavior will be difficult not only because it will require consistency of discipline but because it will be difficult for them to alter the child-rearing methods to which they and the child have become accustomed (Drabman and Jarvie, 1977). Many parents of disobedient children tend to ignore the child when he is behaving acceptably. It is suggested that parents be helped to attend to the child's positive behaviors so that they can reinforce them. Some parents need to learn how to praise their children and also how to give instructions considerately, communicating to the child their trust that the instructions will be followed. Many parents think of reward in terms of material reward, but most authors stress the importance of using praise, approval, and body contact as rewards for compliance with directions and requests (Bernal, 1969; Drabman and Jarvie, 1977; Bugental, et al., 1977; Forehand and King, 1977).

Parents are often not aware that although some misbehavior can be ignored, refusal to obey directions, as opposed to refusal to grant requests, should not be ignored. If it is pointed out to the parent that only necessary rules should be established, the parent can often realize that if the rules are indeed necessary, compliance with them must be enforced. The parent should decide before establishing the rule what he will do if the child does not comply. This will help to prevent the situation where the parent, after bickering with the child who is refusing to comply, finally decides that maybe the rule is not that important and gives in to the child. According to most authors, an important ingredient in effective punishment is an awareness on the part of the child that there will be consequences for disobedience and a further awareness of what those consequences will be (Dreikurs and Grey, 1968; Verville, 1967; Drabman and Jarvie, 1977).

It is suggested that if the parent is consistent, the child will learn that there is a penalty for disobedience. This knowledge may make him reflect before he disobeys. At first, the warning or reminder of the resulting consequence may bring about compliance; later the warning may not be necessary. A warning also has the advantage of putting the responsibility for compliance on the child who can then choose between obeying or disobeying. When, in a clinic setting, the child is asked who is responsible for his punishment if he had been warned prior to the punishment, he admits that he has himself brought about the negative consequence.

Dreikurs and Grey (1968) suggest that wherever possible the punishment should be "natural and logical." They argue that the child who can see the relationship between his behavior and the punishment is less likely to be resentful and angry. It is not always possible to find "logical consequences." Time-out, a term whose root is probably in its use in athletic games and here denoting removal of reward, often the reward of being with others, can be a logical consequence of non-compliance but frequently is not. One can, however, explain to the child that the consequence of not getting along with others is to be by himself. Drabman and Jarvie (1977) suggest putting a small child in a chair facing the wall and sending an older child to his room. Although parents often do tell their disobedient children to go to their room, the technique is frequently haphazard and uncontrolled. The children usually terminate the time-out when they please, successfully elicit a response from the parents while they are in their room, and often have a television set and/or a pleasure-giving toy in their rooms. Isolation, under these conditions, is not an effective time-out procedure.

Drabman and Jarvie suggest that the child remain in his room for time periods which vary according to the child's age and that these time periods be increased each time the same disobedience occurs. For instance, since the preschool child has such a poor sense of time, five minutes or less in a chair or in his room usually seems like an hour while a six- or a seven-year-old can remain in his room for ten minutes, the increments for each further infraction being about five minutes. If the child disobeys in a different way, in order that he not remain in his room too long, the new disobedience should be penalized with the initial time period, not added to the time already accumulated. The authors suggest that the child receive no attention while he is in his room and that if he damages or messes his room, he cannot come out until the room is clean. Making him remain in his room until he cleans it may be unrealistic especially for the younger child. Also, in order to save face, he just may remain in his room for long periods. It might be better to help him clean up the mess and not heap punishment on punishment by forcing a confrontation over what was done in the room while he was being punished. If he emerges from his room, it is necessary to put a latch on the outside of the door. If parents are reluctant to do this even when it is pointed out to them that the latch would be on the door for very short periods, they should be advised not to use the room for discipline since the inability to enforce punishment usually results in greater defiance.

The establishment of rules which must then be obeyed tends to provide some of the structure necessary for the child's well-being. According to Muuss (1969), children brought up in a structured environment were found to be "decisive, confident, self-accepting and achievement-oriented." Those children who were brought up in an unstructured environment were "indecisive, distrustful, pessimistic, and perceived success in terms of luck." Baumrind and Black (1967) suggest that parents should try to strike a balance between being warm and affectionate toward the child and controlling the child's behavior, making demands upon the child and letting him know precisely and clearly what is required of him. A balance between these factors tends to encourage obedience and cooperation.

Temper Tantrums

When parents do not desire to grant a child's wishes, they should be firm in their denial; they should make it clear that tantrum behavior will result in the denial of a request. They should ignore the child when he is having a tantrum. If this is done, the tantrum behavior should cease. Crow (1967) suggests that if the child cannot be ignored, which is the case if he happens to be in a group setting, he should be removed until he has calmed down and is ready to behave in an acceptable manner. The child who has learned in the past that his demands will be met if he has a temper tantrum, when being told that this behavior will no longer result in the fulfillment of his demands, should be made aware that although the tantrum behavior cannot be permitted, his frustration at not being able to have his own way is understandable.

Aggression

Parents are often not aware that temperament may also be a factor in the aggressive behavior of the very active child, who appears to have more difficulty than the less active child controlling his aggressive behavior when he is confronted with frustration (Mussen, et al., 1956). Children whose parents use harsh physical punishment, since they, the children, cannot retaliate against the parents, often express their anger by abusing other children (McCord, et al., 1967; Lefkowitz, et al., 1977; Ingram, 1974; Verville, 1967). Schaefer and Norman (1967) found that boys who are aggressive rationalize their behavior by calling attention to the severe punishment they have received from others. The authors point out that these boys can then defend their behavior, thus reducing their guilt and permitting them to continue to behave aggressively. It should also be considered that often the child's aggressive behavior elicits further punishing behavior from the parent.

Another possible determinant of aggressive behavior is the aura of masculinity which tends to accompany such behavior especially when it is perceived as defensive. Thus, "turning the other cheek" is a sign of weakness. Parents, particularly fathers, may foster aggression by teaching the child to "fight back" (Wittenberg, 1971; Ingram, 1974). The very young preschool child, because he cannot yet differentiate between initiating aggression and counteraggression, may assume that aggressive behavior, in general, is permitted. The older child who may, for some reason, wish to engage in aggressive behavior may provoke aggression, which then permits him to justify his own aggressive behavior.

One of the most potent sources of aggressive behavior is the presence of aggressive models. The models may be the child's parents, other adults, peers, and/or aggressive models on television (Wittenberg, 1971; Ingram, 1974; McCord, et al., 1967; Lefkowitz, et al., 1977). Although there is still considerable controversy over the degree to which viewing aggressive behavior on television results in the imitation of these acts by the viewer, most studies support the conclusion that even though observing violence on television does not inevitably result in violent behavior in all viewers, it can serve as a model of violence for some. Liebert, et al. (1973) in their own studies of the effect of television on children and youth and in their evaluation of the general body of research in this area found that viewing aggressive behavior is not cathartic but, on the contrary, has an "instigating effect" and tends to increase the probability that the viewer will be aggressive.

In looking for predictors of aggression, they found that one of the best predictors of hostile behavior at age 19 was the boy's choice at age eight of television programs which portrayed violence. This finding was unrelated to children management factors. The authors suggest that the child who is already hostile may be stimulated by the violence on television. Television may even give this kind of child suggestions for carrying out his aggression. The authors found that if an adult was with your child when he was viewing television violence, the amount of aggressive behavior in the child was diminished. When a same-sexed friend was present, aggressive behavior increased.

McCord, et al. (1967) argue that permitting a child to behave aggressively is tantamount to a reward for aggressive behavior. In addition, if aggressive behavior is not punished, the child may develop a permissive superego, which, in turn, may reduce the guilt which often inhibits aggressive behavior. Lefkowitz, et al. (1977) found that boys whose parents were either permissive or who used severe physical punishment when their sons behaved aggressively were more aggressive than boys whose parents were neither permissive nor punitive. It should be noted here that Ingram (1974) finds that inconsistency in the management of aggressive behavior tends to result in increased aggressive behavior. Rimm, et al. (1974) point out that an individual may behave in an aggressive manner under certain conditions because his repertory for coping with those conditions is limited. The child who has been exposed primarily to aggressive models and/or who has been permitted to behave aggressively may not be aware of alternative behaviors.

Children who have not been protected from minor normal frustrations of everyday life and who have learned how to delay gratification are more likely to develop a reasonably high tolerance for frustration, thus minimizing aggressive behavior which is often evoked by frustrating situations.

When parents use physical punishment for aggressive behavior, they may temporarily prevent further aggression, but the physical punishment tends to cause the child to feel frustrated and helpless, which, in turn, may generate further aggression. It also reinforces the concept of aggression as an acceptable and effective way to exercise control over others.

Fagen, *et al.* (1975) offer the following suggestions for dealing with aggressive behavior:

1. Parents should encourage their children not only to express their anger verbally rather than acting it out but to learn to think in terms of their own responsibility in anger-arousing situations rather than justifying their behavior by projecting blame onto others.

2. Children need to learn that there are usually a number of alternative ways of handling frustrating or other anger provoking situations. The authors suggest that, for the child who was perhaps protected from frustrations earlier, exposure, at first, to mild stress and later to more moderate stress should teach him how to handle stress more effectively.

3. If parents can scale their demands to fit the child's capabilities, increasing those demands as the child is able to fullfill them, the child will experience success and not the frustration often experienced by children who are asked to perform beyond their capabilities.

4. The authors point out that children will not be as apt to act out aggressively if they can learn to accept their occasional feelings of frustration and anger. They are more likely to look for alternative ways of behaving if they can accept their emotions and their thoughts along with the knowledge that not all behavior resulting from those thoughts and emotions are acceptable.

5. Related to the above is the suggestion that a child can learn to control his aggression if he can become aware of the kinds of situations and conditions which provoke his anger, so that he can, in some instances at least, deal with those antecedents before he becomes angry or at least when the provoking situations occur, this knowledge may serve as a warning to him (Zegans, 1971).

6. Verville (1967) suggests that placing the child in a small group which is well supervised may help him to learn more acceptable ways of relating to others. It may help the child who is already aggressive if, when he has been accustomed to behave aggressively to one or two friends, other children could be substituted for those friends to prevent the relationship from becoming fixed.

As noted in the section on disobedience, punishment which can be perceived as a logical consequence of the behavior tends to be most effective. Thus, some form of isolation from peers, first for short periods of time and then for longer periods as the aggressive behavior persists, seems to follow somewhat logically. Deprivation of privileges is also often effective. As noted earlier, it is the firmness and consistency of the punishment which is more important than whether the child is isolated or deprived of other privileges.

Although the child who is "picked on" is usually fearful and timid rather than aggressive, it is probably relevant to discuss it here since it tends to occur in a situation which could easily erupt into violence and often finally does. Parents find it difficult to believe that, although a child may be "picked on" initially because he has some handicap or is timid and seems fair game, if the child can keep from reacting and can just ignore his adversaries, they will tend to lose interest in picking on someone who does not feed their desire for excitment. Parents also find it difficult to understand that some children, particularly those who do not have many friends, will subtly provoke others to attend to them even if it means that this attention is negative. And the child who does not provoke the attack may respond to being picked on in such a way that he gives pleasure, albeit perverse pleasure, to his attackers.

When children who are picked on are brought into clinics and with their parents present are asked for specific examples of their behavior both before and after they are attacked, it becomes clear to both them and their parents that they bear some responsibility for the fact that they continue to be picked on. Parents also need to learn that they often reinforce this behavior by giving the child a great deal of attention each time he complains that he has been picked on. Sometimes just ignoring the child's complaints with an "oh" or "uh-huh" is sufficient to interrupt the behavior. In other situations, helping the child with social skills, improving his self-image as well as teaching him to ignore verbal attacks, is successful. Some of these children, when trained in one or more of the martial arts, find that this gives them enough confidence so they no longer react in a fearful manner when others provoke them. There is no evidence, that as a result of this training, they become the aggressors.

Sibling Fighting

Suggestions for minimizing sibling rivalry and sibling jealousy have been discussed in previous chapters. Where intense sibling conflict already exists, parents should, in addition to dealing with the conflict, be aware of some of the conditions which tend to generate conflict between siblings. Ihinger (1975) emphasizes the importance of respect for each child's possessions, rewards which are based on age and other factors, and unambiguous and nonnegotiable rules governing privileges. Also crucial in preventing and resolving conflicts is the consistency with which the rules are enforced.

Each child should ask permission of his sibling if he wishes to borrow objects belonging to that sibling, and each child should respect the privacy of his siblings. Why one child is granted a privilege not accorded a sibling should be clarified. For instance, it can be a rule of the household that an older child will go to bed later than his younger sibling. Privileges may also be granted or withheld on the basis of acceptable or unacceptable behavior.

A common parental error is to assume that it is important to determine which child instigated the fighting. When parents are faced with the children blaming each other for initiating the fighting, they tend to pick out one child to punish, often the eldest child, rationalizing that since he is older he should handle the situation in a more mature manner. The eldest child may also be punished because parents tend to overprotect the younger child. Sometimes neither child is punished. Parents who have followed recommendations to ignore the question of who may have initiated the conflict and who, after warning the children, have punished both children, report a diminution of the dissension. Sometimes just separating the siblings for a short period even if they remain in the same room and increasing the time of separation as the conflict continues is sufficient punishment. If this is not effective, separating the children into different rooms, again for short periods and increasing the time, is usually effective. In situations where the children share a room, they can take turns being isolated.

If one child, often the youngest child, is the provocateur, the fighting may persist because he, although punished for fighting, gains sufficient satisfaction from seeing his sibling also punished to make it worth his while to continue initiating conflicts. In this situation, parents should try to watch the children more closely so that they can catch the child who tends to be the instigator. When he alone is then punished consistently, the behavior should cease.

Stealing

Anna Freud (1965) points out that a child under the age of four who takes something that does not belong to him does not really know the difference between what is his and what rightfully belongs to others. In addition, his ability to deal with abstract concepts is still at a rather primitive stage so that the moral aspect of his behavior is beyond his ability to comprehend. Verville (1967) suggests that even young children are more likely to ask permission before taking something belonging to another if, in the home, he has learned that he cannot take something belonging to his siblings or to his parents without first asking permission.

After a child has reached the age where he is aware that stealing is unacceptable, he may steal for reasons other than his desire for the article which his parents would refuse to give him if he asked them for it. According to Verville (1967), children may steal because their parents or older siblings are scofflaws who are not caught for minor infractions of the law. The child may perceive this as implicit or even explicit support for his behavior. He may steal as a retaliation against his parents; a child who feels rejected by his parents may find that he gains considerable attention or even recognition as a result of his behavior. When children steal in order to retaliate against their parents or in order to gain attention and recognition, they tend to leave the stolen objects out where the parents can see them. Punishment tends to be ineffective in these cases. The child who feels rejected by his peers may steal in order to bestow money and/or gifts on others. Some children may want objects which become, for them, substitutes for love and warmth which they perceive as being denied them by their parents. Children who do not have an allowance sometimes stop stealing after they have money which belongs to them alone and for which they are not accountable to their parents.

Overindulgent and overprotective parents will sometimes permit a child to keep the object which he stole instead of insisting that the child himself return the object to its owner or make restitution where this is necessary and that he apologize for his behavior. Where restitution is necessary, the child who is given an allowance can be given the entire allowance and then asked to return part of it each week to the parent or to the owner of the stolen object until either the entire value of the object, if it is a small amount, is repaid or until a reasonable amount is repaid if the object is so valuable that it would be unrealistic to ask the child to pay for its entire worth.

Lying

In addition to his attempt to delay or evade punishment for misbehavior, the child may lie in an effort to boost his self-image or to manipulate others. He is likely to continue to lie if by doing so he is successful in avoiding punishment and if his manipulations do indeed beguile others.

Lying is often made easier when parents ask questions which tend to invite the child to lie. It is suggested that if the parent actually sees the child engaging in unacceptable behavior, he should, after warning him, punish the child without first asking him if he did indeed misbehave. If the parent did not see the misbehavior, he can ask the child if he committed the deed, but then he must accept the child's denial. In situations where the parent has reason to suspect that the child is lying, it may be necessary to supervise the child more closely so that the parent can catch the child and punish him consistently without having to rely on the child to confess his misdeeds.

Parents are often concerned that other children or other adults will complain about misbehavior which their child denies. Here again the relationship between parent and child is likely to be unimpaired if the parents withhold punishment but supervise the child more closely and then punish him only when the evidence is irrefutable. Although it is appropriate to punish a child for lying when it is clear that he has lied, without the supervision necessary to prevent lying, punishment for lying appears to be ineffective.

As with stealing, children under the age of about four do not seem to understand the difference between what is true and what is a lie, probably because the line between reality and fantasy is still blurred for them. Sometimes when the fallacy of what they have said is explained to them in concrete terms related to the level of their cognitive development and to their experience, they can begin to understand that their story is not reality based.

Fire-setting

Verville (1967) cites studies which reveal that fire-setting tends to be an expression of anger and/or anxiety. The behavior tends not to occur by itself. Fire-setters tend also to steal, to be runaways, to have learning problems, and to feel rejected. In addition to dealing with the causes of the fire-setting, and to being certain that matches are not available to the child, Verville suggests that the child not be left alone. She does not agree with those who suggest that the child be permitted to light fires under adult supervision. Dreikurs and Grey (1968), on the other hand, suggest that not only should the child be allowed to light the fire in a fireplace under adult supervision but should be made to strike matches, also in the presence of the parents, until he is satiated and asks not to have to strike them any longer. There are children who do not appear to be angry or anxious and who do not exhibit any significant inappropriate or unacceptable behaviors but who appear to enjoy watching things burn. It is these children who tend not to strike matches when alone if they are allowed to do so under supervision. Those children who have multiple problems of which fire-setting is only one may need to be referred to a mental health professional.

Anxiety

Crow (1967), Mussen, *et al.* (1956), Kagen and Havermann (1968), and Verville (1967) suggest the following as sources of anxiety:

1. Parents who are overprotective and who constantly emphasize the hazards and risks in situations may lead the child to feel constantly worried that something unpleasant may occur.

2. Related to this is the anxiety generated by exposure to a steady diet of stories about monsters, accidents, and other calamities.

3. Children will often worry when a parent encumbers them with adult conflicts.

4. Parents who are extremely punitive or whose demands for good behavior are unrealistically high. The latter creates a situation in which a child must fail.

5. Some parents are not only inconsistent in their child management techniques but are erratic in their emotional responses to the child, responding with love one moment and withdrawing the love shortly after for no apparent reason. If the child cannot predict his environment reasonably well, he will have difficulty learning to cope effectively.

6. A child may feel anxious because he is afraid he will lose his parents' love or because he is afraid he will be separated from them. The former may result from the parents' overreaction to the child's misbehavior or from the parents' preoccupation with their own concerns, which may mean that less attention is given to the child. The latter may be a result of situations such as marital conflict and the attendant fear that the parents will separate and abandon the child or it may be a result of separations for which the child has not been prepared.

7. The immature, overly dependent child tends to be anxious not

only because of separation fears but because of his lack of self-confidence.

8. Children, particularly younger children, who are continuously angry with their parents are often anxious partly because of the intensity of their emotions, partly because of their fear that the parents are aware of the anger and may retaliate, and partly because of their fear that their angry thoughts have magical properties and can harm the parents.

9. A child who is treated as a substitute parent in families where the parents are divorced, where one parent has died, or where one of the parents tends to be extremely passive and takes no responsibility in the home may become anxious because of the fear that he will not be able to fullfill the parent's expectations.

10. Anxiety may be aroused in children who are having difficulty accepting their sex role. (See the section on Sexual Problems.)

In addition to dealing with the antecedents mentioned above, teaching children, as well as parents, to accept some anxiety at times so that the anxiety itself does not stimulate further anxiety may help to prevent the escalation and generalization of fears. Parents can be reassured that if they do not know the root of their child's anxiety, they need not be concerned as long as it is not interfering with the child's functioning. In these instances, after making certain that none of the conditions listed above are present, teaching the child some relaxation exercises may help to alleviate the existing anxiety. Relaxation techniques may vary, but essentially they include diaphragmatic deep breathing exercises, muscle relaxation—tensing and then immediately relaxing the muscles progressively, starting with the toes and moving upward to and including the neck (Wolpe and Lazarus, 1966)—and relaxing thoughts—imagining a relaxing setting such as a pastoral or beach scene. Children can also be taught to exercise some control over their anxious thoughts by counting backwards from a thousand or a hundred, depending on the child's age, and by generally substituting neutral thoughts for anxiety-producing ones, even when they are not doing the muscle relaxation exercises. Relaxation exercises in thought control seem to also help anxious adolescents and children with chronic diseases.

Fears

Although fears tend to be specific, Mussen, et al. (1956) suggest that some children's fears are "symbolic." They may represent a fear of being punished by the parent or a fear of not being loved. In essence, they tend to represent those fears which are anxiety producing but which are anchored to specific situations, unlike diffuse or free-floating anxiety. The authors feel that because these fears are so irrational, it is useless to try to explain to the child that monsters do not exist and that there is no reason to be afraid of the dark or of being by himself.

Following are some suggestions for handling the child's fears:

1. Since anxious children tend to be more fearful than children who are relatively relaxed, it is important, before dealing with the specific fear, to reduce the child's anxiety.

2. Mussen, *et al.* (1956) and Verville (1967) suggest that encouraging a child to verbalize his fears and to describe them as concretely and specifically as possible is helpful in eliminating the fear. Parents should be warned, however, that they may reinforce the fear if they do not, after awhile, distract the child from continuing to discuss the fear and from trying to elicit a reaction from the parents. Dreikurs and Grey (1968) feel that children often express fears because they learn that this elicits the parents' concern and that it may result in special favors. Because of this they suggest that parents indicate to the child that they understand the child's fear, but that once they have done this, they should ignore it.

3. Fear of situations to which the child does not have to adjust can be handled by removing the feared object; for instance, the child who is fearful of watching certain television programs need not watch the programs. In certain fear-provoking situations, as in the fear of the dark, modifications can be made to reduce the fear. A dim light can be left on in the room or the door can be left ajar with a light in the hallway. What might be even preferable for a somewhat older child is the availability of a flashlight so that when the child is fearful, he can flash the light around the room to reassure himself that all is well.

4. Mussen, *et al.* (1956) point out the importance of insisting that the child remain in his bed in situations where the child is fearful of thunder and lightning. Staying with the child for a short period during the greatest intensity of the storm may reduce his fear. If the child is permitted to come into the parents' room and/or the parents' bed, the fear may not only be reinforced, but there is a tacit approval of coming into the parents' room and sleeping with them. Sometimes telling the child what causes the thunder and lightning helps, as does the suggestion that he count the seconds between the lightning and the thunder.

Verville (1967) and Mussen, *et al.* (1956) emphasize the importance of successive approximation to the feared object and, wherever possible, pairing the feared object with pleasure. If a child is fearful of fire engines, he might first remain inside and, while being held by the parent, brought to a window where he can observe the fire engine passing by. Visiting the fire house, touching the fire engine, sitting in the driver's seat, and finally being outside when the sirens are on—all of the time with a trusted adult nearby—tends to reduce the child's fear. The authors suggest that the feared object can be presented to the child simultaneously with the presentation of candy.

Parents should be warned that whenever a reward is continuously paired with a feared object, it can have the effect of reinforcing the fear. This is particularly true in situations where the parent continues to go to the child's bedroom with him because the child is afraid of the dark or where the parent continues to sit with the child who is afraid of a storm. In these situations it is preferable for the parent to gradually lessen the distance from which he accompanies the child to his room and to gradually reduce the length of the time he sits with the child who is afraid of storms. As with the anxious child, relaxation exercises and techniques for thought control are helpful. (School phobia will be discussed in the chapter, School Problems.)

Nail-biting, Rocking, Head-banging, and Tics

The incidence of nail-biting is higher in boys and tends to occur more often in first-born and last-born children. The young child who bites his nails tends also to sleep poorly and to be fidgety. Verville (1967) suggests that these children usually have parents who make unrealistic demands on the child, demands which the child cannot fulfill. Sometimes, however, nail-biting becomes a habit which no longer is related to anxiety. In this latter situation, girls will sometimes give up the habit when they are rewarded for doing so with a manicure set or trips to the beauty parlor which are spaced further and further apart. Where the nail-biting is severe, the child can be gradually deprived for longer and longer periods of privileges like television, an activity which tends to elicit the habit.

Rocking and head-banging are also discussed in the chapters dealing with the newborn and infancy. There it was suggested that a calm, reasonably tranquil, and predictable environment can probably prevent these behaviors. In situations where the child already engages in these behaviors, the parents need help in learning how to structure the child's environment so that it is reasonably organized and relaxed. Some children are more sensitive than others to stimuli even when the stimuli are relatively normal, and they, as well as children who are already habitual rockers, seem to eventually rock less if they have available to them a rocking chair or a rocking horse which permits them to rock appropriately.

Sumpter (1975), in his discussion of head-banging, states that more than half of the children who are head-bangers cease by the time they are four years old although there are children who continue this behavior after entering elementary school. He suggests that children who bang their heads tend to be overactive. For a discussion of the relationship between head-banging and deprivation, see the section on Irritability in the chapter, Newborn at Home. Verville (1967) cites a study where it was found that there was a greater incidence of otitis media in children who banged their heads. Both Sumpter and Verville suggest padding the crib or bed.

The presence of tics tends to be a sign of psychological tension. Here again, one frequently finds that the parents are overly demanding. These children are often engaged in numerous activities, in part, because they perceive their parents are expecting them to be successful socially, academically, and in their general behavior. These children are often perfectionistic and hypersensitive. Dynamically, these children may repress their hostility over the demands made upon them, and the tension generated by this repression may express itself in tics. Sometimes the tic is a representation of repressed material (Kessler, 1966; Verville, 1967; Mussen, et al., 1956).

Most authors suggest that, in addition to reducing the tension in the child's environment, helping the child become aware of the muscle contractions makes it easier for him to try to control them voluntarily. Negative practice, "the intentional and purposeful repetition of the tics," seems to work, possibly because it stimulates the child's awareness of his behavior. Parents are frequently unaware of the degree to which the amount of attention given to the child for the tic is reinforcing. Some parents when they are made aware of this and agree to try to ignore the behavior, complain that the tics are so annoying that, short of keeping the child isolated, they cannot ignore them. One should keep in mind the possibility that once the child has developed tics there may be a secondary gain which reinforces the tic behavior; the child can, albeit sometimes unconsciously, express anger in this manner. When parents become aware that they may also be reinforcing the tics by their angry reaction to them, they are apt to be more motivated to ignore the behavior.

References

Bandura, Albert: The self system in reciprocal determinism. *Am Psychologist,* 1978, **33**(4), 344–358.

Baumrind, Diana and Black, Allen E.: Socialization practices associated with dimensions of competence in preschool boys and girls. *Child Development,* 1967, **38**(2), 291–327.

Bernal, Martha E.: Behavioral feedback in the modification of brat behaviors. *J Nervous and Mental Disease,* 1969, **148**(4), 375–385.

Bowlby, John: *Attachment and Loss, Vol. I: Attachment,* Great Britain, Pelican Books, 1969.

Bugental, D. B., Whalen, C. K., and Henker, B.: Causal attributions of hyperactive children and motivational assumptions of two behavior-change approaches: Evidence for an interactionist position. *Child Development,* 1977, **48,** 874–884.

Crow, Lester D.: *Psychology of Human Adjustment,* New York, Alfred A. Knopf, 1967.

Drabman, Ronald S. and Jarvie, Greg: Counseling Parents of children with behavior problems: The use of extinction and time-out techniques. *Pediatrics,* 1977, **59**(1), 78–85.

Dreikurs, Rudolf and Grey, Loren: *Logical Consequences: A New Approach to Discipline,* New York, Meredith Press, 1968.

Fagen, Stanley A., Long, Nicholas J., and Stevens, Donald J.: *Teaching Children Self-Control,* Columbus, Ohio, Charles E. Merrill Publishing Co., 1975.

Forehand, Rex and King, H. Elizabeth: Noncompliant children: Effects of parent training on behavior and attitude change. *Behavior Modification,* 1977, **1**(1), 93–108.

Freud, Anna: *Normality and Pathology in Childhood,* New York, International Universities Press, Inc., 1965.

Ihinger, Marilyn: The referee role and norms of equity: A contribution toward a theory of sibling conflict. *J Marriage & the Family,* 1975 (Aug), 515–524.

Ingram, Gilbert L.: Families in crisis, in Hardy, Richard E. and Cull, John G. (Eds.): *Therapeutic Needs of the Family,* Springfield, Ill., Charles C. Thomas, 1974.

Kagan, Jerome and Havemann, Ernest: *Psychology: An Introduction,* New York, Harcourt, Brace and World, Inc., 1968.

Kessler, Jane W.: *Psychopathology of Childhood,* Englewood Cliffs, N. J., Prentice-Hall, Inc., 1966.

Lefkowitz, M. M., Eron, L. D., Walder, L. O., and Huesmann, L. R.: *Growing Up to Be Violent,* New York, Pergamon Press, Inc., 1977.

Liebert, Robert M., Neale, John M., and Davidson, Emily S.: *The Early Window: Effects of Television on Children and Youth,* New York, Pergamon Press, Inc., 1973.

McCord, William, McCord, Joan, and Howard, Alan: Familial correlates of aggression in nondelinquent male children, in Medinnus, Gene R. (Ed.): *Readings in the Psychology of Parent-Child Relations,* New York, John Wiley and Sons, Inc., 1967.

Mussen, Paul Henry, Conger, John Janeway, and Kagan, Jerome: *Child Development and Personality,* New York, Harper and Row, 1956.

Muuss, Rolf E.: *Theories of Adolescence,* 2nd ed., New York, Random House, 1969.

Rimm, D. C., Hill, G. A., Brown, N. N., and Stuart, J. E.: Group-assertive training in treatment of expression of inappropriate anger. *Psychological Rep,* 1974, **34,** 791–798.

Schaefer, Judith B. and Norman, Martin: Punishment and aggression in fantasy responses of boys with antisocial character traits. *J Personality & Social Psychology,* 1967, **6**(2), 237–240.

Schulman, Robert E., Shoemaker, Donald J., and Moelis, Irvin: Laboratory measure of parental behavior, in Medinnus, Gene R. (Ed.): *Readings in the Psychology of Parent-Child Relations,* New York, John Wiley and Sons, Inc., 1967.

Sumpter, Edwin A.: Behavior problems in early childhood, in Friedman, Stanford B. (Ed.): *The Pediatric Clinics of North America,* 1975, **22**(3), Philadelphia, W. B. Saunders Co.

Swift, Marshall S. and Spivack, George: *Alternative Teaching Strategies: Helping Behaviorally Troubled Children Achieve,* Champaign, Ill., Research Press, 1975.

Thomas, Alexander, Chess, Stella, and Birch, Herbert G.: *Temperament and Behavior Disorders in Children,* New York, New York University Press, 1968.

Verville, Elinor: Behavior Problems of Children, Philadelphia, W. B. Saunders Co., 1967.

Wittenberg, Clarissa: Alternatives to violence, in Segal, Julius (Ed.): *The Mental Health of the Child,* Rockville, Md., NIMH, Public Health Service Publication No. 2168, 1971.

Wolpe, J. and Lazarus, A.: *Behavior Therapy Techniques,* New York, Pergamon Press, 1966.

Zegans, Leonard S.: Towards a unified theory of human aggression. *Brit J Med Psychology,* 1971, **44**, 355–365.

CHAPTER 15

Speech Problems

The most common speech disabilities are articulation disorders, delayed speech, and stuttering. Somewhat less common is selective or elective mutism.

The most frequent speech disorder is that of articulation. Many of the problems of articulation are related to immature speech. For instance, "l's" and "r's" tend to be articulated at a later age than other sounds so that the child whose problem is immature speech will omit such sounds or distort them beyond the age of seven or eight years, by which time all speech sounds are generally learned. According to Kessler (1966), if a child has reached the age of nine and is still having articulation problems, he is not likely to improve without speech therapy. Kessler suggests that these children may have had poor language models or may have emotional problems which interfere with their language development.

Speech can be considered as delayed in the two or two and one-half year old child who has no vocabulary with which to make his wants known. Kessler suggests the following as possible antecedents of delayed speech:

1. There is a correlation between intellectual functioning and the age at which a child starts talking. Although some gifted children, in a study done by Terman, were found to be delayed in their speech, most of them talked at the age of eleven months. Thus, delayed speech may be a symptom of mental retardation.

2. Delayed speech is frequently found in children diagnosed as autistic. It is sometimes difficult to differentiate autism from aphasia. The aphasic child can interact adequately and appropriately with others; the autistic child cannot. Delayed speech in the latter child is considered to be secondary to his psychological problem. It is also sometimes difficult to differentiate autism from mental retardation;

153

not infrequently both are present in the child. Psychological testing by a skillful examiner can usually distinguish between the two conditions.

3. Mothers who appear to have a need to infantalize their children may perceive the ability to speak as a sign of maturity and may, as a result, discourage speech. These mothers are often overly close to the child and overprotective. Mussen, *et al.* (1956) suggest that twins and triplets are often delayed in their speech development because they do not need words to communicate. Sometimes the youngest child in the family does not need to speak because other family members anticipate his wants. In these situations, helping the mother and other family members change their attitudes and behavior toward the child is often effective.

4. Children who come from poor homes tend to be slow in speech development. It is not clear exactly why this should occur except that poor mothers often do not speak as much or, if they do, they sometimes do not listen to the child who tries to speak. In some large poor families, a child who is less aggressive than his siblings may just not be able to compete verbally. It has also been found that children from bilingual homes speak later. The reason for this is not known.

5. Children who have just begun to learn to speak may regress and stop speaking as a reaction to stress. Separation from mother, the birth of a new sibling, or intense marital conflict may result in loss of speech because the skill has not yet been stabilized and is vulnerable to stress. According to Kessler, this does not happen frequently. Also occurring rarely is delayed speech due to the child's fear that speaking may give expression to his anger.

6. It should be noted that hearing deficits may be the cause of delayed speech.

The selectively mute child is one who speaks well when he is at home with his family and who understands speech, but does not speak in school or in the presence of strangers. The onset usually occurs between the ages of three to five, and the condition is not prevalent. According to Sluckin and Jehu (1969), parents of these children may be perfectionistic, insisting that when the child speaks, he does so properly. These children are described as being "timid and shy." These authors also suggest, as a source of the problem, the child's concerns about speaking because of "family secrets" which he has been warned not to divulge. In order to be sure that he will comply, he may feel it is safer not to talk at all. Since these children tend to be somewhat timid and shy, they often cannot express aggression directly. They may then do so indirectly by being negativistic and oppositional.

Rossenbaum and Kellman (1973) as well as Sluckin and Jehu (1969) suggest using desensitization in treating the child with this condition. In the family situation, the mother and/or family members could be present and close to the child while the stranger is at a distance. When the child speaks to the stranger, rewarding him first for a short whisper and continuing to reward him as he moves closer to the stranger and talks at greater length and in a normal speaking tone until he is gradually alone with the stranger can be effective. The same shaping by successive approximations can be done with a counselor, the counselor rewarding the child first for perhaps just nodding to him, then making one sound, and then putting words together into sentences. This can also be done in the classroom where the child can say first one word in a reading group, and then several words and sentences for longer periods still in the reading group until he can finally speak in the classroom itself. These techniques have been found to be effective, particularly if they are coupled with attempts to reduce tension and anxiety in the home.

The incidence of stuttering among school children has been estimated to be about 1%. A survey done by Brady (1976) revealed, however, that there has been a marked reduction in the incidence. Males outnumbered females about four or five to one, and, in about 90% of the cases, the stuttering began before the age of six, with the peak occurring between the ages of two and four. One of the problems in systematically studying stuttering is that the theories are vague and formulated poorly; in addition, results of treatment are often too general to be of value. This may be why little of the research done during the past 25–50 years has resulted in any definitive results (Webster, 1977; Bloodstein, 1977).

In an effort to organize the large number of factors which may be related to stuttering, Coleman (1964) has grouped them into three major theories:

1. Familial theories. Coleman cited a study which revealed that stutterers had nine times as many parents or siblings who also stuttered. Coleman cautions that although it is tempting, on the basis of this statistic, to assume a hereditary predisposition, it is possible that parents who themselves stutter are more likely to become upset at the normal "disfluent" speech of their small children, a situation to which the child could react with anxiety about speech. This, in turn, could result in stuttering. Kessler (1966) states that, although there is evidence for a hereditary predisposition, this explanation cannot, by itself, account for the symptoms. Sheehan (1977) concludes from an examination of studies of the role of heredity that there is a hereditary factor in about 25% of the cases. In none of the studies, however, have any consistent personality patterns been found among stutterers. Stut-

tering is often an isolated symptom, perhaps because it is an effective defense against the anxiety aroused by conflict.

2. Neurological theories. According to Coleman (1964), some children have had infectious diseases prior to the onset of stuttering, the implication being that the central nervous system was affected. In most cases, however, there are no indications of brain damage, nor is there any evidence to support the "mixed cerebral dominance theory." There are no more left-handed or ambidextrous individuals among stutterers than among nonstutterers, and most of the children who were forced to use their right hand rather than their left do not stutter. In addition, treatment directed at reinforcing "unilaterality" has not been successful.

3. Psychosocial theories. Bloodstein (1977) suggests that stuttering, like most characteristics, is probably a result of both constitutional and environmental factors. Following are some of the suggested psychological and/or social factors which may contribute if not cause stuttering:

a. Some parents become so concerned when they perceive their child as "nonfluent" that they demand perfect speech, a demand which the child may not be capable of fulfilling. Goldman and Shames (1964) in a study comparing parents of stutterers and parents of nonstutterers found that the former set higher goals for their children's speech. Related to this is the tendency of some parents to equate the three- or four-year-old's normal hesitant and sometimes repetitious speech with stuttering, and then to try to improve the child's speech, thus communicating to him their concerns (Mussen, *et al.*, 1956).

b. Goldman and Shames also found in their study that parents of stutterers tended to be unrealistic in their general expectations as well as in their expectations that the child speak perfectly.

c. There is some evidence to suggest that problems in the relationship between the stuttering child and his mother are not infrequent. In some situations where the mother-child relationship is symbiotic, the child cannot verbally express his anger toward his mother because of his dependency on her. This fear of expressing anger verbally may cause the child to fear verbalization in general (Mussen, *et al.*, 1956). Kinstler (1967) suggests that one major factor is "covert or hidden rejection by the mother." Children of these mothers are afraid to express anger verbally because they perceive language as a weapon. Results of a study comparing mothers of stutterers with those of nonstutterers revealed that the former tended to hide their rejection more than the latter and tended to accept their children less than mothers of nonstutterers. It was also found that the latter are more open in their rejection than the former.

d. Coleman (1964) suggests that some stutterers may be "fixated" at the oral stage of development. He suggests that this may be due to overgratification of the child's needs at that psychosexual stage.

e. Some children are overly sensitive to criticism and disapproval, and, because of their intense attempts to gain commendation and acceptance, they may be in a continuous state of stress.

f. An emotional conflict such as an approach-avoidance conflict may be a factor in stuttering. Coleman (1964) and Kessler (1966) suggest that when a child finds himself in a situation where the need to speak and not to speak are "equal in strengths," the child's speech is "blocked" and, therefore, hesitant. When this happens, anxiety is reduced and the reduction of the anxiety reinforces the stuttering.

The child who stutters probably reflects his concerns in disordered speech and increases in stress or anxiety will probably intensify the stuttering. Also reinforcing is the stutterer's tendency to perceive himself and to label himself as a "stutterer."

According to Bloodstein (1977), none of the diverse treatments which have been attempted have been systematically effective. Results vary and, in general, do not seem to bear much relationship to the treatment itself. Kessler (1966) lists treatment suggestions from a pamphlet called "Stuttering is a Family Affair" by Dean Engle, a speech pathologist. Most of the suggestions follow logically from the etiological factors listed above. In addition, Kessler suggests that when adults talk to the child, they not use many words or complex words and that they not overwhelm the child with conversation. In most cases speech therapy is indicated.

References

Bloodstein, Oliver: Stuttering. *J Speech & Hearing Disorders,* 1977, **42**(2), 148–151.

Brady, William A. and Hall, Donald E.: The prevalence of stuttering among school-age children. *Language, Speech & Hearing Services in the Schools,* 1976, **7**(2), 75–81.

Coleman, James C.: *Abnormal Psychology and Modern Life,* 3rd ed., Glenview, Ill., Scott, Foresman and Co., 1964.

Floyd, Susan and Perkins, William: Syllable dysfluency in stutterers and nonstutterers: A preliminary report. *J Communication Disorders,* 1974, **7**(3), 279–282.

Goldman, Ronald and Shames, George H.: Comparisons of the goals that parents of stutterers and parents of nonstutterers set for their children. *J Speech & Hearing Disorders,* 1964, **29**(4), 381–389.

Kessler, Jane W.: *Psychopathology of Childhood,* Englewood Cliffs, N. J., Prentice-Hall, Inc., 1966.

Kinstler, Donald B.: Covert and overt maternal rejection in stuttering, in Medinnus, Gene R. (Ed.): *Readings in the Psychology of Parent-Child Relations,* New York, John Wiley & Sons, Inc., 1967.

Mussen, Paul H., Conger, John J., and Kagan, Jerome: *Child Development and Personality,* New York, Harper and Row, 1956.

Peins, Maryann, Lee, Bernard S., and McGough, W. Edward: A tape-recorded therapy method for stutterers: A case report. *J Speech & Hearing Disorders,* 1970, **35**(2), 187–193.

Rosenbaum, Edward and Kellman, Marianne: Treatment of a selectively mute third-grade child. *J School Psychology,* 1973, **11**(1), 26–29.

Sheehan, Joseph G. and Costley, Marian S.: A reexamination of the role of heredity in stuttering. *J Speech & Hearing Disorders,* 1977, **42**(1), 47–59.

Sluckin, Alice and Jehu, Derek: A behavioural approach in the treatment of elective mutism. *Brit J Psychiatric Social Work,* 1969, **10**(2), 70–73.

Verville, Elinor: *Behavior Problems of Children,* Philadelphia, W. B. Saunders Co., 1967.

Webster, Ronald L.: Concept and theory in stuttering: An insufficiency of empiricism. *J Communication Disorders,* 1977, **10**(1–2), 65–71.

CHAPTER 16

School Problems
Part I—General

Mussen, *et al.* (1956), in their summary of a study of mothers of high need achievement children, found that these mothers praised and otherwise reinforced their childrens' efforts to achieve from infancy onward. These mothers also had a tendency to disregard their children's appeals for help. In their discussion of the differences in achievement between children of middle-class parents and lower-class parents, they suggest that the former are more apt to see their parents reading and engaging in intellectual activities. In addition, children reared in a middle-class environment are more likely to associate with peers reared in a similar environment, resulting in similar "peer group values," which should reinforce the parental values. Lack of high achieving models and the absence of reward by either parents or peers for achievement may predispose a child to the development of school problems.

In addition to these somewhat passive conditions which can result in school problems, situations in which the parent speaks about the school in a disparaging manner, finds fault with the teachers, and/or belittles or scorns scholarly pursuits will make it difficult for the child to perceive school and learning as a positive experience (Swift and Spivack, 1975). Thomas, *et al.* (1968) call attention to two other possible antecedants of school problems: (1) It may be difficult for a child reared in a relatively permissive environment at home to adjust to the more structured environment of the school. (2) The child who, by temperament, tends to be "slow to warm up" may become frustrated if teachers expect him to execute their demands as quickly and readily as other children.

159

School Entrance Age

Bower (1974) found that younger children entering first grade performed more poorly academically than children who had entered at the average age. It was found that these children continued to perform more poorly through their high school years. In another study, however, by Miller and Norris (1967) it was found that, although children entering first grade early did significantly more poorly than the control group, by the time they had entered fifth grade, the average achievement level of these early entrants was not significantly different from the average achievement level of the control group. On the basis of their study, they suggest that children between the ages of five years, eight months and six years may enter first grade, without difficulty. Some of the discrepency between the two studies may be due to a difference in population. Even if the results of the Miller and Norris study are reliable, whether an individual younger child should enter first grade or wait depends on how mature that child is and how effectively he can cope with stress. A child of this age is probably mature enough to enter first grade if he can: (1) separate from mother with ease or with a minimal amount of distress; (2) dress himself without supervision; (3) play with others cooperatively and yet be somewhat assertive when this is appropriate; (4) adapt with relative ease to new situations; (5) in most instances foresee the consequences of his behavior so that he can exercise impulse control; and (6) be exposed to normal frustrations without having temper tantrums.

School Phobia

Most writers report that school phobia occurs more frequently in girls despite the fact that, in the general population of child guidance clinics, boys outnumber girls. Children who become school phobic are often described by their parents as having more incidences of illness which have kept them from school, as tending to be absent more at the beginning of the school year than in the spring, as having more difficulty going back to school after holidays, and as having almost no somatic symptoms on weekends and in the summer.

It may be possible to prevent school phobia by the early identification and treatment of minor problems which, although not inevitable sources of the phobia, may be contributing factors. Some of the problems commonly seen in school phobic children are: persistent separation anxiety; overprotection by parent(s); fear that something will happen to the parent while they are away from home; related to this, fear of the power of their angry thoughts against the parent(s); a weak ego; and an overanxious reaction to school, school work, and/or teachers.

McDonald and Sheperd (1976) point out that separation problems alone cannot cause school phobia because the highest incidence occurs between the ages of 10 and 11 years. They do agree, however, that separation anxiety is an important factor. They, Kessler (1966), and Mussen, *et al.* (1956) all concur that the separation problem is one involving both the mother and the child and not the child alone. It is suggested that by accepting his somatic complaints without question, by frequently oversleeping herself, by writing excuses to the school when the child doesn't wish to go, by keeping him out of school if she is not well, and by depreciating the school, teacher, and/or education, the parent may subtly communicate to the child her desire to keep him at home. Kessler states that mothers of school phobic children appear to have an unresolved dependency relationship with their own mothers and seem to fear that their children will not be dependent on them. Although, as has been noted earlier, it is normal for very young children to experience separation anxiety, the symptoms usually disappear after about a week or 10 days. The normal early separation anxiety in school phobic children, however, tends to last longer and to be more intense.

Mussen, *et al.* (1956) argue that mothers of school phobic children often perceive school as a "cold, forbidding place from which they must protect the child." Nader, *et al.* (1975) describe the child of overprotective parents as either one whose parents are older than usual, as having been born prematurely, or as having had a large number of illnesses as an infant. Parents also tend to overprotect the child who has a life-threatening illness or an illness which they perceive as lifethreatening. Even when the phobia is not caused by a mother's need to be overprotective, the overprotective mother's reaction to the phobia may reinforce the child's refusal to go to school.

A child may be unwilling to go to school because he fears that some harm will come to the parent while he is at school. If there is considerable family strife accompanied by physical violence, there may be an element of reality to his fear. Kessler (1966) suggests that the child may be fearful that his hostile wishes against the parent will be realized by some force outside himself. And a younger child may be unwilling to go to school because of his concern that while he is at school, the mother is spending her time with his preschool sibling. Nader, *et al.* (1975) suggest that in situations where the parent has been ill and/or hospitalized, the child may be fearful that when he is at school, the parent will again become ill. It is almost as if the child feels a responsibility to protect the parent.

The child who overvalues himself may have difficulty remaining in school where his unrealistic self-concept is threatened. His anxiety is alleviated when he is at home where his perception of himself is reinforced. Szyrynski (1976) suggests that some children, for whatever reason, have a weak ego and a "low threshold for anxiety." This kind of child may become school phobic under conditions where his ego is further weakened by unusual stress. Marital conflict and/or a new sibling, both of which may result in decreased attention from parents, can compel the child to cling to the parent for support and security. The child who tends to be shy and timid and who is devastated when he perceives himself as being spurned or criticized, the child who makes unrealistically high demands upon himself, or the child who just fears that he will not be able to succeed may find school threatening. The child who is afraid that he will not succeed is often a middle-class child who is achievement-oriented because of the pressure, either subtly or overtly, by his parents to succeed or because he has developed a superego which demands success. Although he is bright, enjoys school, and earns excellent grades, he perceives his performance as inadequate. He may then develop psychosomatic or "pseudo-somatic" complaints which are more acceptable than going to school and achieving less than he feels he should achieve.

Although there are situations in which one might consider that the child is justified in being afraid to go to school, it is frequently the child's and/or the parents' reactions to these situations which lead to school phobia rather than the situations themselves. For instance, the child who tends to fail in school may find the constant exposure to failure anxiety producing and may thus try to avoid the situation. If his parents reinforce his refusal to attend school, he becomes susceptible to the development of school phobia. The same risk is involved in situations where the child's refusal to attend school because he is "picked on" is abetted. The child who is stressed by pressures such as examinations and having to hand in assignments may not be school phobic because of these demands but because the demands are sufficiently stressful to trigger an anxiety reaction which may actually be based on some of the factors noted above. Szyrynski (1976) points out that sometimes school phobia is intensified by school personnel who cannot differentiate between school phobia and truancy.

The school phobic child frequently exhibits what Szyrynski calls "pseudo-somatic manifestations": headaches, dizziness, muscle and joint pains, and most frequently gastrointestinal tract symptoms. Dreikurs and Grey (1968) suggest that unless the parent is convinced that the child is really ill, the child should not be permitted to remain home. Nader, *et al.* (1975) suggest that in situations where the school is concerned that the child may be really ill, the pediatrician can confirm that the child can attend school. Parents should be cautioned against reinforcing the child's physical complaints by discussing his health. If mother is not sure whether the child should stay home or not, she can take him to the pediatrician early in the morning, and, if he is all right, he can go directly to school. In situations where the school nurse sends the child home, the mother can take the child straight to the physician and from there directly back to school if the child is not ill. The school nurse should be informed of the child's problem.

All of the authors cited agree that returning the child to school as soon as possible is crucial. Although in the treatment of many of the other psychological problems there is some disagreement over whether the symptoms should first be relieved before the causes are treated, in school phobia the consensus is that if the child is not returned to school as quickly as possible, the phobia may continue for months and even years. Even when the original cause of the phobia is somewhat minor, any delay in returning the child to school relieves his anxiety, and he becomes even more reluctant to leave the comfort and security of home. Kessler (1966) does not advise using physical force to return the child to school; other authors do not specifically adivse against it. In situations where children have been brought to a mental health clinic for school phobia, it has frequently been necessary to use force when no other method has been effective, and it has been decided that any temporary trauma due to the use of force was preferable to the possible long term effect of permitting the child to remain at home.

If the problem is identified early, if the parents are cooperative, and if treatment is instituted immediately, systematic desensitization is often successful, and it is then not necessary to resort to force. The child would gradually approach closer and closer to school, finally stopping with the counselor before going on into the school room where he would remain. He can be rewarded with tokens, for instance, which can then be redeemed for something he desires. Some phobic children will attend school but only if the parent takes them to school. In these instances, the parent can gradually let the child out of the car farther and farther away from the school, again using tokens as a reward, until the child can finally go alone.

Nader, *et al.* (1975) suggest that the child be encouraged to talk about his fears, and particularly to try to describe in concrete and specific terms what he anticipates will occur if he goes to school. They as well as Kessler, however, warn against reasoning with the child and against giving him too much attention when he is at home, particularly when he is at home during the school hours. Adults should reassure the child that although they understand his fears, he must return to school.

McDonald and Sheperd (1976) suggest family therapy and/or therapy for the mother at first to relieve some of the symptoms and later, if this is not adequate, to deal with some of the underlying causes. Nader, et al. (1975) and Szyrynski (1976) suggest that the problem is a family one. They caution against permitting the parent to continue to place the blame for the child's phobia on the teacher or the school. Where it is quite clear that the major cause is a separation problem, for instance, counseling for the parent in behavioral methods of gradually separating from the child can alleviate the symptoms. In this same way, if the mother is overprotective, or if the child's ego needs strengthening or the parent is overreacting to some school situations, the parent may respond to suggestions for changing her child rearing methods.

McDonald and Shepard (1976) identified two different groups of school phobic children between the ages of 12 and 17. The children in one group were chronically absent from school, and the cause of their poor attendance appeared to be related to the attitude of their parents and to their environment. The children in the second group suddenly after consistent attendance refused to attend school for no apparent reason, and, although they realized that their behavior was inappropriate, they were unable to do anything about it. Children in the former group tended to have a number of adjustive problems which made it difficult for them to function in general. They may already have developed personality disorders. Children in the latter group, on the other hand, may have functioned reasonably well in other areas and had a history of consistent school attendance and average or above average school performance. Since the onset of the phobia in these latter children is sudden, it may be possible to return them to school successfully if this is done immediately. If, however, the cause cannot be ascertained and removed, there may be a recurrence of the phobic reaction.

As noted earlier, sometimes school personnel do not distinguish between school phobia and truancy, an oversight which can aggravate the phobia. The school phobic tends to enjoy school and to be a good student. This latter characteristic can contribute to the development of the phobia. In his efforts to achieve, the child may make unrealistic demands on himself and may then become anxious if his grades are less than perfect. The phobic child when he absents himself from school hurries either to be with his mother or, if he is an adolescent, to be by himself. The younger child, if he is permitted to remain home, once the morning wrangling over going to school is over, is quite normal in his behavior.

The truant, in contrast to the phobic, has a history of poor academic performance and of disliking school. When he leaves school, instead of going home, he tends to roam the streets with his peers. It is not unusual to find that the habitual truant is limited in his intellectual functioning, and has always had learning problems. Not only are there no separation problems, but children who are truant tend to be alienated from their families.

The Distractible Child

If the child is to learn, he must pay attention and be able to concentrate. Thomas, *et al.* (1968) caution against perceiving distractibility as undesirable in all areas. They suggest that the distractible child is capable of responding to a variety of stimuli which, in some situations, can be a positive attribute. On the other hand, they emphasize its negative properties. The distractible child is not perseverant and so tends not to finish his work without close supervision. Crow (1967) and Verville (1967) suggest that the distractible child is often bored and indulges in frequent daydreaming. There are indications that some children seem temperamentally to become easily bored because they adapt so quickly to stimuli.

Other possible sources of distractibility besides temperament are:

1. Few demands on the child to assume responsibility for finishing tasks at home. This may cause the child to be insufficiently persistent in completing his school work both at home and at school.

2. Immaturity and inappropriate dependency. According to Verville (1967), immature and inappropriately dependent children tend to daydream. They are also accustomed to having things done for them and have rarely if ever been given the responsibility for doing disagreeable or difficult chores.

3. Premature learning. Verville suggests that children who were compelled to learn academic material during their preschool years sometimes rebel. They permit themselves to be distracted by extraneous stimuli and, thus, do not attend to the work at hand.

4. Anxiety. Some children are distracted by family problems. Anxieties over marital conflicts and/or feelings of rejection may interfere with their ability to concentrate.

In considering the appropriate treatment, causes other than those suggested above should first be ruled out. A child may be unable to concentrate because he is not getting sufficient sleep, because nutrition is inadequate or faulty, because he is intellectually limited, or because he has a visual or hearing problem. The distractible child seems to work more effectively if, when doing his school work, he does not have to sit still for long periods at a time. He can assume responsibility for short rest periods if he is given a timer or an alarm clock to warn him to return to his work. This is preferable to constant reminders that he complete his task. Thomas, *et al.* (1968) suggest that if the child does not return to his work and/or complete his task, he should have to accept certain consequences. He can be deprived of privileges, increasing the length of the deprivation as he continues to ignore the demand that he finish his assignment. It can be suggested to his teacher that if he does not attend in school, he should be deprived of group activity or recess until the task is completed. He can then be rewarded with praise for finishing his work.

Some children are distracted when working in a group and do better if they can work alone. They can do their homework in the quiet of their own room, and it can be suggested to teachers that, where possible, a carrel or a screen be provided so that the amount of extraneous stimulation is minimized. According to Swift and Spivack (1975) distractible children are more apt to successfully complete their work if they are given only one task at a time. In addition, if the tasks are relatively short and uncomplicated, the child becomes less bored. Longer and more complicated tasks can be added as the child achieves success on the more simple ones. Mothers and teachers who insist that children repeat instructions given to them report an increase in attentiveness.

The child who appears to be distracted by family problems can often benefit from talking about his anxieties. Swift and Spivack (1975) suggest that the child learn to monitor himself so that he becomes aware when he is not paying attention to the task at home and that he write out what he is thinking about at that time. This may help him to exercise some control over his thoughts.

Kater (1975) and Braud, *et al.* (1975) suggest that control of breathing and control over attention are related and that, by helping the child to decrease his respiratory rate, he can reduce muscle activity and thus increase attentiveness. This same exercise can be used for overactive children.

Conduct Problems Related to School

The typical history of the child who is referred to a mental health clinic because he is having behavior problems in school reveals that he has always been a very active child with poor impulse control. Stewart

(1976) suggests that how the parent handles an irritable infant will have an effect on how this child conducts himself later. The parent can reinforce the behavior by reacting to it with an inordinate amount of attention or the parent may further frustrate the child by ignoring the behavior without making efforts to reduce the irritability. (See the chapter Newborn at Home.) Stewart implies that anticipatory guidance to parents of these children may help to prevent misbehavior in school. Berlin (1974) warns against reassuring parents when the child is still very young that the child's misbehavior, because it does not appear to be serious at that time, should be ignored. If parents are given the impression that, if ignored, the problem will disappear, it is sometimes difficult when the child begins to have problems in school to help them see that it is not entirely a school problem.

Parents can be advised that, in general, even if they are not having any present problems with their very young children, they may prevent conduct problems in school if there is a reasonable amount of peace and tranquility in the home and if the environment is organized, structured, and predictable (Swift and Spivak, 1975; Fagen, *et al,* 1975; Benson, *et al.,* 1977; Berlin, 1974).

Most authors imply that the primary cause of conduct problems in school is related to the use of ineffective management techniques in the home. If parents do not set limits on the child's behavior or if they do set limits and these limits are not enforced, if they permit the child to behave at home in a manner which cannot be tolerated in school, the child will tend to have problems both at home and in school. Parents may, however, not be concerned when the undesirable behavior is confined to the home. If when at home the child can interrupt, talk constantly, be inattentive and disobedient, he will tend to behave in this same manner in the classroom. The child who tends to be the center of attention at home or who was the center of attention until the birth of a new sibling, often engages in attention-getting behavior in school. Fagen, *et al.* (1975) suggest, however, that some children may misbehave as a defense against their fear that they will not be able to achieve success in learning. They may feel less anxious if the attention is focused on their conduct rather than on their academic inability.

Bugental, *et al.* (1977) argue that self-discipline is a result of consistent discipline applied externally. Thus, if a child is to behave appropriately and acceptably outside the home, behavior characteristics which require self-discipline, he must have been disciplined consistently in the home for the behavior to generalize and persist. Sometimes parents and teachers are afraid to insist on desirable behavior from an impulsive child because their demands may precipitate an angry reaction. They should be given suggestions for handling the child's anger and cautioned against protecting him from the consequences of his outbursts.

O'Leary and Pelham (1978) suggest that parents reward the child with praise for acceptable behavior, that they ignore trivial disturbances, and that they use "time-out" for punishment. They suggest that the parents ask for a daily school report so that punishment will not be delayed. Fagen, et al. (1975) suggest that, wherever possible, teachers be advised to handle the disruptive child in this same way. Urging children to learn to repeat to themselves what they are doing when they are controlling their behavior should help them to be more reflective. In general, it is suggested that children can more easily control their behavior by talking to themselves out loud, if possible, at first and then silently as they become proficient in talking aloud. These authors also emphasize the need for the child to learn to delay gratification if he is to develop self-control. And they stress the importance of introducing structure at home and in the classroom. Some parents and teachers are fearful that somehow structure will block the development of creativity. Ryckman, et al. (1976) cite the results of a study which revealed that a "highly structured teacher controlled reading program" did not interfere with a task requiring divergent thinking.

Some parents and teachers are resistant to recommendations that the child with behavior problems be placed in a special class. The rationale for their resistance is the fear that the child will be stigmatized. Apparently, however, improvement in learning can result from special class placement. A study reported by O'Leary and Schneider (1977) revealed that when first graders were assigned in a random order to a regular class or a special class for behavior problem children, the latter, when returned to the regular class after eight months in the special class, scored higher in reading achievement than the controls.

In anticipation of the discussion of learning disabilities as a separate topic, it is important to call attention to the relationship of conduct problems, particularly those involving poor impulse control, to learning. This relationship is reflected in the results of a study by Epstein, et al. (1977). These authors found that children with learning disabilities were more impulsive than normal children and that severely learning disabled children were more impulsive than children with mild learning disabilities.

CHAPTER 17

School Problems
Part II—Learning Disabilities

Learning Disabilities

According to the National Advisory Committee on Handicapped Children, children with specific learning disabilities are "those who have a disorder in one or more of the basic psychologic processes involved in understanding or in using language (spoken or written) which disorder may manifest itself in an imperfect ability to listen, think, read, write, spell, or do mathematical calculations. These disorders include such conditions as perceptual handicap, brain injury, minimal brain dysfunction, dyslexia, and developmental aphasia." Adelman (1974) points out that in actual practice children labeled as learning disabled are a heterogeneous group in relation to etiology. The major problem in diagnosis is what Fagan, *et al.* (1975) call the "circular interacting relationship between thoughts and feelings such that cognitive experience affects emotional experience affects cognitive experience, etc." The child who has difficulty learning may react by developing emotional problems, and the child who has emotional problems may have learning problems. It is not always possible to know which problem came first. Chalfant and Flathouse (1971) argue that since it is impossible to see how information is being processed, one can only infer how the child learns. Behaviors which tend to be perceived as symptoms of a learning disability may also result from emotional problems.

Individuals who work with children tend to use a variety of terms such as hyperkinesis, hyperactivity, brain damage, cerebral dysfunction, minimal brain dysfunction, visual-perceptual-motor problems,

169

and dyslexia, all of which are equated with the term, "learning disability." In spite of the government's efforts to develop a circumscribed definition of learning disability, the term continues to be interpreted in different ways (Beatty, 1977; Denhoff, 1976).

In 1966 a study by Pasamanick and Knobloch revealed that one of five disorders significantly correlated with complications of pregnancy and prematurity was dyslexia (Leong, 1977). Since 1974, there have been a number of studies with essentially similar results. Wilborn and Smith (1974) found that about eight out of ten learning disabled children had "at least one perinatal and/or developmental abnormality." Steg and Rapoport (1975) report a number of studies which show a "higher incidence of anomalies in children with either a primary severe learning disability or with severe difficulty in impulse control." They also report studies of learning disabled children in which the family history and/or the prenatal history suggest that these children may suffer from "a genetic disorder or a congenital defect induced by prenatal insults." And Smith and Wilborn in 1977 found that prenatal and perinatal factors such as "blood incompatibility, induced labor, post maturity, hand-eye dominance, type of birth, prematurity, convulsions, toxemia of pregnancy" were related to later problems in the "speech, reading, visual motor" areas.

Behaviors which can be identified early as predictors of school problems include restlessness, not paying attention, difficulty in handling frustration, and low frustration tolerance (Schrager, et al., 1967). The authors also found that when these children were in kindergarten, they tended to be absent more than those children who did not exhibit these behaviors, and the absence was unrelated to health. The authors suggest that, in addition to the behaviors mentioned above, the frequent absences would tend to hinder the learning process. Bellak (1976) adds to the foregoing indicators of possible school problems those such as delayed language development, poor spatial abilities, poor coordination, and difficulty with impulse control. The results of a study by Forness, et al. (1977) revealed that the one most significant predicator of potential school problems is inattentiveness, which can be readily identified early and, if handled effectively, can prevent many learning problems. The two-year-old should be able to attend to a task for about 15 minutes, the three-year-old for about 30 minutes, and the four-year-old for about 45 minutes. If inattentiveness can be identified early, it may not be necessary to deal with the other symptoms.

Although rarely are hard neurological signs found in children diagnosed as learning disabled, soft signs such as perceptual and spatial problems, and poor fine and/or gross motor coordination are quite common. Whether poor coordination is directly related to learning disability or whether it is just often found in learning disabled children is not clear.

Leong (1977) cites Satz and Nostrand who suggest that dyslexia is due to "a lag in the maturation of the brain." They argue that perceptual-motor skills will be retarded in the young child and that conceptual and linguistic skills are more likely to be retarded in the older child who is immature. Jani (1973) also suggests that, whether due to a consititutional or genetic defect, there appears to be a developmental delay in dyslexic children, even though there may be no actual symptoms of brain damage. There is also some evidence that learning disabled children have increasing difficulty recalling material as the time between the original presentation of the material and the recall is increased (Bauer, 1977).

Although it is not clear that overactivity and distractibility are causes of learning problems, 40% of learning disabled children tend to be "over-active and distractible" (Silver, 1976). As noted previously in the discussion of early identification, young children who tended to be overactive and inattentive were more likely to develop school problems later.

Also as was noted previously, the circularity of the relationship between emotional and cognitive factors makes it imperative that where there are emotional or child rearing problems, they be considered as possible causative factors and not accepted as secondary to the learning disability without clear evidence that they are secondary. Barton, *et al.* (1974) found that children with very strict fathers and physically punitive mothers tend to be underachievers in school and that children with parents who are not profuse in rewarding or praising the child but who merely encourage achievement tend to be achievers. Adelman (1969) found that boys who are underachievers do not expect to be successful while boys who are achievers assume they will succeed.

There are two conditions involving emotional factors which frequently result in learning problems. One is a fear of failure, which is often seen in children who are perfectionistic, but which is more commonly seen in children who are slow developers or whose intellectual functioning is in the low average or borderline range. These children are too bright to be placed in a slow learning class but too dull to compete successfully with children in a regular class. They are frequently labeled as "lazy," and teachers become annoyed at them because they, according to the teacher, "sit and do nothing." Fagen, *et al.* (1975) suggest that a child who is continually faced with failure will, in order to defend himself against anxiety, avoid situations which may

force him to be faced with his inabilities. By denying his possible inadequacies, he can reassure himself and sometimes his parents that if
he were to apply himself, he would succeed.

A second condition which can interfere with learning is test anxiety.
Mussen, *et al.* (1956) suggest that test-anxious children lack confidence
in their ability to succeed; they then give up easily, and the combination of their anxiety and lack of persistence causes them to do poorly on
examinations. Verville (1967) suggests that the test-anxious child
tends to be perfectionistic and it is this which causes him to be anxious
during tests. Parents of test-anxious children tend, in addition to making unrealistic demands on the child, to emphasize the importance of
scholastic achievement.

Most authors agree that parent counseling can be effective even in
those situations where the learning disability appears to be primarily
due to neurological factors. As has been noted, emotional and/or behavioral factors are common in these children, and changes in parent
management may reduce the seriousness of the learning disability.
Where there are no apparent emotional problems, support for the parent and counseling concerning school placement, for instance, may
reduce the parents' anxiety. Following are some suggestions for dealing with learning disabilities, both those clearly related to neurological problems and those in which emotional factors are apparent and
neurological involvement is ambiguous:

1. Children with perceptual problems, with defective spatial
abilities and/or poor eye-hand coordination, who have received training in these areas, manifest improvement in language skills (Bellak,
1976; Elkind and Deblinger, 1969; Zietz, 1970). Zietz includes in her
paper concrete suggestions for remediations of eye-hand coordination
and perceptual abilities. It should be noted that the effectiveness of
this treatment is controversial. In order to improve the child's ability
to recall information, Silver (1976) suggests teaching the child in such
a way that he overlearns the material. That is, he continues to practice
the material after he can recall or reproduce it perfectly. Silver stresses
the importance of differentiating between a visual-perceptual problem
and an auditory-perceptual problem. The child who suffers from the
former will have difficulty learning to read by the look-say method
while the child with the latter problem would have difficulty learning
to read by the phonic method. In general, the child with the auditory-
perceptual problem may have more difficulty learning in a situation
where the teacher may talk too fast or indistinctly.

2. Because test-anxious children are often diagnosed as learning
disabled and because it is often not clear until treatment has been
instituted that they are not learning disabled, it seems appropriate to

discuss their treatment here. Parents of these children may need to become aware of their child's capabilities and to learn how to calmly encourage the child without pressure. Verville (1967) suggests that since speed tests tend to be anxiety producing, test-anxious children do better if they are given fewer tests where speed is a factor. These children may also become less tense if their assignments are shorter. Swift and Spivack (1976) advise that test-anxious children try, for a while, to ignore the time and read all of the items before starting to answer them, answering first only those to which they know the answers and then, if time is left, to go on to items whose answers are not as obvious. They also suggest that these children go over the answers carefully if there is time. It is possible that as these children begin to perform well on tests and their anxiety is reduced, they can begin to try to work faster without becoming anxious.

3. Occasionally, a child's learning problem may be related to unpleasant experiences associated with learning. For instance, a child may avoid reading because of the anxiety it produces. Word and Rozinko (1974) report success in using desensitization to reduce the child's fear of reading.

4. Where learning problems are associated with impulsivity and distractibility, stimulation should be reduced; the child should be praised or otherwise rewarded for achievement, and external controls should be consistently applied in a generally structured environment (Bellak, 1976; Swift and Spivack, 1976).

5. Kagan and Havemann (1968) suggest that some learning disabled children do not improve in their academic performance because of the often long delay between what they learned and the grade they finally received following a test. It has been shown that feedback is most effective in improving learning if it is given as soon after the learning as possible.

6. As noted above in the discussion of test anxiety, emotional problems which may, after investigation, prove to be the source of learning difficulties are frequently, albeit mistakenly, considered to be secondary to a learning disability. Because of the difficulty sometimes in determining whether the emotional problems are the cause or the result of underachievement (see beginning of this section), it is important to begin treatment of the emotional problem, which, if effective, will clarify the basis for the learning difficulty. It is because of the circularity of emotional and neurological factors that the discussion of emotional problems which may interfere with learning is relevent to the discussion of learning disabilities.

The child who exhibits symptoms of fear of failure may benefit from being praised for what might ordinarily be perceived as insignificant improvements. Frequently the child who continues to fail is discouraged when he is still receiving a failing grade with no recognition of improvement because the improvement was so slight that it had no effect on his grade. Swift and Spivack (1975) point out that one can almost always find something to praise in the child's work in order to encourage him to continue to try to improve.

It should be noted here that very occasionally a child may develop learning problems because of an inability to appropriately express anger toward his parents. When he learns, usually inadvertently, that his parents become upset when he does not do well in school, and that he can elicit their anger by not doing his work, he may continue to achieve below his capability. This is not to say that he consciously sets out to fail. A somewhat similar situation is that in which the parent punishes a child so severely for one poor grade that the child feels he might as well be shot for a sheep as for a lamb. In these situations, other reasons for the learning problem should be explored. If the child has a learning disability, praising him for improvement, teaching him to express his anger appropriately, and/or teaching the parents to temper their reaction to his grades may solve the learning problem.

7. Learning disabled children, because they tend to be distractible, should do their homework in a quiet place with minimal extraneous stimulation. These children also do better if a routine for doing their homework has been established and is rarely broken. Dreikurs and Grey (1968) suggest that the child not be permitted to watch television or to play until his homework has been completed. Many children who do not have school problems can postpone doing their homework and still complete it before bedtime. Learning disabled children, however, because they are distractible and because schoolwork is often so laborious for them usually require more time for completing their assignment.

8. Although considerable controversy has been generated by the question of whether learning disabled children should be placed in a special class or remain in a regular class, the general consensus seems to be that the former is preferable. Silver (1976), Briard (1976), Bellak (1976), and Decker and Decker (1977) all suggest that special education is the treatment of choice. Although, ideally, it might be better for the learning disabled child to remain with his peers in a regular classroom, his needs usually cannot be met in the typical class environment. Most of the teachers teaching a regular class are not specifically trained to help the learning disabled child, and, even if they were, there are so many children in the regular classroom that it would be difficult for them to spend as much time with the learning disabled child as he usually requires. In addition, he may be humiliated by

those classmates who perceive him as being "different" and, thus, fair game for ridicule. In any case, "mainstreaming" should be considered only on an individual basis and/or during parts of the day for subjects which the child can handle. Daniel Ringleheim of the Department of Health, Education, and Welfare states that "there are children who do need to be in special classes and private facilities, and these settings may very well constitute the least restrictive environment for those children."

The Effects of Medication on Children With School Problems

The effects of medication on children with learning and/or behavioral problems are not entirely clear and will probably remain inconclusive until more definitive studies have been done. According to Freeman (1976) and Pope (1970) one of the problems is the difficulty measuring activity level, particularly when the important criterion of "hyperactivity" is the absence of "appropriate direction" to the activity rather than the amount of activity.

Yahraes (1971), in his summary of three studies done by Dr. Leon Eisenberg using tranquilizers on children with behavior problems, reports that none of the studies yielded any evidence of improvement which could be attributed to the drugs. The results of one study revealed that children with behavior problems who were given a placebo and psychotherapy for seven weeks were as apt to show improvement as those given tranquilizers and psychotherapy.

Stimulants, however, according to Yahraes did seem to be effective for children labeled as "hyperkenetic." It is suggested that the stimulants improved learning because they increased the child's attention. Barkley (1977) in his review of the research on the use of stimulants found that only a small number of children did not improve after being given stimulant drugs. He suggests that the medication appears to affect the central nervous system in such a way as to improve the child's ability to concentrate and to decrease his impulsiveness. He does report, however, that follow-up studies reveal that "psychosocial adjustment of these children in the long term are not affected by treatment with stimulant drugs." Freeman (1976) and O'Leary and Pelham (1978) found that there were also no long term effects on scholastic achievement.

Rie, et al. (1976) in their study using a placebo and a stimulant drug found that children who received the stimulant were less active, more attentive, less distractible, and more highly motivated than children who received the placebo. The drug had no effect, however, on measures of reading, mathematics, and spelling. The authors suggest that, because of this, the drug is not appropriate for those children who are learning disabled but have no behavior problems. Cole and Moore (1976) suggest that the drug does nothing more than make the child "compliant." They agree with Rie that there is no evidence that stimulant drugs improve the child's ability to reason or to succeed in learning material which does not require rote learning. In studying the effects of stimulants on social adjustment, Stewart (1976) cites short term studies which suggest considerable improvement in social adjustment as a result of treatment with stimulant drugs. Follow-up studies after five years, however, reveal that the effects were not significant.

There are a small number of children—mental health workers report that they comprise less than 0.1% of the child guidance clinic population—who have no behavior problems and are referred solely because they have no control over their movements which, in contrast to most children labeled as "hyperactive," are not movements of intention. Parents and school personnel report a marked decrease in these extraneous movements resulting from treatment with stimulant drugs.

All of the authors cited express concern over the side effects. Barkley, in his review of the research, points out that although many of the side effects are temporary, "suppressed weight and height gain may remain problematic throughout treatment." Rie, et al. argue that diminished affect and "spontaneity" may really hinder learning rather than improve it.

Most authors agree that if a drug is used, it should be used for only short periods of time and in combination with other treatment methods. Rie, et al. (1976) and Conrad, et al. (1971) suggest that if other means of intervention are not used, the medication may conceal the learning problem because the child is no longer a behavior problem. Related to this is the concern by Bugental, et al. (1977) that children who are given drugs will learn to ascribe the beneficial effects on their behavior to sources that are not under their control, and this can result in a continued dependency on outside help for the solution of problems. Some parents tend to reduce their attempts to teach the child to control his behavior when they find that the drug will do the job.

O'Leary and Pelham (1978) and Stableford, et al. (1976) report success in controlling the child's behavior without medication by teaching the parents effective child management techniques. In one study some children were taken off medication while others continued to take the drug. The teacher handled the behavior of the children in the former group by applying management techniques which have been effective in the past. It was then demonstrated to the parents of these children that their behavior was no different than that of the children still on medication. Parents whose children have been taking stimulant drugs and who bring their children to mental health clinics either because the drugs are not sufficiently effective or because they do not want the children on medication find that they can, after following suggestions for handling the child's behavior more effectively, discontinue the medication.

Feingold's Diet

Most of the studies of the effect of the Feingold diet on children who have a short attention span, who are restless, distractible, and evidence learning problems, are not double-blind studies and are, therefore, inconclusive. In addition, the experimenters have not controlled for such factors as the added attention the affected child is likely to receive as a result of his need for a special diet. Harley (1976), in a double-blind study using control subjects, randomly assigned children to either the Feingold diet or one which was "comparable in appearance, variety, nutritional value and palatability." Results of the study did not substantiate the claim that the Feingold diet causes improvement in these children. What was significant was that children on both diets scored better on tests when compared to their baseline performances. Some of the improvement could have been due to the practice effect of having been tested repeatedly. It is possible, however, that the greater amount of attention and improved nutrition may have contributed to the results. In any case, at present, there is no reliable evidence to support claims that the Feingold diet is effective.

References

Adelman, Howard S.: Reinforcing effects of adult nonreaction on expectancy of underachieving boys. *Child Development,* 1969, **40**(1), 111–122.

Adelman, Howard S.: Learning problems, in Williams, Gertrude J. and Gordon, Sol (Eds.): *Clinical Child Psychology: Current Practices and Future Perspectives,* New York, Behavioral Publications, 1974.

Barkley, Russell A.: A review of stimulant drug research with hyperactive children. *J Child Psychology & Psychiatry,* 1977, **18**, 137–165.

Barton, K., Dielman, T. E., and Cattell, R. B.: Child rearing practices and achievement in school. *J Genetic Psych,* 1974, **124**, 155–165.

Bauer, Richard H.: Short-term memory in learning disabled and nondisabled children. *Bull Psychonomic Soc,* 1977, **10**(2), 128–130.

Beatty, James R.: Identifying decision-making policies in the diagnosis of learning disabilities. *J Learning Disabilities,* 1977, **10**(4), 13–21.

Bellak, Leopold: A possible subgroup of the schizophrenic syndrome and implications for treatment. *Am J Psychotherapy,* 1976, **30**(2), 194–205.

Benson, H., Kotch, J. B., Crassweller, K. D., Greenwood, M. M.: Historical and clinical considerations of the relaxation response. *Am Scientist,* 1977, **65,** 441–445.

Berlin, Irving N.: Minimal brain dysfunction: Management of family distress. *J Am Med Assoc,* 1974, **229,** 1454–1456.

Bower, Eli M.: The three-pipe problem: Promotion of competent human beings through a pre-school kindergarten program and sundry other elementary matters, in Williams, Gertrude J. and Gordon, Sol (Eds.): *Clinical Child Psychology: Current Practices and Future Perspectives,* New York, Behavioral Publications, 1974.

Braud, L., Lupin, M. N., and Braud, W. G.: The use of electromyographic biofeedback in the control of hyperactivity. *J Learning Disabilities,* 1975, 8(7), 421–425.

Briard, Fred K.: Counseling parents of children with learning disabilities. *Social Casework,* 1976(Nov), 581–585.

Bugental, D. B., Whalen, C. K., and Henker, B.: Causal attributions of hyperactive children and motivational assumptions of two behavior-change approaches: Evidence for an interactionist position. *Child Development,* 1977, **48,** 874–884.

Chalfant, J. and Flathouse, V.: Auditory and visual learning, in H. Myklebust (Ed.): *Progress in Learning Disabilities, Vol. 2,* New York, Grune and Stratton, Inc., 1961.

Cole, Sherwood O. and Moore, Samuel F.: The hyperkinetic child syndrome: The need for reassessment, *Child Psychiatry & Human Development,* 1976, 7(2), 103–112.

Cole, W. G., Dworkin, E. S., Shai, A., and Tobiessen, J. E.: Effects of amphetamine therapy and prescriptive tutoring on the behavior and achievement of lower class hyperactive children. *J Learning Disabilities,* 1971, 103–112.

Conrad, W. G., Dworkin, E. S., Shai, A., and Toblessew, J. E.: Amphetamine therapy and prescriptive tutoring on the behavior and achievement of lower class hyperactive children. *J Learning Disabilities,* 1971.

Crow, Lester D.: *Psychology of Human Adjustment,* New York, Alfred A. Knopf, 1967.

Decker, Robert J. and Decker, Lawrence A.: Mainstreaming the LD child: A cautionary note. *Academic Therapy,* 1977, **12**(3), 353–356.

Denhoff, Eric: Locating young children with learning problems. *New York State J Medicine,* 1976, **76**(12), 2007–2010.

Dreikurs, Rudolf and Grey, Lorew: *Logical Consequences: A New Approach to Discipline,* New York, Meredith Press, 1968.

Elkind, David and Deblinger, Jo Ann: Perceptual training and reading achievement in disadvantaged children. *Child Development,* 1969, **40**(1), 11–19.

Epstein, M. H., Cullinan, D., and Sternberg, L.: Impulsive cognitive tempo in severe and mild learning disabled children. *Psychology in the Schools,* 1977, **14**(3), 290–294.

Fagen, Stanley A., Long, Nicholas J., and Stevens, Donald J.: *Teaching Children Self-Control,* Columbus, Ohio, Charles E. Merrill Publishing Co., 1975.

Forness, S. R., Hall, R. J., and Guthrie, D.: Eventual school placement of kindergartners observed as high risk in the classroom. *Psychology in the Schools,* 1977, **14**(3), 315–317.

Freeman, Roger.: Minimal brain dysfunction, hyperactivity, and learning disorders: Epidemic or episode? *School Review,* 1976 (Nov), 5–30.

Harley, J. Preston: Diet and behavior in hyperactive children: Testing the Feingold hypothesis. Paper presented at American Psychological Association 84th Annual Convention, Washington, D. C., September, 1976.

Harlow, H. and Suomi, S. J.: Social recovery by isolation-reared monkeys. Proc Nat Acad Sci, 1971, **68**(7), 1534–1538.

Jani, Subhash N.: Dyslexia: A summary of representative views. *J Assoc Study of Perception,* 1973 8(2), 80–87.

Kagan, Jerome and Havemann, Ernest: *Psychology: An Introduction,* New York, Harcourt, Brace, and World, Inc., 1968.

Kater, Donna: Biofeedback: The beat goes on. *The School Counselor,* 1975, **23,** 16–21.

Kessler, Jane W.: *Psychopathology of Childhood,* Englewood Cliffs, N.J., Prentice-Hall, Inc., 1966.

Leong, C. K.: Detection of children with learning problems: Some considerations. *Mental Retardation Bulletin,* 1977, **5**(1), 3–8.

McDonald, James E. and Sheperd, George: School phobia: An overview. *J School Psychology,* 1976, **14**(4).

Miller, W. Duane and Norris, Raymond C.: Entrance age and school success. *J School Psychology,* 1967 **6**(1), 47–60.

Mussen, Paul Henry, Conger, John Janeway, and Kagan, Jerome: *Child Development and Personality,* New York, International Universities Press, Inc., 1956.

Nader, Philip R., Bullock, Dorothy, and Caldwell, Bill: School phobia, in Friedman, Stanford B. (Ed.): *The Pediatric Clinics of North America,* 1975, **22**(3), Philadelphia, W. B. Saunders Co.

O'Leary, Susan G. and Schneider, Marlene R.: Special class placement for conduct problem children. *Exceptional Children,* 1977, **44**(1), 24–30.

O'Leary, Susan G. and Pelham, William E.: Behavior therapy and withdrawal of stimulant medication with hyperactive children. *Pediatrics,* 1978, **61**(2), 211–217.

Pope, Lillie: Motor activity in brain-injured children. *Am J Orthopsychiatry,* 1970, **40**(5), 783–794.

Rie, Herbert, Rie, Ellen D., Steward, Sandra, and Ambuel, J. Philip: Effects of ritalin on underachieving children: A replication. *Am J Orthopsychiatry,* 1976 **46**(2), 313–322.

Ryckman, David B, McCartin, Rosemarie, and Sebesta, Sam: Do structured reading programs hamper intellectual development? *Elementary School J,* 1976 **77**(1), 71–73.

Schrager, J., Lindy, J., Harrison, S., and McDermott, J.: The hyperkinetic child; some early indicators of potential school problems. Paper presented at American Orthopsychiatric Association Annual Conference, Washington, D. C., March, 1967.

Silver, Archie A. and Hagin, Rosa A.: Fascinating journey: Paths to the predication and prevention of reading disability. *Bull The Orton Society,* 1975, **25,** 24–36.

Silver, Larry B.: The playroom diagnostic evaluation of children with neurologically based learning disabilities. *J Am Acad Child Psychiatry,* 1976, **15**(2), 240–256.

Slater, Barbara R.: Perceptual development at the kindergarten level. *J Clinical Psychology,* 1971, **27**(2), 263–266.

Smith, Don A. and Wilborn, Bobbie L.: Specific predictors of learning difficulties. *Academic Therapy*, 1977, **12**(4), 471–477.
Stableford, W., Butz, R., Hasazi, J, Leitenberg, H., and Peyser, J.: Sequential
withdrawal of stimulant drugs and use of behavior therapy with two
hyperactive boys. *Am J Orthopsychiatry*, 1976, **46**(2), 302–312.
Steg, John P. and Rapoport, Judity L.: Minor physical anomalies in normal,
neurotic, learning disabled, and severely disturbed children. *J Autism &
Childhood Schizophrenia*, 1975, **5**(4), 299–307.
Stewart, Mark A.: Is hyperactivity abnormal? and other unanswered ques-
tions. *School Review*, 1976, **85**(1), 31–42.
Szyrynski, Victor: School phobia, its treatment and prevention. *Psychiatric J
Univ Ottawa*, 1976, **1**(4), 165–170.
Swift, Marshall S. and Spivack, George: *Alternative Teaching Strategies: Help-
ing Behaviorally Troubled Children Achieve*, Champaign, Ill., Research
Press, 1975.
Thomas, A., Chess, S., and Birch, H. G.: *Temperament and Behavior Disorders
in Children*, New York, New York University Press, 1968.
Torgesen, Joseph K.: Memorization processes in reading-disabled children. *J
Educational Psychology*, 1977, **69**(5), 571–578.
Verville, Elinor: *Behavior Problems of Children*, Philadelphia, W. B. Saunders
Co., 1967.
Wilborn, Bobbie L. and Smith, Don A.: Early identification of children with
learning problems. *Academic Therapy*, 1974, **9**(5), 363–371.
Word, Penny and Rozynko, Vitali: Behavior therapy of an eleven-year-old girl
with reading problems. *J Learning Disabilities*, 1974, **7**(9), 27–30.
Yahraes, Herbert: Brief psychotherapy vs. drugs: Fitting the treatment to the
illness, in Segal, Julius (Ed.): *The Mental Health of the Child*, Rockville,
Md., National Institute of Mental Health, 1971.
Yepes, L. E., Blaka, E. B., Winsberg, B. G. and Bialer, I.: Amitriptyline and
methylphenidate treatment of behaviorally disordered children. *J Child
Psychology & Psychiatry*, 1977, **18**, 39–52.
Zietz, Sister M. Bernetta: Developmental Visual Perception for Reading. *The
Slow Learning Child*, 1970, **17**(1), 16–25.

CHAPTER 18

Psychosomatic Symptoms

Psychological effects of physical problems were discussed in the chapter on chronic illness. The focus in this chapter will be on the emotional or psychological antecedents of physical symptoms. Kessler (1966) divides these into:

1. Transient somatic symptoms resulting from acute emotional distress. In these situations when the distress has been alleviated, the somatic symptoms also disappear, and there are usually no residual physical symptoms.

2. Physical symptoms which appear to reflect emotional distress in "symbolic form." In these situations the child's condition resembles an adult hysterical conversion reaction. The child cannot move or see, for instance, because an anxiety-producing unconscious desire is for him associated with movement or vision.

3. Physical illness brought about, in part, by chronic psychological stress. It is possible that somatic symptoms initially resulting from emotional stress may eventually result in a modification in the tissues with concomitant organic symptoms. Examples of diseases which may be psychogenic are ulcers and some forms of dermatitis.

Most authors agree that for serious psychosomatic disease to be present, one of the important factors in the etiology is "physiologic vulnerability." Which organ will be affected then will depend on the child's "constitutional predisposition." It may also explain to some extent why some children respond somatically to stress while others do not. Temperament may be a factor in how the child responds to stress. The child who is constitutionally hypersensitive or hyperreactive may be more apt to respond to stress with somatic symptoms (Minuchin, *et al.*, 1975; Pinkerton, 1974; Kessler, 1966).

Although constitutional predisposition appears to be important in the development of psychosomatic symptoms, other factors may pre-

181

cipitate the problem. Minuchin, *et al.* (1975) suggest family structure as a factor. In some cases the child's illness may serve to preserve that family structure. The authors suggest that some of these families are unable to effectively resolve their conflicts and the child may be used as a scapegoat for the family conflicts, which then do not have to be faced.

Green (1975) mentions other family situations which may precipitate or maintain psychosomatic symptoms: the death of a significant person in the child's life; separation or divorce of the parents or the anticipation of these events; and persistent separation of parent and child. A very common source of somatic symptoms are similar symptoms, especially symptoms of gastrointestinal distress, in the parents.

Some authors believe that the maternal role is a crucial factor in the development of psychosomatic symptoms. Green provides evidence that mothers of children with psychosomatic symptoms tend to be inadequate and ineffective in satisfying the child's needs for "body care and pleasurable stimulation." It should be noted here that the interviews from which these results were obtained were held five to ten years after the illness, suggesting that the information may not be entirely reliable. One can, however, infer a trend. There are also indications that these children tend to have a symbiotic relationship with the mother although this can be an effect rather than a cause if, as a result of the mother's anxiety over the child's illness, she becomes overly protective.

Although the theory that closeness may be an antecedent to psychosomatic symptoms may seem contradictory to the theory of rejection, it need not be if one considers that not infrequently a mother's defense against the anxiety aroused by her rejection of a child is to be overprotective. If the child and mother are overly close prior to the onset of the symptoms, the symptoms may be a result of a necessary change in that relationship such as may occur after the birth of a sibling, the starting of school, or the illness of the mother. Some mothers are neither rejecting nor overly close but are inconsistent, rejecting the child at times and expressing affection at other times. In this situation the child may be frustrated and angry but cannot express his feelings because of the fear of more persistent rejection. The stress resulting from this situation may produce somatic symptoms (Mussen, *et al.,* 1956).

Laybourne and Churchill (1972) point out that the child who has been ill or who has observed the treatment of others who have been ill may become aware that illness can reduce the demands made on the individual and that through illness one can escape from situations which are frustrating, unpleasant, or threatening. This awareness may have the effect of producing somatic symptoms in the child who has a minor physical ailment. When he is exposed to threatening circumstances, he may withdraw to the relative security of illness. This is not to imply that the child is malingering. It may be a true conversion reaction. Kessler (1966) points out, however, that preadolescent children are rarely considered to have hysterical reactions possibly because their behavior is so variable. Adolescents, on the other hand, are more frequently considered to be suffering from a conversion reaction.

It is, of course, important to help the parents become aware of the relationship between the symptoms and the child's emotional problems. The parents can be counseled to encourage the child to express his concerns verbally, in addition to being given suggestions for reducing the stress. Pinkerton (1974) emphasizes the importance of not allowing the family to deny the significance of the symptoms as symptoms of emotional problems. Related to this is the concern of Laybourne and Churchill (1972) that parents may reinforce the somatic symptoms by insisting that they are physically based rather than psychogenic. They also emphasize the importance of making certain that the symptoms are not rewarded by unusual attention or gifts. Hartman and Boone (1972) stress the desirability of helping parents become aware of the dangers of having an overly close relationship with the child. Family therapy, in order to alter the family structure is recommended by Minuchin, *et al.* (1975). Some families respond well to concrete and specific suggestions for changing relationships within the family, for reducing specific stressful situations, and for handling the somatic symptoms when they emerge.

References

Green, Morris; A developmental approach to symptoms based on age groups, in Friedman, Stanford B. (Ed.): *The Pediatric Clinics of North America,* 1975, **22**(3), Philadelphia W. B. Saunders Co.

Hartman, B. H. and Boone, Donald R.: The benevolent overreaction. *Clinical Pediatrics,* 1972, **2**(5), 268–271.

Kessler, Jane W.: *Psychopathology of Childhood,* Englewood Cliffs, N. J., Prentice-Hall, Inc. 1966.

Laybourne, Paul C. and Churchill, Stephen W.: Symptom discouragement in treating hysterical reactions in childhood. *Int J Child Psychotherapy,* 1972, **1**(3), 111–123.

Minuchin, Salvador, Baker, Lester, Rosman, Bernice, Liebman, Ronald, Milman, Leroy, and Todd, Thomas; A conceptual model of psychosomatic illness in children. *Arch General Psychiatry,* 1975, **32**, 1032–1038.

Mussen, Paul H., Conger, John J., and Kagan, Jerome: *Child Development and Personality,* New York, Harper and Row, 1956.

Pinkerton, Philip: Symptom formation reconsidered in psychosomatic terms. *Psychotherapy & Psychosomatics,* 1974, **23**, 44–54.

CHAPTER 19

Sexual Problems

Many of the sexual problems which will be discussed are more often social problems rather than problems for the children. The behaviors involved may, however, be symptoms of problems in the child and/or in the family and they can, if permitted to continue, create problems.

Sex Role Confusion

One of the problems may be described as sex role confusion. Biological predisposition, family structure, and the sex role assigned to the child by the parents are factors which may be related to confusion in sex role. In discussing the topic, Tiefer (1971) suggests that a biological predisposition, if it does exist, can be "modified, overcome, channeled or suppressed." Rutter (1970) cites studies by Money and the Hampsons which indicate that there is evidence for the opinion that biological factors do affect sex role. Doerr, *et al.* (1976), in the discussion of male homosexuality, suggest that it is a "spectrum of interrelated hormones" and not just one hormone that may be related to the reversal of sex role. In a study done by scientists at the Reproductive Biology Research Foundation in St. Louis, Missouri in 1971 it was found that "the blood testosterone level of men who are exclusively or perdominantly homosexual is only 40% of the level of men who are predominantly heterosexual." It was also found that "60% of the homosexuals tested had below normal sperm levels."

There are a number of theories concerning the role of family structure in sexual identification problems. Probably the most common theory involving males implies that sexual role confusion is more apt to occur in families where, for some reason, the mother is the dominant figure and the father assumes a passive role. Because, in these situations the mother usually makes most of the decisions in the household

184

and takes most of the responsibility, it is easier and more expedient for the male child to turn to the mother for help in making decisions. Some fathers may themselves have problems in sexual identification and may marry "masculinized" wives. In any case, the child does not have an adequate masculine model with which to identify (Rosen and Teague, 1974). Coleman (1964), on the other hand, suggests that the dominant father who is a severe disciplinarian without tempering his severity with some closeness hinders his son from forming a relationship with him which would encourage masculine identification. Instead, as in the situation previously described, the child will turn to the mother. Stringer and Grygier (1976) warn, however, that, even though the family structure is important, it is neither a necessary nor a sufficient condition for sex role disturbance.

Some authors believe that the sex role assigned to the child by his parents is crucial. Except in cases where physical characteristics are ambiguous, parents may inadvertently masculinize a girl or feminize a boy because of their disappointment in the child's sex. Dupont (1968) reports a case of transvestite behavior which followed a boy's discovery that his mother had been disappointed at not having a girl. His behavior was reinforced by the negative attention it received.

Treating feminized boys or masculinized girls, although involving the entire family, often eventually requires marriage counseling to help father become more responsible and more involved in decision making and to help mother relinquish many of her responsibilities to father. This is sometimes easier for mother if she can involve herself in activities outside the home and if she can permit father to make decisions without being critical of those decisions.

Compulsive Masturbation

Masturbation as a normal behavior was discussed earlier. As was noted during that discussion, there are times when a child is masturbating excessively and/or compulsively, and, at times, the behavior can be considered pathological. (See section on Sexual Activity in the chapter, Some Nonspecific Topics.) Kessler (1966) suggests that it may reflect a conflict between Oedipal desires which may have been stimulated either by the child's observation of the "primal scene" or by sleeping with the opposite sex parent and the child's inability to discharge these feelings verbally. In other words, the child may have learned that sexual expression is "bad," and yet the child cannot successfully repress these feelings when they are stimulated.

Gordon (1974) suggests that masturbation may become excessive when it is motivated by an attempt to avoid reality. Some children who

are friendless, and who feel rejected, may engage in excessive masturbation in their search for gratification (Coleman, 1964). Another possible source of compulsive masturbation is general tension in the home
which may be due to marital conflict or intense sibling rivalry. Satterfield (1975) suggests that it may continue if the child begins to see
that it annoys the parent. It is felt that some psychotic or brain-
damaged children masturbate excessively because they have been deprived of stimulation or have been overstimulated.

Sexual Abuse

Statistics concerning the incidence of sexual abuse in general reveal
that in 93% of the reported cases the child is female and in 7% the child
is male. The age of the child is between two years and 18 years, and, in
75% of the cases, the offender is known while in 25% the offender is a
stranger. The sex of the offender is male in 99% of the cases and female
in 1% and in only 3% of the cases are there any injuries (Berliner,
1977). Despite the preponderence of female victims, Swift (1977) warns
that young boys are also victims of sexual molestation.

Meiselman (1978) and Berliner (1977) point out that the child who
has been nonviolently sexually molested on one occasion by a stranger
appears to be affected very little emotionally, while a child who has
been exposed to a violent attack or to a situation where he has been
molested for a long period may become emotionally disturbed. If a child
is abused sexually by a stranger rather than by a family member she is
less likely to be affected, probably because the stranger does not have
an ambiguous role vis-a-vis the child. In the case of sexual abuse by a
stranger the child has the support of the family and is not given the
impression that she may somehow be at fault.

After the young child has been abused sexually, he or more probably
she may have difficulty sleeping, have nightmares, become irritable,
and cling to the parent. There may be some regression reflected in
behaviors such as enuresis, thumb sucking, and irrational fears. Berliner (1977) suggests that these symptoms usually disappear in a very
short time. It is suggested that the parents may also need help because
of their guilt over not having adequately prevented the incident. Verville (1967) cites a study in which none of the children, at least at the
time that they were molested, showed any anxiety. A follow-up study
revealed that, as adults, they appeared to function normally.

It has been suggested, as noted earlier in the discussion of the prevention of problems resulting from molestation, that it is frequently
the adults' reaction or more properly overreaction to the incident
rather than the incident itself which often creates anxiety in the child.

If the families are aware of this and are advised to respond as casually and calmly as they can, the child may be able to perceive the
occurrence as just one more unpleasant experience along with other
experiences which may be somewhat confusing and displeasing.

It is not clear why incest appears to occur more frequently than
previously. Rosenfeld (1977) suggests that present day frankness in
admitting sexual activity may account for the disclosure of incest
which previously would have been hidden, although the possibility of
an actual increase in the incidence cannot be discounted. Statistics
reveal that, at present, in 95% of the cases the child is female and the
age of onset is 12 years or younger in 81% of the cases. In 13% of the
cases the incest involves one isolated incident, in 20% of the cases the
duration is up to six months, and in 67% of the cases the duration is
from one to 14 years. In 75% of the cases the offender is the father or
stepfather; in 7% of the cases it is mother's "live-in" boyfriend, in 18%
uncles, grandfathers, brothers, or grandmothers. Ninety-nine percent
of the offenders are male and 1% are female (Berliner, 1977).
Homosexual incest occurs in only about 5–15% of the incest cases, and
more homosexual incest is reported by males than by females. Meiselman (1978) cautions that statistics concerning the incidence of incest
usually refer to those cases involving the law and in some cases involving conviction of the offender. If this is true, then the actual incidence
might be considerably greater than the published figures. In evaluating the statistics, one must also consider that the reports may not be
true. Meiselman emphasizes the fact that incest is still relatively un-
common.

There is considerable evidence that, in families where incest occurs,
the offending parent may have come from a disadvantaged home, in
some cases a fatherless home. Some of the offenders, probably because
of their disadvantaged backgrounds, are not as interested in social
conformity as they are concerned with gratifying needs which were
unfulfilled previously. It has also been suggested that fathers coming
from fatherless homes are unconcerned with society's perception of the
relationship between child and parent and may thus perceive the
daughter as just one more female and not different than other female
sex objects. It is possible that if the father has been deprived of love
from his parents, he may obtain affectional gratification from the incestuous relationship with his daughter.

There are also indications that many of these fathers observed incestuous relationships in their own families. It is interesting to note that
fathers who came from relatively healthy families tended to begin the
incestuous relationship with the daughter when she was younger. It is
also suggested that mothers in families where incest occurs are not as

concerned because their family backgrounds may have exposed them to incestuous relationships (Rosenfeld, 1977; Meiselman, 1978).

Rosenfeld (1977) points out that, in general, incest is increasingly being viewed as a symptom of disturbed family relationships rather than as the cause of individual and/or family problems. This is not to say that there are no ill effects resulting from incest, only that in the past incest as a symptom tended to be ignored.

Meiselman reports that the incestuous father is either authoritarian and dominates the family or is a "sociopath" who perceives the family members as having the function of satisfying his needs. If the father assumes the former role, the daughter is fearful of defying him or of telling her mother because she may be punished. In any case, she may just be accustomed to obeying the father.

It was found that incestuous families were frequently symbiotic, and it was as though the incestuous relationship kept the family together. In these families when the father had a poor sexual relationship with his wife, unlike some men who would seek their sexual gratification outside the home, they sought sexual fulfillment within the family.

In a number of cases studied, there was no mother in the home. She had either abandoned the family, had died, or was chronically ill. Related to this is the finding that, although the mother may be physically present in the home, she tends to be so passive that she feels incapable of interfering with the incestuous relationship. Sometimes these passive mothers relinquish their responsibility for the household and for the younger children to the eldest daughter who is perceived as the "little mother" and becomes the object of incest. Some mothers tend to be masochistic and enjoy perceiving themselves as the injured party in the situation. One finding which runs through almost all the studies is that there is a poor sexual relationship between father and mother. Either mother is frigid or she may submit to father's advances out of feelings that it is her "duty" to do so (Meiselman, 1978).

Usually the incest is initiated by the father, but there are some situations where apparently the daughter has been seductive. According to Meiselman, this appears to be true in only a small number of cases. Some children, however, especially those under the age of 13 appear to enjoy what they perceive as a sign of affection from their father; sometimes they enjoy their role of father's pet, or they may just care for the father as a parent too much to report him. The possibility that incest continues for a long period of time because the child is herself gaining sexual satisfaction should not be discounted. When the incest lasts for a long period of time, it usually ends when the child becomes an adolescent and is eager to form relationships with peers. In some cases, the father then initiates an incestuous relationship with a younger daughter. Sometimes the incest is terminated by either party because of hostility involving situations that have nothing to do with the incest.

Some of the factors related to brother and sister incest are: little or no supervision of the children; older brothers who have been assigned the role of father where the father is not present in the home; and homes where the mother tends to be very strict and prudish about sex. In brother and sister incest, there is usually agreement to engage in sexual activities, and the siblings tend to enjoy what they are doing. In general, the activity is temporary. Mother-son incest is very rare. Meiselman cites two cases, one in which the son who initiated the incest was psychotic and the other where the mother and son had not seen each other for a long period of time. In father-son incest, the son usually acquiesces until he enters adolescence when he terminates the relationship apparently because of his fear that he may be or may become a homosexual.

Because few of the studies on the effects of incest on the child have included control groups and because the number of subjects studied have frequently been small, the studies are, for the most, unsatisfactory. Some studies revealed that the sexually abused child may complain of pain or discomfort in the thighs and/or in the genital area. Sometimes the child's anxiety is reflected in symptoms of conversion hysteria. The adolescent may be more profoundly depressed than usual and may make a suicide attempt in an effort to obtain help. When compared with the younger child, the adolescent, perhaps because he is more cognizant of community standards, is more likely to be disturbed. Even though the child may seem unaffected, the adverse effect of the experience may not manifest itself until later when there is an attempt to become involved in a relatively mature sexual relationship. At this time the effects of the earlier incest may be reflected in sexual dysfunction. Meiselman cites a study which revealed that incest may have resulted in "personality disturbance in 35% of the cases, exacerbated pre-existing symptoms in 27% and had no traceable relation to personality problems in the remaining 38%."

According to Sarles (1975), fathers who have been offenders in an incestuous relationship tend to be upset only when they are exposed. They tend to excuse their behavior as being motivated by their desire to shelter their daughters from strange men and teach them the "facts of life." How the family copes with the situation once it has been revealed depends to some extent on where the loyalties lie. If, for instance, the mother cares for her husband, she may actually blame the daughter, particularly if the father insists that the daughter is lying. If, however, the mother and daughter are close and if the mother does not have to rely on the father, she may insist that the father leave the home.

When incest is discovered, in order that the child should not be abused further, it may be necessary to report the situation to the child protective services. It is suggested that the disclosure of the incest be accepted as true until it has been fully investigated and found to be false (Berliner, 1977).

Parents should be advised not to interrupt the child's regular habits and to insist that responsibilities regularly assigned to the child be carried out as usual. They should be warned not to overprotect the child and to respond to her questions or to her verbal expressions of her emotions in a casual manner. Adults should not insist that the child talk about her experience. It is important, however, that she be directed to report at once any efforts on the part of the offender to resume the sexual activity. It is also important that the child be reassured that she is not to blame for the situation. In those cases where the parents need help in restructuring the family situation so that the family will become more functional, a referral should be made for family therapy.

The Sexually Active Child

There are indications that young people are more sexually active today than they were in the past (Bender, 1973). Whether or not they also become sexually active at younger ages has not been documented. Experience in child guidance clinics, however, where it is not unusual to see not only sexually active adolescents but sexually active 10-, 11-, and 12-year-olds, suggests that this may be a trend. What advice to give parents who seek counseling for handling their sexually active child depends to some extent on what Spanier (1975) calls "sexualizing influences." His study revealed that the onset and frequency of dating and exposure to sexual activity were important in accounting for the differences in sexual activity. Formal sex education in the schools appeared to have little influence. Spanier points out that, although parents do play a role in the "sexualization" of their children, parental values seem to have little influence on sexual behavior. He suggests that the "pressures and demands of the dating relationship" are apt to weaken the parental influence.

If the above has any validity, it would appear that preventing the sexually active pre-adolescent and early adolescent child from dating and controlling the frequency of the dating in the later adolescent could minimize the opportunities for further sexual behavior. Parents have also found that they can exercise greater control over the child's behavior if they are aware of the identity and acceptability of their child's friends, and if they forbid relationships which appear to stimulate sexual behavior. Occasionally, a girl will become sexually active in order to impress her father with her womanliness. In these situations, a referral for family and/or individual psychotherapy is indicated.

References

Bender, S. J.: Sex and the college student, *J School Health,* 1973 (May), 1–9.
Berliner, Lucy: Child sexual abuse: What happens next? *Victimology: An International Journal,* 1977, **2**(2), 327–331.
Coleman, James: *Abnormal Psychology and Modern Life,* Chicago, Scott, Foresman and Co., 1964.
Doerr, Peter, Pirke, Karl M., Kockott, Gotz, and Dittmar, Franz: Further studies on sex hormones in male homosexuals. *Arch Gen Psychiatry,* 1976, **33**, 611–614.
Dupont, Henry: Social learning theory and the treatment of transvestite behavior in an eight year old boy. *Psychotherapy: Theory, Research and Practice,* 1968, **5**(1), 44–45.
Gordon, Sol: Second thoughts about sex education in the schools, in Williams, Gertrude J. and Gordon, Sol (Eds.): *Clinical Child Psychology: Current Practices and Future Perspectives,* New York, Behavioral Publications, 1974.
Kessler, Jane W.: *Psychopathology of Childhood,* Englewood Cliffs, N. J., Prentice-Hall, Inc., 1966.
Meiselman, Karin C.: *Incest: A Psychological Study of Causes and Effects with Treatment Recommendations,* San Francisco, Jossey-Base, 1978.
Mussen, Paul H., Conger, John J., and Kagan, Jerome: *Child Development and Personality,* New York, Harper and Row, 1956.
Reproductive Biology Research Foundation, St. Louis, Mo., *New England J Medicine,* 1971, **285**, 1170.
Rosen, Alexander, and Teague, James: Case studies in development of masculinity and femininity in male children. *Psychological Rep,* 1974, **34**, 971–983.
Rosenfeld, Alvin A.: Sexual misuse and the family. *Victimology: An International Journal,* 1977, **2**(2), 226–235.
Rutter, Michael: Normal psychosexual development. Paper presented at the British Psychological Society Meeting at Leeds, England on November 6, 1970.
Sarles, Richard M.: Incest, in Friedman, Stanford B. (Ed.): *The Pediatric Clinics of North America,* 1975 (Aug.), **22**(3), 633–641.
Satterfield, Sharon: Common sexual problems of children and adolescents, in Friedman, Stanford B. (Ed.): *The Pediatric Clinics of North America,* 1975, **22**(3), Philadelphia, W. B. Saunders Co.
Spanier, G. B.: Sexualization and premarital sexual behavior. *The Family Coordinator,* 1975(Jan), 33–41.
Stringer, Peter and Grygier, Tadeusz: Male homosexuality, psychiatric patient status, and psychological masculinity and femininity. *Arch Sexual Behavior,* 1976, **5**(1), 15–27.
Swift, Carolyn: Sexual victimization of children: An urban mental health

center survey. *Victimology. An International Journal,* 1977, 2(2), 322–327.
Tiefer, Leonore: Hormones, sexual differentiation, and sexual behavior in primates. American Association for the Advancement of Science, 138th meeting, 1971.
Verville, Elinor: *Behavior Problems of Children,* Philadelphia, W. B. Saunders Co., 1967.

CHAPTER 20

Communicating with Parents

Some parents, even those who themselves request the help for their child, are resistant to carrying out the recommendations made to them. They may have a conflict between their desire to do what they have been told is best for the child and their desire to indulge and over-protect him. The latter may fulfill their need to feel close to the child as well as their need to be loved by him. They are often unable to see the consequences for the child's later development of their present child management behavior, and they want the child to be "happy now." They may also be resistant because the child is filling a void left by an absent spouse, and they fear that by following advice to separate from the child, they will lose what has become for them a satisfying rela-tionship. They may be resistant because the child reminds them of someone, usually a relative, whom they do not like and there is almost a compulsion to fulfill their prophecy that this child must continue to resemble his prototype. Related to this is resistance due to general negative feelings toward the child. Finally, some parents are resistant because they perceive the physician as an authoritarian parental figure against whom they must rebel in an effort to prevent feelings of dependency and helplessness.

The parent who argues about the suggestions and/or who returns to say that the suggestions do not work is probably manifesting some resistance. Parents who are seeking help because the school has suggested they do so and parents who are given advice because the physician suggests that it is indicated may be more resistant than those who seek help because they are themselves concerned over the child's behavior. Sometimes ascertaining the source of the referral for

parental guidance and evaluating the strength of the parents' motivation can prevent or at least minimize the resistance.

Giving parents an opportunity to ventilate their apprehensions, em-
pathizing with their frustrations and concerns, reassuring them as
much as possible, and praising them for their successes as well as for
their efforts should help to overcome their resistance. If parents continue to be resistant even after they have been warned concretely and
specifically of the dangers of overindulgence, overprotectiveness, and
symbiosis, if they have been made aware that they may be, albeit
inadvertently, fulfilling a prophecy that their child will act out, if they
do not even attempt to carry out the recommendations which if im-
plemented could result in a better relationship with the child, and if
the empathy and reassurance does not break down resistance due to
perceiving the advisor as authoritarian, referral to a mental health
practitioner is indicated (see Chapter 13). It is advised that parents be
provided with counseling even if resistance is overt. It is not unusual to
find that resistant parents, at some later date, have, in fact, carried out
recommendations made to them previously.

Communicating to parents confidence in the efficacy of the advice as
well as in the parents' ability to effectively carry it out can be reassuring to the parents. Minimizing the parents' responsibility in creating
the problem by emphasizing concern for the child's well-being rather
than focusing on past child-rearing errors will help to assuage parental
guilt. Parents should be assured that problems can be caused by for-
tuitous events or by unintended acts of others. Providing encourage-
ment and reassurance to parents should, of course, be an integral part
of parent counseling. Some parents, however, may appear confident
perhaps as a reaction to their insecurity and their need for reassurance
is not obvious. Clues to this need may include expressions of concern
for what neighbors or relatives have told them about the child's problem, concerns that the child will develop major problems which they
see in adults who, as children, had similar problems, concern with
what they have learned from reading about the problem, and their
tendency to constantly watch the child's movements while they are in
the office.

Praise can be considered as an important element in reassuring parents that they are doing well. As has been noted earlier, one significant
advantage of having parents treat their children is the gratification
they can experience of having themselves essentially solved the problem. When the child has improved, parents can be reminded that the
improvement was, primarily, a result of their efforts. Perhaps more
importantly parents who are having difficulty implementing the recommendations need praise for what may appear to be insignificant

gains in their ability to manage the child more effectively. As with parents who do not appear to require reassurance, some parents do not seem to need to be praised. Again, it is possible to infer from certain of their behaviors that they are seeking recognition for their efforts, possibly because they are not certain that they are achieving success. In addition to the clues which imply a need for reassurance, the parents who by their manner seem indifferent to praise, but who may need it, will manifest anxiety even after the child has improved. They may either deemphasize the successful solution to the problem or, on the other hand, overemphasize the improvement, or they may report opinions of relatives and/or neighbors that the child has improved or, conversely, that he has not improved sufficiently.

Finally, parents are often relieved to learn that the solution of the presenting problem does not preclude the development of problems at a later date and that, should this occur, they can again request help.

Name Index

Subject Index